Presented to

Jim & Frances Clark

Compliments of

Curt Tompkins

Best wishes to a
wonderful couple!
Curt

August 2, 1999

See esp. pp. 290-91.

MICHIGAN

CELEBRATING A CENTURY OF SUCCESS

Sand Dunes Lighthouse juts up from Benton Harbor. © Charles Benes/FPG International LLC

MICHIGAN

CELEBRATING A CENTURY OF SUCCESS

CAROL MALIS

CHERBO PUBLISHING GROUP, INC.

ENCINO, CALIF.

Dodge Fountain, the stainless-steel masterpiece designed by sculptor Isamu Noguchi, is the centerpiece of Philip A. Hart Plaza in Detroit. The Detroit Renaissance Center can be seen in the background. © Jay Lurie/FPG International LLC

CHERBO PUBLISHING GROUP, INC.

PRESIDENT **Jack C. Cherbo**

EXECUTIVE VICE PRESIDENT **Elaine Hoffman**

EDITORIAL DIRECTOR **Christina M. Beausang**

MANAGING FEATURE EDITOR **Margaret L. Martin**

FEATURE EDITOR **Maria A. Collis**

PROFILES EDITOR **J. Kelley Younger**

ESSAY EDITOR **Tina G. Rubin**

PROFILES WRITERS **Barbara Beckley, Paul Lavenhar, Brian K. Mitchell, Tina G. Rubin, Stan Ziemba**

SENIOR DESIGNER **Mika Toyoura**

CONTRIBUTING DESIGNER **Mary Cameron**

PHOTO EDITOR **Catherine A. Vandenberg**

SALES ADMINISTRATOR **Joan K. Baker**

PRODUCTION SERVICES MANAGER **Ellen T. Kettenbeil**

ADMINISTRATIVE COORDINATOR **Jahnna Biddle**

REGIONAL DEVELOPMENT MANAGER **Merle Gratton**

PUBLISHER'S REPRESENTATIVES **Terry A. Grady, John Lofgren, Patricia A. Stai**

Cherbo Publishing Group, Inc., Encino, CA 91316

© 1999 by Cherbo Publishing Group, Inc.

All rights reserved. Published 1999

Printed in the United States of America

Visit CPG's Web site at www.cherbo-publishing.com.

Library of Congress Cataloging-in-Publication Data

Malis, Carol

A pictorial guide highlighting 20th-century Michigan lifestyle and economic history.

98-71770

ISBN 1-882933-23-0

ACKNOWLEDGMENTS

Heartfelt appreciation goes to Jack Cherbo for his interest in Michigan; to Maria Collis, coach, advocate, and cheering section; to Andrea Sunderman and Elisabeth Weston at the Michigan Chamber of Commerce, and Sheila Middaugh at the Michigan Jobs Commission, for their assistance and support; to the Rochester Hills Public Library for its excellent Michigan collection; to Crain's Detroit Business, an invaluable resource for who's who and what's what in these parts; to kind folks, including Jim Lionas and John and Nancy Haskin, who volunteered key research materials; to Gary Barfknecht and Mary and Don Hunt, whose books are the first and last word on what's special about Michigan; and to whatever Web wizards maintain the indispensable "Welcome to Michigan!" site. My gratitude also goes to family and friends for managing to manifest perpetual interest in the barrage of Michigan facts and trivia with which they were bombarded over the course of the year.

Magnificent multicolored sandstone cliffs characterize Pictured Rocks National Lakeshore on Lake Superior. © John P. George

DEDICATION

For Tony, Bess, and Julie

Thanks for the love, support,

and uninterrupted computer time.

Lake Superior reflects the tranquility of Isle Royale in this view from the deck of Rock Harbor Lighthouse, built in 1855. © Bob Firth/Firth Photobank

STATE OF MICHIGAN

OFFICE OF THE GOVERNOR

LANSING

Dear Reader:

In the past 100 years, Michigan has established itself as a national and international business leader. From forestry, agriculture, and the automotive industry to medical technology, environmental services, and the energy industry, our state has become the center for new innovation. That innovative spirit is the driving force behind Michigan's businesses and it is what draws new companies here each year.

The last decade of the century is one of which we are particularly proud. Michigan has undergone a phenomenal transformation. Michigan's new reputation as one of the most attractive business locations in North America is well earned. We have worked hard to build a successful business climate, with twenty-four tax cuts and an approach that truly promotes growth.

Along with the presence of fabulous business opportunities and exciting technology, there are many other elements that make life in Michigan great. The restructuring of public education has made our schools the best in the nation, while the development of unique job training programs is helping prepare our children for the working world. Michigan's natural beauty is something else that sets us apart. No other place can boast the variety of natural elements that can be found in Michigan. The beautiful beaches, countless lakes and rivers, rugged forests, and quiet offshore islands offer endless pleasure to native Michiganians and visitors alike.

Michigan proved itself a success during the twentieth century. As we enter the twenty-first century, we will continue to work hard to build a prosperous way of life for our citizens. Join me in watching Michigan take on the next 100 years.

Sincerely,

John Engler
Governor

CONTENTS

Mackinac Island's Grand Hotel balcony seemingly stretches to infinity. © Vito Palmisano/Tony Stone Images

THE FOLLOWING COMPANIES AND ORGANIZATIONS, WHOSE PROFILES APPEAR IN
THIS BOOK, HAVE MADE A VALUABLE COMMITMENT TO THE QUALITY OF THIS
PUBLICATION. CHERBO PUBLISHING GROUP GRATEFULLY ACKNOWLEDGES THEIR
PARTICIPATION IN *MICHIGAN: CELEBRATING A CENTURY OF SUCCESS.*

Bete Grise Light looks solemnly out on the Mendota Ship Canal. Both are remnants of the Upper Peninsula's late-nineteenth-century copper boom. © Bob Firth/Firth Photobank

CHERBO PUBLISHING GROUP WOULD LIKE TO THANK THE FOLLOWING INDIVIDUALS, LISTED BY SECTOR, FOR CONTRIBUTING ESSAYS TO *MICHIGAN: CELEBRATING A CENTURY OF SUCCESS:*

INTRODUCTION

Four hundred million years ago a species of coral thrived in the warm Devonian seas that covered Michigan. The fossilized remains of these five-sided organisms continue to wash ashore from the Great Lakes. Called Petoskey stones, they are the official stone of Michigan, a state which is as many-sided as the coral and bears equally strong ties to the water that formed it.

To most of the world today, Michigan means cars. While it is true that Michigan's automobile industry is pivotal to the state and to the nation, the Great Lakes State is so much more. It is unique—two peninsulas completely separated by water, their borders defined by four of the five Great Lakes. Thick forests cover half the state. More than 50,000 farms dot the fertile land whose lake-protected climate places Michigan among the top five agricultural states. Michigan supplies the nation with automobiles, but it is also the world's major source of black beans, blueberries, breakfast cereal, and baby food. Trucks, yes, but also tart cherries, magic tricks, and top-ten hits.

Chippewa, Ottawa, and Potawatomi were the first to call Michigan home, but beginning in the 1600s the French led an influx of immigrants from around the world. With more than one hundred racial and ethnic groups contributing to a culturally rich community, Michigan is the most ethnically diverse of the fifty states. And people continue to come, drawn by the state's strong economy; top-ranked educational institutions; renowned medical facilities; thriving high-tech, chemical, and manufacturing industries; and the unique beauty of this land known as the Great Lakes State.

The Chippewa word manistee *means "spirit of the woods." That spirit is still palpable in the winter hush covering the Nordhouse Dunes Wilderness Area of Michigan's Manistee National Forest. © Terry Donnelly*

HISTORICAL HIGHLIGHTS

AREA: 58,527 square miles
POPULATION: 9,594,300
STATE CAPITAL: Lansing
STATE MOTTO: Si Quaeris Peninsulam Amoenam Circumspice (If You Seek a Pleasant Peninsula, Look About You)
STATEHOOD: Admitted as the twenty-sixth state in 1837
STATE BIRD: American robin
STATE FLOWER: Apple blossom
STATE NICKNAMES: Auto State, Great Lakes State, Wolverine State

© Hilber Nelson

PEOPLE

TIM ALLEN (b. 1953), actor, stand-up comic, author, and star of TV's hit series *Home Improvement,* was born Tim Allen Dick, a fact he claims molded his personality. Allen grew up in Birmingham.

WILLIAM EDWARD BOEING (1881–1956) started as a lumberman before forming a series of companies that would later become United Aircraft, United Airlines, and Boeing Aircraft (a major manufacturer of military and civilian aircraft).

RALPH BUNCHE (1904–1971), Nobel prize–winning African American diplomat and statesman, persuaded the Arabs and Jews to sign an armistice while serving as acting mediator for the United Nations in 1949.

FRANCIS FORD COPPOLA (b. 1939), film director, was born in Detroit and began his career as an apprentice to the B-movie director Roger Corman. Coppola's masterpieces include *The Godfather* (Parts I and II) and *Apocalypse Now.*

EDNA FERBER (1885–1968), novelist, born in Kalamazoo, is best remembered for *So Big* (1924, Pulitzer Prize), *Giant* (1952), and *Show Boat* (1926), which was adapted into a now-classic musical.

GERALD R. FORD (b. 1913), thirty-eighth president of the United States and former first lady **BETTY FORD** (b. 1918 Elizabeth Warren) are natives of Grand Rapids. Michigan Congressman Ford replaced Spiro Agnew as vice president in 1973, then moved up after Richard Nixon's resignation the next year.

BERRY GORDY JR. (b. 1929). After serving in the army and running a record shop in Detroit, Gordy started writing songs for local singing groups. He founded Motown Records in 1959 and went on to make music history.

ROBERT HAYDEN (b. 1913) was the first African American named Poet Laureate by Congress. His powerful work includes *The Night-Blooming Cereus* (1972).

ROBERT JARVIK (b. 1946), artificial heart inventor/surgeon, was born in Midland.

EARVIN "MAGIC" JOHNSON (b. 1959) led Michigan State University to an NCAA basketball championship in 1979 before becoming a guard for the Los Angeles Lakers. He played on the

gold medal–winning 1992 Olympics "dream team."

JOE LOUIS (1914–1981), 1937 heavyweight boxing champion and longtime resident of Detroit, was called the "Brown Bomber" for his ambidextrous killer punch. His nearly twelve years as heavyweight champion is still the longest reign in history.

MADONNA (b. 1958 Madonna Louise Ciccione), singer/actress, dropped out of the University of Michigan and moved to New York, where she worked as a dancer before switching to music and breaking into the club scene, catching the eye of record producers.

MALCOLM X (1925–1965, b. Malcolm Little), African American activist, grew up in Lansing. He became a Black Muslim recruiter in 1952, gaining national attention for his militant approach to civil rights, and stirring racial pride among blacks with his speeches. Before his assassination at age forty he formed the Organization of African American Unity, hoping to cooperate with progressive white groups.

TED NUGENT (b. 1949), rock singer, hunter, radio personality, has been called the "Motor City Madman" for his outrageous presence—both on- and offstage.

JOYCE CAROL OATES (b. 1938), novelist/poet, is best known for her violent and visionary novels.

ROSA PARKS (b. 1913), activist and longtime Detroit resident, is known as the mother of the modern civil rights movement for helping to incite the Montgomery bus boycott of 1955–1956 when she refused to move to the back of a city bus.

This page, top to bottom, first column: © Kosta Alexander/Fotos International/Archive Photos; © Chris Felver/Archive Photos; second column: © Archive Photos/Scott Harrison; third column: © Sonia Moskowitz/Archive Newsphotos; © Archive Photos; © Archive Photos/George Dabrowski

SUGAR RAY ROBINSON (1929–1989, b. Walker Smith Jr.), five-time middleweight boxing champ, often considered "pound for pound, the greatest boxer in history," got his name by using a friend's birth certificate to fight when he was underage.

DIANA ROSS (b. 1944), born in a Detroit housing project, was led to stardom as lead singer of The Supremes by Motown's Berry Gordy. Gold and platinum records followed, as well as an Oscar nomination for her title role in the 1972 film *Lady Sings the Blues.*

GLENN T. SEABORG (1912–1999), Nobel prize–winning physicist and former head of the U.S. Atomic Energy Commission, was born in Ishpeming.

DANNY THOMAS (1912–1991, b. Muzyab Rakhoob), comedian, is best known for

his portrayal of a beleaguered father in *Make Room for Daddy*, which won him an Emmy in 1954. Thomas later founded a research hospital for children. His daughter, actress/political activist **MARLO THOMAS** (b. 1938), paved the way for independent career women on the small screen with her 1960s series *That Girl.*

LILY TOMLIN (b. 1939), Tony Award–winning actress/comedian, was born in Detroit. Working as an office temp, Tomlin moonlighted in cabarets before winning audiences' hearts with her irascible characters on television's *Laugh-In* (1969–1973).

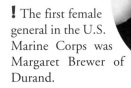

CHRIS VAN ALLSBURG (b. 1949), children's author/illustrator, graduated from the University of Michigan and the Rhode Island School of Design before working as a fine artist, sculptor, and creator of children's books such as *Jumanji* and the award-winning *Polar Express.*

STEVIE WONDER (b. 1950 Steveland Judkins Morris), singer/ musician, blind since birth, was kept off Detroit streets

by his worried mother and passed time banging on household objects to songs on the radio. By age ten he could play several instruments and was a hit at his local church, where Berry Gordy saw him and signed him on the spot.

DID YOU KNOW...?

! The nation's first licensed driver was Dearborn's Henry Ford.

! The first female general in the U.S. Marine Corps was Margaret Brewer of Durand.

! Bertha Van Hoosen (1863–1952), a Rochester physician, was the cofounder and first national president of the American Medical Women's Association.

! Rose Will Monroe, a worker at Ford's Willow Run plant, became World War II's "Rosie the Riveter" when actor Walter Pidgeon heard about her while making a promotional film for war bonds at the plant and invited her to appear in the film. Kay Kyser's song, inspired by another Rosie, was already a hit,

and the famed "We Can Do It" poster was everywhere.

! General Motors engineers helped build a series of electric vehicles used by Apollo astronauts for driving on the moon.

! The first girl in the country to play in the Little League was twelve-year-old Carolyn King of Ypsilanti, who beat out three boys to win a spot on the Ypsilanti Orioles in 1973. Resulting court cases eventually forced the Little League to drop its boys-only policy.

! In 1929 one out of every six U.S. jobs was related to car production, a statistic that still holds true today.

! Howard Miller Company of Zeeland is the world's largest maker of grandfather clocks. Established in 1926, the company is still family owned and operated.

! Eugene Power of Ann Arbor, founder of University Microfilms (UMI), first developed the use of microfilm, now a standard in information technology.

! Grand Rapids is the tenth-best city in the United States in which to do business according to an article in the 23 November 1998 issue of *Fortune* magazine.

! Bronner's in Frankenmuth is the world's largest Christmas shop, with more than 6,000 ornaments and 500 nativity scenes on display.

! Zehnder's Restaurant in Frankenmuth seats 1,500 diners, making it the nation's largest family-owned restaurant.

! Michigan boasts 56 of the 842 champions on the National Register of Big Trees.

HISTORICAL HIGHLIGHTS

MEMORABLE MOMENTS IN MICHIGAN HISTORY

1854 The Republican Party is formed at a convention held in Jackson of more than 1,500 Michigan Whigs, Democrats, and Abolitionists.

1872 Elijah McCoy, perhaps the most famous African American inventor of the nineteenth century, invents the first practical automatic lubricating cup for steam locomotives while working for the Michigan Central Railroad. Many lubrication systems were developed for trains, but McCoy's was the best, and many engineers would accept no substitute. His invention spurred the phrase, "The Real McCoy."

1886 Billy Durant starts the Flint Road Cart Company and sells 4,000 buggies.

1900 The world's first heavyweight title fight is held in Detroit. James Jackson Jeffries knocks out John Finnegan in the first fifty-five seconds of the first round.

1901 Roy Chapin, a young Oldsmobile engineer, drives from Detroit to New York in seven and a half days at an average speed of fourteen miles per hour.

1901 The Detroit Tigers host the Milwaukee Brewers for the first American League baseball game.

1902 The University of Michigan wins the first Rose Bowl, defeating Stanford 49–0.

1903 The Buick and Cadillac Motor companies begin making cars.

1905 Burroughs Adding Machine Company begins production near Detroit, heralding the dawn of the computer age.

1906 Will Kellogg starts a breakfast cereal company based on brother John Harvey Kellogg's ideas.

1906 The first Yellow Pages is issued in Detroit.

1908 Having purchased Buick and thirty other existing auto companies, carriage maker Billy Durant forms General Motors.

1911 Chevrolet Motor Company begins operation.

1916 Michigan's annual copper production peaks at 133,500 tons.

1919 Michigan is the first state to ratify the nineteenth amendment, giving women the right to vote.

1922 The Detroit Symphony Orchestra plays the first complete symphony concert over the radio, broadcast by Detroit News Radio WWJ.

1925 Chrysler Corporation organizes.

1927 Final construction is completed on Ford's River Rouge Complex, the largest industrial operation in the world.

1928 Detroit's convention center is the site of the nation's first aircraft show, where forty manufacturers exhibit sixty-three different aircraft.

1933 *The Lone Ranger* debuts on Detroit's WXYZ. By 1940 more than 400 stations across the nation will carry the program.

1936 The United Auto Workers and the Congress of Industrial Organizations join to form the UAW-CIO.

1937 Joe Louis, Detroit's "Brown Bomber," wins the heavyweight boxing championship.

1939 Detroiters and drivers across the nation welcome air-conditioning to automobiles, thanks to the Packard Motor Car Company.

1941 The University of Michigan opens the nation's first heredity clinic. U-M researchers will go on to find the genes responsible for cystic fibrosis, neurofibromatosis, and Huntington's Disease.

1948 The Cadillac V-8 sprouts tailfins, and a new era in automobile fashion begins.

1950 Preston Tucker is acquitted of charges of fraud in the failure of his $28 million automobile business.

1951 The 100-millionth car is built in the United States.

1951 Ishpeming's Glenn Seaborg shares the Nobel Prize for chemistry for discovering ten new elements, including seaborgium, the only element named for a living person.

1954 Ann Arbor–born Thomas Weller shares the Nobel Prize for physiology and medicine for cultivating the polio virus in a laboratory.

1957 The Mackinac Bridge opens, linking Michigan's Upper and Lower Peninsulas.

1959 Kalamazoo becomes the first community in the United States to close off city streets for a pedestrian mall.

1965 Jackson resident James McDivitt becomes the first of many Michiganians in space when he commands NASA's *Gemini 4* mission. Later he will blast off again, as commander of *Apollo 9.*

1969 Alfred Hershey of Owosso shares the Nobel Prize for physiology and medicine for his research into genetic mutations.

1970 Cornelia Kennedy of Detroit becomes the first female federal judge.

1973 Peter Karmanos Jr. and two partners start a company with $9,000 and the mission statement, "We will help people do things with computers." Compuware Corporation will go on to become one of the largest independent software vendors in the world.

1987 The People Mover monorail opens in downtown Detroit, with 2.9 miles of track connecting thirteen passenger stations.

Each station has its own unique artwork. The entire system is wheelchair-accessible.

1990 Michigan automakers make driver-side air bags standard on every car built in the United States.

1994 The Pontiac Silverdome hosts the World Cup soccer tournament, becoming the first indoor venue to receive that honor.

1995 University Microfilms International's state-of-the-art on-line information system, ProQuest Direct, is added to the Smithsonian Institution's Permanent Research Collection on information technology innovation.

1995 GM forms Saturn, the corporation's first new car company since Chevrolet.

1995 Kalamazoo-based Upjohn merges with European pharmaceutical firm Pharmacia to become the ninth-largest prescription drug firm in the world.

1996 The new world-class Detroit Opera House opens to rave reviews.

1996 Michigan becomes the most Internet-connected state in the Midwest, with 90 percent of the state's population able to dial the Internet by a local phone call.

1998 Michigan-born and -bred Chrysler merges with German automaker Daimler-Benz, creating the third-largest car manufacturer in the world in terms of revenue. (Michigan's General Motors and Ford rank first and second, respectively.)

1998 Michigan ranks first nationally in  getting its state institutions of higher learning "wired" for the twenty-first century according to the Progress and Freedom Foundation's report on the "Digital State."

1998 Keep America Beautiful awards Ford Motor Company its Vision for America award, recognizing the company's environmentally responsible manufacturing processes.

1998 Tara Lipinski, who trains at the Detroit Skating Club, wins the Olympic gold medal in the ladies' freestyle skating competition at the winter games in Nagano, Japan.

1998 The U.S. auto industry produces fifteen million units for the fifth year in a row.

1998 Michigan's own Stroh's beer is selected as the world's best-tasting lager beer in the biennial Brewing Industry International Awards competition.

1998 Detroit's Red Wings win the National Hockey League Stanley Cup for the second year in a row (the ninth year overall).

FIRSTS AND INNOVATIONS FROM THE GREAT LAKES STATE

1817 The University of Michigan, the first large public institution governed by the people of the state, is founded.

1822–1830 Dr. William Beaumont discovers the gastronomic action of pepsin while conducting experiments on a gunshot patient at Fort Mackinac.

1834 The first patent for a combination harvester and thresher goes to Hiram Moore of Kalamazoo County.

1857 Michigan Agricultural College, which will become Michigan State University, opens as the nation's first state college of agriculture.

1857 The world's first successful underwater telegraph cable is laid across the Detroit River between Detroit and Windsor.

1866 Pharmacist James Vernor of Detroit introduces the world's first carbonated soft drink, Vernor's Ginger Ale.

1874 Silas Overpack introduces "Big Wheels" for transporting lumber overland without the need for snow.

1875 Melville Bissell patents the carpet sweeper. After Bissell's death in 1889, his wife, Anna, becomes America's first female corporate CEO.

1880 The world's first international telephone line opens between Detroit and Windsor.

1881 The nation's first high school music course is developed for Ann Arbor schools by Dr. Francis York.

1883 The Industrial Browhoist Corporation of Bay City builds the world's first wrecking crane.

1894 Detroit's Parke-Davis is the first firm in the nation to market an antitoxin for diphtheria.

1896 Henry Ford builds a gas-powered Quadricycle in a Detroit storage shed.

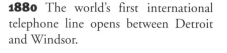

1897 Ransom E. Olds and a group of Lansing investors form the first operating automobile company, The Olds Motor Vehicle Company.

1898 Charles Post produces his first box of Grape Nuts in Battle Creek.

1899 The Olds Motor Works is erected in Detroit, becoming the first factory built in America for the manufacture of automobiles.

1901 Parke-Davis introduces a pure form of adrenaline, the first hormone to be isolated in pure form.

1901 Bay City schoolteacher Annie Edson Taylor becomes the first person to survive a barrel ride over Niagara Falls.

1904 The nation's first freshwater aquarium opens on Detroit's Belle Isle.

1908 Ford begins producing the Model T, the first low-priced, mass-produced automobile with standard, interchangeable parts.

1910 The world's first pontoon airplane, improvised by the Alger brothers, successfully lands on the Detroit River.

1912 The first electric starter appears in Cadillac cars.

1913 Ford introduces the moving assembly line, where workers stand in one place and perform one task, with parts coming to them on a moving belt. Production time for one automobile is cut from twelve hours and eight minutes to one hour and thirty-three minutes.

1914 Henry Ford stuns the world when he institutes the eight-hour, five-dollar day for Ford workers.

1915 The world's first traffic light is installed in Detroit at the corner of Woodward and Grand Avenues.

1920 Detroit's WWJ transmits the nation's first commercial radio broadcast.

1922 For the first time, the automobile can be considered all-weather transportation when Hudson manufactures the first closed car, the Essex.

1926 The eight-passenger Ford Trimotor, an all-metal aircraft produced in Dearborn, is the nation's first successful transport plane.

1927 Dan Gerber invents commercial baby food and sells one-half million cans.

1929 The Ambassador Bridge spans the Detroit River between Detroit and Windsor, Ontario, becoming the first bridge to connect two countries.

1936 Ty Cobb becomes the first player to be inducted into the Baseball Hall of Fame. Cobb played twenty-two years for the Detroit Tigers.

1939 Two Michigan Department of Health physicians, Dr. Pearl Kendrick and Dr. Grace Eldering, develop the first DPT vaccine, which protects against diphtheria, whooping cough, and tetanus.

1941 Ford Motor Company makes the first experimental plastic automobile. Henry Ford demonstrates the car's durability by taking an ax to the trunk lid.

1941 Chrysler delivers the first M-3 twenty-eight-ton General Grant tank to the army. By the end of World War II Chrysler will produce 25,000 tanks.

1942 The first mass-produced B-24 Liberator Bomber emerges from Ford Motor Company's Willow Run plant. At peak production the plant can assemble a plane in 59.3 minutes, producing 8,500 planes in World War II.

1942 The world's first urban freeway, the Davison, is completed in Detroit.

1946 Percy Jones Hospital in Battle Creek puts into use the nation's first microfilm projector. Made by University Microfilms and Argus Cameras, both of Ann Arbor, the machine entertains bedridden patients by projecting enlarged images onto the ceiling over their beds.

1950 Detroit's Dr. Ralph Bunche is the first black man to win the Nobel Peace Prize.

1953 The first Corvette, called America's only true production sports car, rolls off the Flint assembly line.

1954 Northland, the nation's first shopping mall, opens in Southfield.

1960 Michigan's own Farm Bureau Insurance introduces the nation's first farmowners insurance policy.

1969 As prime food contractor for NASA's Apollo missions, Whirlpool Corporation of Benton Harbor provides the first meal ever eaten on the moon. The menu: bacon squares, peaches, sugar cookie cubes, pineapple-grapefruit drink, and coffee.

1969 Dr. Alfred B. Swanson of Grand Rapids designs and perfects the first silicone rubber joint implant to replace damaged human joints.

1971 A sixty-three-year-old Warren man receives the nation's first mechanical heart pump at Detroit's Sinai Hospital.

1975 The nation's first black-owned television station, WGPR/Channel 62, begins broadcasting from Detroit.

1976 Detroit's Sheila Young becomes the first American to win three medals in one

winter Olympics, winning a gold, a silver, and a bronze in speed skating events at Innsbruck, Austria.

1977 The country's first bikepath along an interstate freeway is constructed beside thirty-seven miles of Interstate 275 from Monroe County to southern Oakland County.

1980 Lansing's Ingham Medical Center opens the first arthroscopic surgery center in the United States.

1981 The world's first superconducting cyclotron smashes its first atom at Michigan State University.

1983 Michigan's Court of Appeals orders an attorney to pay his ex-wife $20,000 over a period of ten years because she helped put him through law school, becoming the first court in the nation to rule that a professional degree can be considered marital property.

1983 Squirt and Company of Holland markets the first U.S. soft drink sweetened only with aspartame.

1984 The Holocaust Memorial Center, the nation's first museum dedicated to the holocaust, opens in West Bloomfield Township.

1992 The groundbreaking Michigan Telecommunications Act makes Michigan the first large state to deregulate its business telecommunications services, allowing for increased competition and pricing flexibility.

1996 Michigan automakers are the first in the world to offer a crash-activated automatic S.O.S. signal, which uses a vehicle's cellular phone and Global Positioning Satellite (GPS) technology to alert public safety agencies when and where a crash occurs.

WATER, WEALTH, AND WONDER

PART ONE

If all that makes Michigan spectacular and unique could be reduced to a single word, that word would be water. Carved by the last Ice Age 150 centuries ago, Michigan is cradled by four of the five Great Lakes. Its very name comes from the Chippewa *michi-gama*, meaning "great water."

Michigan is the largest state east of the Mississippi River, and two-fifths of it lies underwater. Nearly 40,000 square miles of Great Lakes fall within the state's borders. Michigan has more freshwater coastline than any other state—more coastline period than any state except Alaska. With 11,000 inland lakes and 36,350 miles of rivers, no spot in the state is more than six miles away from water. There are more than 150 waterfalls in the Upper Peninsula alone. Boats and bridges are a fact of life, as are summer visits to the lakeshore and outings to ski slopes and ice shanties, when winter turns some of that water to snow and ice.

Michigan's two peninsulas, one 300 miles north to south, the other 300 miles east to west, cover a surprising expanse of territory. It is farther from Detroit to Houghton in the Upper Peninsula than it is from Detroit to Baltimore. A land of diversity, Michigan is a national leader in manufacturing, yet forests cover half the state. More species of trees grow in Michigan than in any other state and in all of Europe. With the surrounding lakes protecting the land from harsh weather extremes, the state also is an agricultural Eden. In spring orchards burst with cherry, peach, and apple blossoms, a display rivaled only by the forests' fiery autumn pyrotechnics. The state motto is well chosen: If you seek a pleasant peninsula, look about you.

Lake Superior's immense surface waits beyond the rocks of Union Bay like a sleeping giant, subject not to man or beast, but only the changing sky. © Terry Donnelly

RICH PAST, BRIGHT FUTURE

CHAPTER ONE

ITS ENVIABLE GREAT LAKES LOCATION GUARANTEED MICHIGAN'S ECONOMIC SUCCESS FROM THE VERY BEGINNING. LOW-COST WATER TRANSPORTATION, ENHANCED BY A WEALTH OF NATURAL RESOURCES AND THE HAPPY COINCIDENCE OF HOMEGROWN GENIUS, HAVE PRODUCED A FLOURISHING AND DIVERSE ECONOMY. TODAY MICHIGAN COMPANIES HEAD UP THE FORTUNE 500, AND MICHIGAN PRODUCTS ARE FOUND IN EVERY AMERICAN HOME.

Furs drove the state's first major economic boom. Beginning in the 1600s stylish European gentlemen developed a passion for beaver hats. For 150 years Michigan produced a steady supply of pelts, creating some notable fortunes in the process. Recognizing great real estate when he saw it, John Jacob Astor headquartered his American Fur Company on Mackinac Island in 1816 on his way to becoming the richest man in America.

Virgin white pine forests, vast iron ore deposits, and the largest native reserve of copper in the world next fueled the state's growth. As settlers moved into the Midwest in ever-growing numbers beginning in the 1830s, they used Michigan's trees to build their new towns and cities, and to rebuild Chicago after its Great Fire of 1871. Lumber was Michigan's "green gold," producing at least a billion dollars more revenue than did California's yellow gold.

America's first mining boom occurred in the Upper Peninsula, which led the nation in copper and iron ore production for more than a century. Then, just as the timber and mining booms began to wane, Henry Ford, Ransom E. Olds, and others created a new industry that would change the face of Michigan and the world forever.

Not only did Michigan put America on wheels, it also introduced the assembly line and the eight-hour workday, the traffic light, and the freeway. As Michigan inspired America's love affair with the car, the automobile also changed Michigan—from a rural state to an urban one. The last year that more Michiganians lived on farms than in cities was 1910. From then on the automobile meant good times for everyone, from the auto baron in his European-style manor on the outskirts of Detroit, to the guy on the assembly line with his benefits package and new car parked in the driveway.

OPPOSITE: The Mackinac Bridge opened in 1957, joining Michigan's Upper and Lower Peninsulas. Five miles in length, the "Mighty Mac" is one of the world's longest suspension bridges. © George E. Stewart/Dembinsky Photo Associates. ABOVE: Native Americans in Saint Ignace don traditional costumes for a ceremonial dance. © Ron Goulet/Dembinsky Photo Associates

In 1924 Henry Ford stands between the ten-millionth Model T and his earlier invention, the Quadricycle. Both vehicles were instrumental in the automobile's change from a luxury item into practical and affordable transportation. © UPI/Corbis-Bettmann

The automobile drove Michigan's economy to prosperity until the early 1970s, when foreign competition and rising gasoline prices warned of a need to diversify. Michigan took the hint, and its economy is more varied today than it has been in a century. Having suffered the nation's highest unemployment rate in 1980, Michigan now has one of the lowest, and accounts for a whopping 20 percent of new manufacturing jobs nationwide. Michigan is the home of industry leaders in pharmaceuticals, furniture, chemicals, telecommunications, utilities, health care, food processing, and retail. The auto industry has made a comeback, too. Michigan-based General Motors, Ford, and the Chrysler division of DaimlerChrysler together produce 65 percent of all cars sold in the United States and more than a third of all cars sold in the world.

Detroit is the country's largest free-trade zone, the busiest stopping-off point for foreign and domestic goods entering and leaving the United States. Michigan has four free-trade zones, reflecting the global nature of the state economy. Each year Michigan ports handle 100 million tons of cargo. In their eight-month navigational season the Soo Locks handle more shipping tonnage than the Panama Canal handles all year.

Michigan is not just an industrial state. Its 52,000 farms bring in $3.8 billion in annual revenues, making Michigan the most diverse agricultural state after California, thanks to the Great Lakes State's unique climate and exceptional diversity of soils.

Michigan blueberries, ripe for picking . © John Gerlach/Dembinsky Photo Associates

Western Michigan is one of the best places on the continent to grow fruit, and Michigan leads the nation in the production of tart cherries and blueberries, as well as five other commercial crops. The state ranks fifth or higher in twenty-five crops.

Michigan has a larger gross product than most countries, ranking twenty-fifth in the world in products and services. The state currently enjoys one of the highest credit ratings in the nation. Its per capita income is above the national average, while its consumer price index is below. That makes Michigan a financially comfortable place to live, a fact reflected in its 72 percent home own-

The Keweenaw Peninsula is the longest of Michigan's many "pleasant peninsulas" stretching out into Lake Superior. The tiny town of Kearsarge lies near the Keweenaw's northern shore. © Greg Ryan–Sally Beyer

ership rate, the third-highest in the nation. Michiganians have an investment in their communities, evidenced by a history of ardent involvement in local government and schools. Grassroots efforts led by community groups such as the Michigan PTA have resulted in statewide neighborhood Child Watch programs, twenty-five-mile-an-hour school speed zones, playground safety measures, and tobacco-free schools.

ONE STATE, MANY PEOPLES

Michigan's riches began drawing people more than 10,000 years ago and continue to draw them today. Some of the first Native Americans to come to the region settled in the forests of southeastern Michigan. Others went to the Upper Peninsula where they found copper just a few inches beneath the earth's surface and became the Western world's first coppersmiths.

When the French began exploring the area in the early 1600s they identified nine tribes, falling into three main groups: the Hurons, the Ottawa, and the Chippewa. The heritage of these first inhabitants continues in the names of Michigan cities and rivers, and in descendants, many of whom live on reservations across the state.

After Michigan became a state in 1837, and thanks largely to the opening of the Erie Canal, a flood of settlers chose Michigan as home. These included immigrants from all over Europe and African Americans from the South. Today the state is a melting pot of more than one hundred racial and ethnic groups, making Michigan's cultural diversity the greatest in the nation.

This blend of cultures has shaped and enriched the state's personality. "Yoopers"—people who live in the Upper Peninsula, or "U.P."—are mostly from Scandinavia, particularly Finland. But a significant number are English, descended from the Cornish miners who brought their expertise to the northern copper and iron ore mines. The U.P. remains a land of saunas and the Cornish meat pies called pasties.

"Trolls"—people who live below the mighty Mackinac Bridge, which ties the two peninsulas together—are a United Nations of ethnic groups. Phonebooks in the western part of the state are chock-full of "Van's" thanks to the Dutch who settled around Grand Rapids and founded the city of Holland. The Tulip Festival held in Holland each May ranks with New Orleans's Mardi Gras in national popularity. When it's Mardi Gras in Louisiana, it's Paczki (poonch-key) Day in Detroit, named for the traditional Polish doughnuts that appear everywhere the day before the start of Lent. German culture is evident in the Bavarian-style village of Frankenmuth, which draws three million visitors each year, making it Michigan's number one tourist attraction. Irish settled in the south-central part of the state, now a vacation region called the Irish Hills, popular for Indy car racing and Saint Patrick's Day celebrations.

Detroit holds a series of ethnic festivals on its waterfront all summer long, including one that celebrates Detroit's Arab American community, the largest Arab community outside the Middle East. The African American Festival showcases the vibrant community that created Detroit's second-most-famous export. The Motown Sound was born in 1957 when Berry Gordy set up a recording studio in a tiny brick house on West Grand Boulevard and became the first person to market black music and artists on a world scale.

Wooden shoe–clad dancers pose proudly in front of a Holland windmill. © Ron Goulet/Dembinsky Photo Associates

ABOVE: *Edison Fishery operates on Isle Royale, the nation's only island national park.* © Layne Kennedy. BELOW LEFT: *Children enjoy painting the great outdoors at one of Michigan's many festivals.* © Leavenworth Photographics/Great Lansing Convention & Visitors Bureau. BELOW RIGHT: *Detroit's Greek Town is famous for its friendly, boisterous waiters as well as its great food. "Opa!"* © Layne Kennedy

OPPOSITE: *The old Quincy Mine near Hancock recalls the early 1900s glory days of Michigan's copper boom.* © Greg Ryan–Sally Beyer. ABOVE: *Picturesque Mackinac Island got its name from the Chippewa* michilimackinac, *meaning "great turtle."* © Layne Kennedy. BELOW: *The Upper Tahquamenon Falls are among the many breathtaking water formations in Tahquamenon State Park.* © John P. George

ABOVE: *Hitsville, U.S.A., once the recording home of Motown greats such as the Jackson Five, is now a hit museum. © Layne Kennedy.*
BELOW: *A hardworking tugboat tools through Betsie River Harbor on Lake Michigan near Frankfort. © Greg Ryan–Sally Beyer.*
OPPOSITE: *The site of the historic iron-smelting town of Fayette on Snail Shell Bay is now a state park. © Tom Algire/FPG International LLC*

THE GOOD LIFE

CHAPTER TWO

MICHIGAN'S POPULATION CONTINUES TO GROW AT A COMFORTABLE, SUS-
TAINABLE RATE, WITH THE AVERAGE AGE OF ITS CITIZENS SLIGHTLY YOUNGER
THAN IN NEIGHBORING STATES. PROJECTIONS SHOW THAT MICHIGAN WILL
HOLD ITS POSITION AS THE EIGHTH MOST POPULATED STATE WELL INTO THE
TWENTY-FIRST CENTURY. JUST ABOUT HALF THE STATE'S RESIDENTS LIVE IN
GREATER METROPOLITAN DETROIT. THIS AREA HAS A STRONG BLUE-COLLAR

heritage, but the auto industry's increasing emphasis on high technology and advanced engineering, coupled with the presence of world-class research universities, has resulted in a booming professional class.

Michigan schools are addressing the need for new skills through mandatory periodic testing to meet rigorous state standards and an innovative statewide program that uses special mathematics and science centers for curriculum enhancement and advanced study. The state is committed to a cutting-edge initiative aimed at giving students the necessary skills not only to be well-rounded, intelligent citizens, but to compete effectively in a twenty-first-century job market.

Michigan has always had a strong commitment to education. It was the first state to guarantee a tax-paid high school education for every child, and the first to provide library service for its citizens. In 1817, while Michigan was still a territory, its voters established the University of Michigan, predating all other state universities. In 1867 U-M became the first university to be supported by a direct property tax. Michigan State University was the first land-grant college and the first college devoted to teaching scientific agriculture. Today Michigan has fifteen four-year universities, sixty-six independent colleges, and twenty-nine community colleges, with more than a half million students. Each year Michigan graduates more than 4,000 engineers, one of the largest figures in the nation.

Michigan colleges and universities are consistently rated among the country's best and are recognized worldwide for their research programs. The University of

OPPOSITE: *A couple enjoys the sunset from Sand Point, one of many such tranquil spots found along Lake Superior and the inland lakes and streams of Pictured Rocks National Lakeshore. © Layne Kennedy.* ABOVE: *Across the bowsprit of a tall ship sailing from Windsor, Ontario, the Detroit skyline beckons, offering adventures of a cultural and culinary kind. © Andre Jenny/International Stock*

Michigan spends more money on research than any other public university in North America. Michigan State University is unique in the nation in having three medical schools on its campus. The country's first university hospital opened at the University of Michigan in 1869, and today the medical school and three hospitals in the University of Michigan Health System rank among America's top health care institutions. These and other world-renowned medical facilities, with nearly 900 of their 20,000 full-time physicians listed in *The Best Doctors in America,* make Michigan a national leader in health care.

A WATER-WINTER WONDERLAND

Welcoming thirty-two million visitors each year, Michigan is one of the top-ten tourist states. For visitors and residents alike, Michigan offers a range of delights as varied as its seasons.

In spring, the maple syrup flows, the tulips bloom, and from across the country people come to the Michigan woods in search of the famous morel mushroom. The area around Mesick is the only place in the world where all five varieties of morel can be found—before they appear on the menus of the nation's best restaurants.

Summer is camping, boating, and fishing season. Although by the late 1800s loggers had virtually decimated Michigan's virgin forests, the trees have returned

The world-renowned University of Michigan has been the centerpiece of Ann Arbor life and culture since 1837. © SuperStock

and now cover half the state—18.4 million acres—thanks to one of the world's most successful reforestation programs. These forests offer a wealth of recreational possibilities. Michigan leads the nation in the number of state parks and prepared campsites, among them the Upper Peninsula's 58,000-acre Porcupine Mountains Wilderness State Park.

Water, naturally, is the state's top draw. Michigan has about a million registered pleasure boats—more than any other state—and its nearly 100 harbors mean that no boat is ever more than fifteen shoreline miles away from a safe place to tie in. Out of Michigan's 149 types of native fish, 25 are game fish, making the state an angler's paradise. Among the most popular game fish are the salmon that were introduced into the Great Lakes and their Michigan tributaries in the 1960s. Today more and larger chinook salmon are caught in Great Lakes waters than in their native Washington.

Summer is also golf season. Michigan has more championship golf courses and more public courses (720 and counting) than any other state, making it an international golf destination. It is the site of annual pro and senior golf circuit events on top-rated courses, several designed by the pros themselves.

When the forests put on their magnificent fall colors, the state's 100 cider mills become the focus of weekend pilgrimages. About this time the deer population—thought to be the largest in the country outside of Texas—runs for cover as thousands of hunters take to the woods.

It's safe for the deer to come out again once the hunters have put away their bows and rifles and taken out their snowmobiles. Michigan has more than 4,200 miles of marked and groomed snowmobile trails, many of them traversing the most scenic state-owned and national forestland in the region. For those who like to burn a few more calories there are 2,400 miles of Nordic ski trails and forty-five fully developed downhill ski areas. Cabin fever is not an option with Tip-Up Town, USA, Houghton Lake's annual shanty-mania, when ice anglers have slippery tug-of-war tournaments and softball matches while waiting for the walleyes to hit. The Polar Ice Cap Golf Tournament challenges duffers to drive and putt across frozen Spring Lake near Grand Haven, and the North

American Snowmobile Festival covers ice-capped Lake Cadillac with ten thousand screaming snowmobiles.

GRAND FANS AND CULTURE VULTURES

Michigan is big on sports. Grayling is home to the Archery Hall of Fame, Ishpeming boasts the National Ski Hall of Fame, and the American Power Boat Association is headquartered in Detroit. An Olympic training center is located at Northern Michigan University in Marquette, and the Detroit Skating Club in Bloomfield Hills grooms figure skating stars such as 1998 Olympic gold medalist Tara Lipinski, men's national champion Todd Eldredge, and ice dancers Elizabeth Punsalan and Jerod Swallow. Big Ten sports are a state obsession—Michigan holds the record for highest attendance at college sport events. Through thick and thin, Michigan fans cheer their professional teams, too: Tigers (World Series champions 1935, 1945, 1968, 1984); Pistons (National Basketball Association champions 1989, 1990); Red

The Carp River wriggles from tiny Lake of the Clouds to giant Lake Superior through a cavern of foliage in Porcupine Mountains Wilderness State Park. © Larry Ulrich/Tony Stone Images

Olympic gold medalist Tara Lipinski trains on the ice at the Detroit Skating Club. © Shaun Botterill/Allsport USA

Wings (Stanley Cup champions 1936, 1937, 1943, 1950, 1952, 1954, 1955, 1997, 1998); Lions (National Football League champions 1935, 1952, 1953, 1957, and still trying hard to get to the Super Bowl); and the new Women's National Basketball Association's Shock. The Vipers represent Detroit in the International Hockey League; the Rockers are Detroit's professional soccer team; and cities across the state support minor league baseball, hockey, soccer, and lacrosse teams.

The hottest tickets in town are not just for sporting events. Detroit is home to the largest theater district in North America outside New York City—twenty-two thousand seats within a 1.5-mile radius. These venues offer a wide variety of entertainment including traditional repertory, alternative theater, comedy, and big-name entertainers, as well as world-class symphony, jazz, and opera. Michigan's rich cultural scene extends beyond the stage. With a permanent collection numbering more than forty thousand works, the Detroit Institute of Arts is the largest municipally owned art museum in the country. Among its treasures are the second-largest Dutch-Flemish collection (including several Rembrandts) and third-largest Italian Renaissance collection outside of Europe. Bloomfield Hills's Cranbrook Academy museum and graduate school of art, design, and architecture has an unparalleled international reputation; and Interlochen, near Traverse City, is the largest, best-known, and most successful fine arts camp in the

United States, as well as a year-round arts academy. Interlochen graduates include newsman Mike Wallace, opera star Jessye Norman, actors Tom Hulce and Meredith Baxter, cartoonist Cathy Guisewite, and singer Jewel. "Interlochen," said pianist Van Cliburn, "is a magic word in the music world."

ON THE ROAD

Another reason visitors like Michigan so much is that it is easy to get to and easy to get around. The state's 9,500-mile highway system offers ready mobility within 500 miles of half the population of the United States. Michigan is so proud of its scenic highways it was the first state to install roadside parks and picnic tables. The highways take visitors to sites of incredible beauty and historical interest. There are four national forests, two national lakeshores, and the country's only island national park—Isle Royale. Mackinac Island was initially designated the country's second national park, following Yellowstone by just three years, but was turned over to Michigan again in 1897, becoming its first state park. Mackinac Island continues to be one of Michigan's most popular tourist destinations, a step back in time to a place without cars, where the air is filled with the clip-clop of horse and buggy and the scent of the island's famous fudge.

OPPOSITE: Ice-encrusted Scott Falls in Hiawatha National Forest releases only a fine spray until spring comes to melt its frosty prison. © John P. George. RIGHT: Golfers take advantage of a perfect day for teeing off in Garland. © Jerry Amster/SuperStock

University of Michigan home football games fill the stadium's nearly 105,000 seats—a number almost equal to the population of Ann Arbor. © Stephen Graham/Dembinsky Photo Associates

Dearborn's eighty-one-acre Greenfield Village is the nation's largest outdoor museum. The more than eighty historic buildings relocated there by Henry Ford include Thomas Edison's Menlo Park laboratory and the Wright brothers' bicycle shop. Detroit's new Museum of African American History is being hailed as the largest and best museum of black culture in the United States. Across the state there are countless other sites where Michigan's history and natural beauty unite to please the eye and engage the imagination.

A GREAT PLACE TO LIVE

"The people here are so friendly—very welcoming, very family-oriented, very grounded," is how one new resident, a former New Englander who also has lived in the South, describes Michigan. "There's all the natural beauty—the water, the bike paths, the parks—plus there are theaters, sports, museums. Our interests have been so much more piqued here than anywhere we've ever lived."

In some ways, not much has changed since the first settlers arrived. "This country, so temperate, so fertile, and so beautiful," wrote Antoine de la Mothe Cadillac, founder of Detroit, in 1702, "that it may justly be called the earthly paradise of North America."

Welcome to the Great Lakes State!

Moonlight and lamplight meet to create an other-worldly glow on the escarpment above Lake of the Clouds in Porcupine Mountains Wilderness State Park. © Layne Kennedy

ABOVE LEFT: *Ice fishing is a family affair in Kensington.* © Joe Sroka/Dembinsky Photo Associates. ABOVE RIGHT: *Detroit's Fox Theatre blazes with neon light.* © Cliff Hollenbeck/International Stock. BELOW: *Three Detroit artists sculpted these figures of enslaved Africans encased in the center section of an eighty-foot ramping platform representing a small ship used to transport African captives to the Americas.* Tight Pack *is part of the core exhibit at Detroit's Museum of African American History.* © Felecia Hunt-Taylor/Museum of African American History

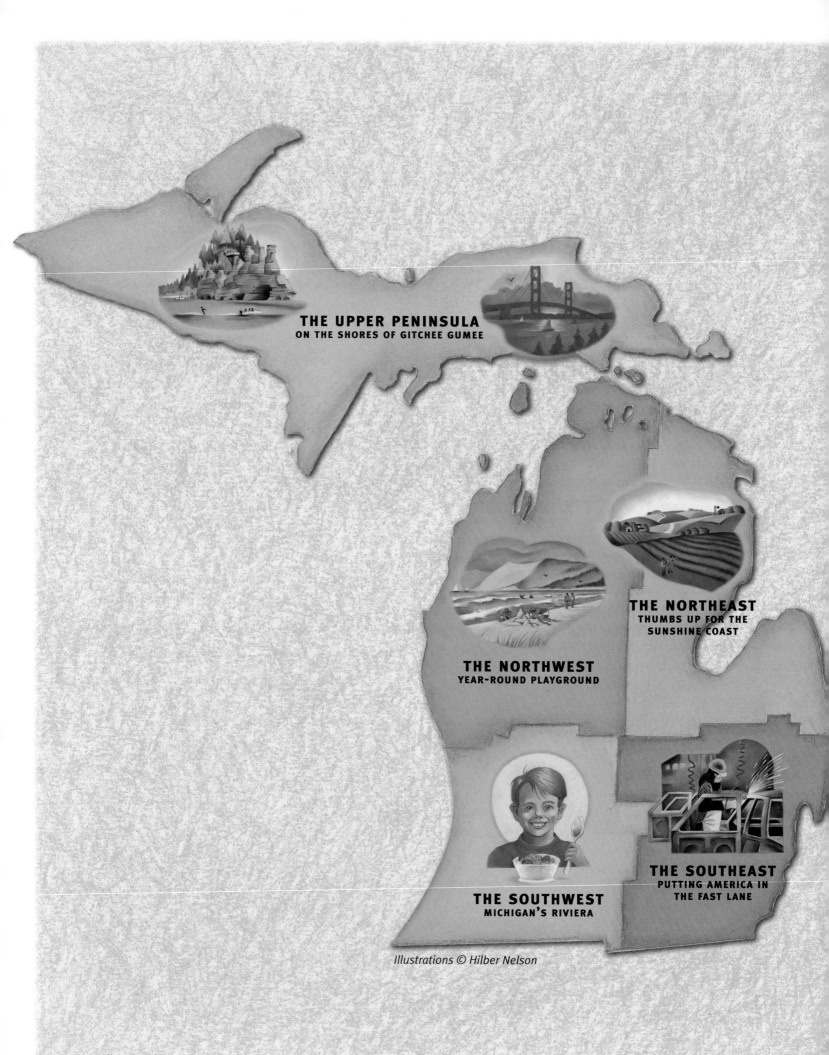

THE UPPER PENINSULA
ON THE SHORES OF GITCHEE GUMEE

THE NORTHEAST
THUMBS UP FOR THE
SUNSHINE COAST

THE NORTHWEST
YEAR-ROUND PLAYGROUND

THE SOUTHWEST
MICHIGAN'S RIVIERA

THE SOUTHEAST
PUTTING AMERICA IN
THE FAST LANE

Illustrations © Hilber Nelson

PART TWO
FROM MOTOWN TO MACKINAC

From the upper reaches of Paradise on the shores of Lake Superior, to Hell downstate, Michigan embraces a world of peoples, landscapes, occupations, and diversions. Each of the state's varied regions offers its own unique physical beauty, recreational amenities, cultural richness, and economic diversity. At the 1887 meeting of the Pioneer Society of Michigan, one member suggested a new twist to the state motto—"If you seek a beautiful peninsula, here's a couple of 'em. Take your pick." A century later, the pickings are even better. Whether for a beautiful vacation spot or a great place to call home, deciding among Michigan's distinctive regions remains a delightful dilemma.

CHAPTER THREE
THE SOUTHEAST
PUTTING AMERICA IN THE FAST LANE

MOTOR CITY

Southeast Michigan is the dynamo that powers not only the state but much of the entire Great Lakes region. The city of Detroit is located here, along with more than half the state's residents. This area is the auto industry's world headquarters, boasting the historic "Big Three," most of the world's auto suppliers, and just about every American automotive research center. The southeast also is home to Michigan's two major universities, one of the world's most extensive medical complexes, the nation's largest free-trade zone, one of America's busiest airports, and the seat of state government.

The Detroit River, which connects the Upper and Lower Great Lakes, first attracted Europeans to the area 300 years ago. Shipping from Detroit wharves was crucial to the region's economy until the early 1900s. Then the handy presence of shipborne raw materials and the ready know-how from Detroit's extensive stove-manufacturing industry created the Motor City, center of the new automobile industry. Hundreds of thousands of workers from across the country and around the world poured into the area. So did money. Lots of it. The combination transformed the region into the rich, vibrant, and diverse megalopolis it is today.

On maps, greater metropolitan Detroit is a three-county area, but in fact the auto industry extends Detroit's reach much farther—all the way to Flint, home of Buick and Chevrolet; and Lansing, land of Oldsmobile. This region felt the economic slump of the late 1970s more acutely than anywhere in the nation, but the 1990s saw a marked turnaround. Detroit has entered a period of vigorous growth in commerce, housing, and the arts. The Renaissance Center, once the failed centerpiece of Detroit's urban renewal, is General Motors' new world headquarters, a financial and emotional investment felt throughout the city. A new stadium for the Detroit Tigers is planned in the restored theater district. The year 1996 saw the opening of the new world-class Detroit Opera House, an event that drew opera luminaries such as Luciano Pavarotti. Within the next few years casino gambling will come to Detroit, with three major hotel-casinos slated to compete with the casinos cur-

Detroit's Renaissance Center is home to General Motors' world headquarters. Here, the center looms above a stretch of the 2.9-mile People Mover, an elevated rail system that runs through the central business district. © H. G. Ross/FPG International LLC

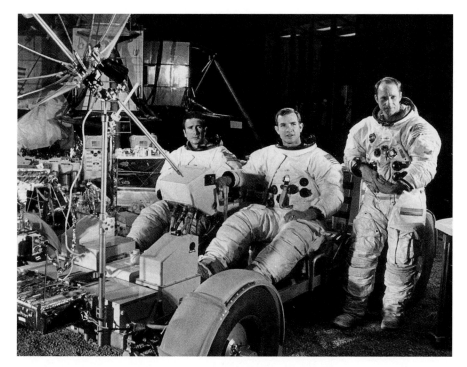

weekend to see the premier event of the hydroplane circuit. Detroit's Grand Prix, held each summer on Belle Isle, is considered one of the world's best road courses by the internationally known drivers who race their 850-horsepower turbo-charged engines around the scenic track.

Detroit's suburbs have been enjoying ever-growing prosperity since the 1920s, when John Dodge's widow built Meadow Brook Hall, America's fourth-largest residence, in the rolling hills of Oakland County. Today Oakland is the third-richest county in the nation, home to a roster of luminaries, from "Queen of Soul" Aretha Franklin to mall magnate and Sotheby's chairman A. Alfred Taubman to renowned author Elmore Leonard.

But the southeast is not just Detroit. After the War of 1812, state legislators grew uneasy over their capital's proximity to a foreign country, so they decided to move

rently operating across the river in Windsor, Ontario. And Detroit Metropolitan Airport, a major hub for Northwest Airlines, is embarking on a $1.6 billion expansion and renovation project.

People are enjoying the city again. Not since the heyday of Motown, when artists such as Smokey Robinson, Marvin Gaye, Martha Reeves, the Temptations, and the Supremes put the city on world music charts, has there been such excitement and optimism downtown. The restored Fox and State Theatres impress new audiences with their opulent 1920s picture-palace splendor. Tickets to watch the Stanley Cup Champion Red Wings play hockey at Joe Louis Arena are blue-chip commodities. The Spirit of Detroit Thunderfest Gold Cup brings one-half million people to the riverfront each Memorial Day

Every August 15,000 athletes come from all over the world to participate in Flint's Crim Festival of Races. Courtesy, Crim Festival of Races

it from Detroit. To avoid giving any one politician a hometown advantage, they agreed on a dot in the middle of nowhere, reachable only by a Native American trail, consisting of nothing more than a small sawmill and a single log cabin. Today Lansing is the seat of state government and home of the Oldsmobile, America's first mass-produced car. The state's largest university, Michigan State, is in neighboring East Lansing.

Flint was the hometown of carriage-maker Billy Durant, who used his stock market winnings to create General Motors. Flint claims the highest concentration of autoworkers of any metropolitan area in the United States. The Flint Institute of the Arts is the state's

RIGHT: *Modelers at General Motors apply clay to an armature, preparing to sculpt a new prototype.* © *Kevin Horan/Tony Stone Images.* BELOW: *The city of Flint, long a transportation center, gave birth to General Motors.* © *Gary Bublitz/Dembinsky Photo Associates*

second-most-prominent art museum, boasting an exceptional collection of nineteenth-century French paintings. Ann Arbor, home of the University of Michigan, is one of the nation's pre-eminent academic and cultural centers, and is considered one of the best places in the country to shop for books and records. Jackson is the town where several thousand Michigan Whigs, Democrats, and Abolitionists gathered on 6 July 1854 and formed the Republican Party. Today visitors gather in Jackson to see the *Apollo 9* command module, a lunar rover vehicle, and moon rocks at the Michigan Space and Science Center. The hands-on museum examines the space program of the 1960s and 70s, and honors the eleven astronauts who came from Michigan.

The Michigan Opera Theatre performs on the stage of the splendidly renovated Detroit Opera House. Shown here is a scene from Aida. *© Michigan Opera Theatre*

Brilliant colors festoon the sunken garden at Cranbrook Educational Community in Bloomfield Hills, an institution known for its excellent art programs. © Cranbrook

Dearborn's Henry Ford Museum & Greenfield Village covers ninety-three acres and 350 years of American culture, industry, and technology. ABOVE: The Automobile in American Life *exhibit shows how cars impacted life in the twentieth-century United States.* BELOW: *Greenfield Village contains Thomas Edison's original Menlo Park, New Jersey, laboratory, where more than 400 inventions were created, including the electric lightbulb. Both photos © Henry Ford Museum & Greenfield Village.* OPPOSITE: *Lansing's state capitol building, with its beautiful rotunda, was built in 1879 to resemble the nation's capitol in Washington. © Vito Palmisano/Tony Stone Images*

CHAPTER FOUR

THE SOUTHWEST
MICHIGAN'S RIVIERA

With the longest stretch of freshwater sand dunes in the world, and a temperate climate that is the best in America for growing fruit, southwest Michigan profits from the benevolence and protection of neighboring Lake Michigan. In the early nineteenth century this favored location attracted settlers from the east and from Europe who established lovely towns and prosperous, often innovative, businesses across the region. Later the area's reputation expanded, as it became the premier resort area of the Midwest.

That the region has not forgotten its past, but has built upon it with respect, gives the southwest its charm. Marshall contains the nation's largest registered historic district— a Victorian showplace of Gothic and Greek Revival homes from the 1840s and 1850s. The town also has a remarkable museum of magic, a place of pilgrimage for the likes of David Copperfield, who combines his regular visits with a stop in Colon. This tiny town forty miles southwest of Marshall, once the summer home of famed magician Harry Blackstone, remains the "magic capital of the world," thanks to the presence of Abbott's Magic Manufacturing Company, the world's largest maker of magic tricks and accessories.

BATTLE CREEK

People who sew probably are aware that every Simplicity pattern is printed in Niles, also the hometown of retailer Montgomery Ward and writer Ring Lardner. Battle Creek is well known as Cereal City, site of Dr. John Harvey Kellogg's famous sanitarium and still the home of Kellogg, Post, and Ralston Foods' Chex facility. Less known is the town's history as a major stop on the Underground Railroad. Battle Creek provided a safe haven for more than 1,000 runaway slaves in the 1840s and 1850s. Sojourner Truth, a vocal champion for abolition and women's rights, was the first person to bring fame to Battle Creek, her longtime home and final resting place.

Kalamazoo County was once the world's largest grower of celery, responsible for a national celery craze in the early part of this century, and is now a prosperous wine-producing region. Kalamazoo, recognized as a center for art and music, is the birthplace of

Holland was settled in the mid-1800s by Dutch immigrants, and still retains the look and feel of a Netherlands town. Visitors especially like to visit in May, when Holland's famous tulips are in bloom. © Vito Palmisano/Tony Stone Images

Checker cabs and Gibson guitars. It is home to the research and production facilities of Pharmacia & Upjohn pharmaceutical company, manufacturer of Rogaine, Cortaid, and PediaCare. Benton Harbor is headquarters for Whirlpool, which not only produces major appliances, but also supplied the first meal eaten on the moon.

Grand Rapids is the economic and political hub of the region. Once synonymous with furniture production, the Grand Rapids area is now the nation's major manufacturer of office furniture and clocks, and the U.S. center for religious publishing. The city is the site of favorite son Gerald Ford's presidential museum and the home base of the Amway direct sales empire. The Dutch who settled this region established the town of Holland in 1847 and proceeded to turn their cultural heritage into big business. Holland's phenomenally popular Tulip Festival features millions of blooms in breathtaking displays throughout the community.

The South Haven area grows more blueberries than any other place in the world, but fruit is a secondary industry here. Beginning in the 1880s, Chicagoans led a tourist invasion that continues to this day. Luxury resorts and lakeside cottages mushroomed along the magnificent beaches, and folks from the Windy City still follow in the footsteps of Richard Daley and Al Capone, using "Michigan's Riviera" as a getaway.

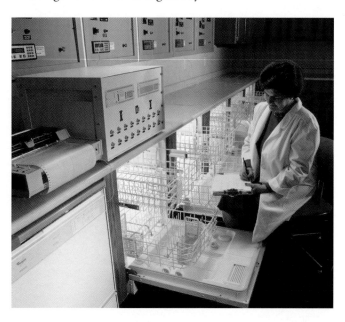

ABOVE: *A Whirlpool technician tests dishwashers. © Whirlpool Corporation.* BELOW: *The sun sinks into Lake Michigan, making a dreamscape of Grand Haven Pier. Grand Haven's beaches are among a few in the world where the sand "sings," giving off a musical whistle when walked on. © Terry Donnelly*

ABOVE: *South Haven straddles the mouth of the Black River on Lake Michigan. The maritime museum here chronicles the history of Great Lakes boating.* © Andre Jenny/International Stock. BELOW: *Michigan has more public beaches and more lighthouses than any other state. Here, Holland Harbor Lighthouse presides over the dunes.* © Terry Donnelly. OPPOSITE: *Holland's many attractions include a wooden shoe and delftware factory, tulip gardens, a local history museum, and a Dutch village with canals, gardens, and windmills.* © K. D. Dittlinger

OPPOSITE: *Grand Haven Pier's proud red lighthouses are a landmark for boats coming into its busy port. © Darryl R. Beers/Dembinsky Photo Associates.* ABOVE: La Grande Vitesse *sculpture in Grand Rapids' Vandenberg Center is Alexander Calder's tribute to the rapids that gave the city both its name and its start as a trading post in 1826. © Andre Jenny/International Stock.* BELOW: *This wood plaque hangs at Warner Vineyards in Paw Paw, reputed to be the Midwest's largest winery. © Greg Ryan–Sally Beyer*

CHAPTER FIVE
THE NORTHWEST
YEAR-ROUND PLAYGROUND

Proceeding north along the Lake Michigan shore, industry becomes noticeably scarcer as the summer homes and resorts grow more luxurious. This is the North Woods Gold Coast, where moneyed midwesterners have summered for more than a century.

SLEEPING BEAR DUNES NATIONAL LAKESHORE

An industrial belt, unique in character, extends across the southern edge of the region. Muskegon's magnificent Victorian mansions hint at its history as the lumbering center of western Michigan. Today the city's Brunswick factory makes most of the nation's bowling pins, which is appropriate since Michigan leads the country in registered bowlers. Shelby, north of Muskegon, is the world's largest manufacturer of synthetic diamonds, rubies, sapphires, and emeralds, gems identical to and in some ways better than those created by nature. Hush Puppies shoes come from Rockford. Tun-Dra Kennels, in the tiny and not particularly snowy town of Nunica near Grand Rapids, is the world's leading dogsled maker and a major distributor of arctic gear. Mount Pleasant is the state's center for gas and oil exploration, and Fremont is famous as the home of Gerber baby food.

North of this belt, the keyword is recreation. State and national forestlands stretch to Traverse Bay. Along Lake Michigan, thirty-five miles of towering sand dunes have been preserved as Sleeping Bear Dunes National Lakeshore, named for the Chippewa legend that tells of a mother bear and her two cubs who swam across Lake Michigan to escape a forest fire. Only the mother made it safely to land, and there she remains, a great dune waiting for her cubs, which became the Manitou islands a few miles offshore.

Traverse is cherry country, where more than two million trees produce 40 percent of the tart cherries grown in the United States. The climate and soil conditions that favor cherry growing proved perfect for grapes, too, so the Leelanau and Old Mission peninsulas are now home to a number of successful wineries. But fruit growers must vie with developers for the beautifully situated land, in high

The Hackley home is one of many Victorian estates built when Muskegon was the Lumber Queen of the World. Visitors can tour the site from Thanksgiving through December. © Layne Kennedy

44

ABOVE: *The Muskegon Harbor Lighthouse in Muskegon State Park endures the ravages of winter.* © Terry Donnelly. RIGHT: *The quaint town of Glen Arbor welcomes visitors to nearby Sleeping Bear Dunes National Lakeshore.* © Greg Ryan–Sally Beyer

demand for second and retirement homes. Beachcombers hunting Petoskeys, the mosaic-like fossil that is the state stone, once had long stretches of the northern Lake Michigan shoreline almost to themselves. Today upscale resort towns extend from Traverse City to the Mackinac Bridge. Old families such as the Fords and Gambles have been joined by newer basketball legends and rock stars who are snatching up the Queen Anne cottages or building sprawling modern residences here in Hemingway country. The Nobel Prize–winning author spent his first eighteen summers on Walloon Lake, the inspiration for his Nick Adams stories. In Petoskey he recovered from wounds suffered in World War I, and he married his first wife in Horton Bay. Hemingway might be hard-pressed to recognize his rustic paradise, today a land of championship golf courses, busy ski resorts, exclusive shopping districts, and million-dollar condos.

OPPOSITE: *Early morning fog obscures a corner of Lake Michigan near Empire.* ABOVE: *Ghost trees lie in the sand of Sleeping Bear Dunes National Lakeshore. Thousands of years ago, the dunes covered living forests, then moved on, leaving these bleached remains. Both photos © Greg Ryan–Sally Beyer.* BELOW: *The Big Sable River feeds Hamlin Lake in Ludington State Park. Here, fishermen at Hamlin Dam take advantage of the annual salmon run. Salmon also can be caught in nearby Lake Michigan. © Layne Kennedy*

ABOVE LEFT: *Sunlight plays on the candles at The Candle Factory in Traverse City. © Layne Kennedy.* ABOVE RIGHT: *Most of the fresh fruits and vegetables used to make Gerber baby food are grown right here in Michigan. © Gerber Products Company.* BELOW: *This farm is typical of the sights in Leelanau County, a pastoral peninsula surrounded by popular water resorts. © Terry Donnelly*

ABOVE: *The village of Leland is flanked by Lake Michigan on the west and Lake Leelanau on the east, making it an ideal place to catch a fishing boat or lake cruise. © Andre Jenny/International Stock.* BELOW: *The Lyman Building in Manistee contains historical exhibits that include the interior of an 1870 drugstore and general store, Civil War displays, and pioneer mementos. © SuperStock*

CHAPTER SIX
THE NORTHEAST
THUMBS UP FOR THE SUNSHINE COAST

FARMING

Cross Interstate 75 and prices drop, population thins, and visitors can get a clearer sense of what Michigan was like before cars and cash. From the "Thumb" north along the Sunshine Coast of Lake Huron there is less development than on the Lake Michigan side of the state. While the northwest is trendy, the northeast is low-key and unpretentious. Here life centers on a simpler appreciation of the great outdoors.

Industry is important in the area. Huge automotive parts plants and a gray iron foundry, all part of General Motors, are located in Saginaw. Dow Chemical was founded in Midland in 1897 and remains the backbone of the city. Alpena is home to the world's largest cement plant as well as the world's leading producer of machinery for making concrete blocks. The world's largest limestone quarry operates in Rogers City, whose port is always busy with freighters loading limestone for delivery worldwide.

Despite these pockets of industry, the northeast remains distinctly rural. For more than fifty years the area played an important role in the Michigan timber boom. Bay City alone once boasted thirty-two sawmills. But by 1880 the trees were largely gone, and a devastating 1881 fire in the Thumb area finished the job. The first emergency aided by the newly formed American Red Cross, the fire left 15,000 people without homes. Fortunately, this tragedy had some unexpectedly positive consequences. Burned-off forestland proved an excellent growing environment for beans, potatoes, and sugar beets, three crops which make the Saginaw Valley one of the most important agricultural areas in the nation today.

While ending one chapter of Michigan history, the great forest fire exposed another: a twenty-by-forty-foot piece of sandstone engraved with more than one hundred Native American carvings dating back perhaps 10,000 years. Located on the banks of the Cass River in Sanilac County, these carvings of birds, animals, and humans, done by ancient artists using stones, bones, and antlers, are the only known set of prehistoric Native American carvings in Michigan.

The Thumb forest fire had a third happy result. It inspired the establishment of the Huron

Bavarian missionaries established Frankenmuth in 1845. Other Germans followed, and Frankenmuth retains its cultural heritage through its architecture and annual events such as the Bavarian festival shown here. © Gary Bublitz/Dembinsky Photo Associates

National Forest in 1909, the first step in reversing the damage done by lumbering. Today the upper northeast is covered with state and national forests, which offer four seasons of recreation to those serious about finding their fun outdoors, be it boating, canoeing, fishing, hunting, camping, birdwatching, skiing, snowmobiling, or golfing.

The northeast offers all manner of adventures. In Grayling, the daring can plunge 3,000 feet at speeds of up to 100 miles an hour on the state's longest toboggan run. This rustic river town is the starting point for the Au Sable International Canoe Marathon, a 240-mile test called the toughest in the country. Birdwatchers flock to the region in May and June to catch a glimpse of the endangered Kirtland warbler. The tiny, yellow-breasted bird winters in the Bahamas but will breed only in the young Jack pines around Grayling and Mio.

Alpena County is a center for sports such as boating, diving, fishing, snowmobiling, cross-country skiing, and hunting. Shown here is a stretch of beach in Negwegon State Park.
© Darryl R. Beers/Dembinsky Photo Associates

Divers can explore eighty shipwrecks in the 288 square miles of protected water in the Thunder Bay Underwater Preserve off Alpena. Fifty acres, just about all that's left of the virgin white pine forests that once covered the state, are preserved in Hartwick Pines State Park. Colonial Michilimackinac in Mackinaw City is the oldest ongoing archaeological site in the United States. Since 1959 archaeologists have excavated millions of artifacts and the foundations of the stockaded fur-trading post, restored and reconstructed to the mid-1700s. Costumed interpreters answer visitors' questions in the fort and in the Native American encampment outside the palisades, brought to life by members of Michigan tribes.

OPPOSITE: *Ice fishermen steal a few more minutes on the Saginaw River, aided by the sunset's fiery mirrored glow.* © Gary Bublitz/Dembinsky Photo Associates. ABOVE: *A father helps his children get ready to cast off in Grayling.* © Mark E. Gibson/Midwestock. BELOW LEFT: *This Native American archer was carved into the Cass Riverbank some 10,000 years ago.* © Scot Stewart. BELOW RIGHT: *A researcher studies a specimen at Midland-based Dow Chemical Company, the world's fifth-largest chemical firm.* © Gary Bublitz/Dembinsky Photo Associates

CHAPTER SEVEN
THE UPPER PENINSULA
ON THE SHORES OF GITCHEE GUMEE

The "Mighty Mac," the world's longest suspension bridge, closes the land gap between the Upper and Lower Peninsulas, but now and then Yoopers still talk about forming their own state and calling it Superior. After all, the U.P. is a different bioregion than its lower sibling, and much of it is in a different time zone. It's a long way, both geographically and in character, from Detroit and Lansing where most of the state's power is flexed. And U.P. residents believe that, in most ways, their region is better.

Life in the Upper Peninsula is a step back in time—simpler, more relaxed, free from urban stress. This is the land of Hiawatha, where the Lake Superior vistas—Longfellow's Gitchee Gumee—are largely unchanged since the days of the legendary brave. Forests still cover more than 90 percent of the land. Water is clean, air is pure, and the Milky Way and northern lights are fixtures in the night sky. The copper-rich rocks near Houghton, responsible for the U.P.'s short-lived population explosion in the late 1800s, are among the earth's oldest rock formations. The deer, bears, coyotes, porcupines, bobcats, beavers, owls, and eagles survived the copper, iron, and timber booms and continue to share the peninsula with its 300,000 permanent human residents.

MACKINAC BRIDGE

PICTURED ROCKS NATIONAL LAKESHORE

Finns are the dominant ethnic group in the western U.P., a rugged land whose ancient mountains once towered higher than the Rockies and formed the core of the first American continent. Mining is still important here, and the earth produces enough gemstones and agates to make the area a national destination for rock hounds. French remains the major ethnic influence in the flatter east, a fishing and logging region. The east and west are divided by the Au Train basin, a series of lakes and streams through which, geologists believe, Lake Superior once emptied into Lake Michigan.

Logging continues to be an important industry. U.P. timber is shipped throughout the country year-round. Three large paper mills operate in the region, and nearly all the bird's-eye maple flooring played on by the National Basketball Association comes from Ishpeming. The Soo Locks make shipping another major segment of the economy. But the locks are a bigger tourist attraction than they are an employer. Tourism is what brings the most dollars over the Mackinac Bridge.

Its throngs of visitors consider Mackinac Island, a short boat ride from Saint Ignace, to be Michigan's crown jewel. The picturesque island is a snapshot of an earlier era: The mansions are Victorian, cars are banned, and the air is scented with fudge. (The Christopher Reeve/Jane Seymour romance *Somewhere in Time* was filmed here.)

Sault Sainte Marie is Michigan's oldest city, first visited by Europeans in 1618 and settled as a mission by Father Jacques Marquette in 1668. Today its Kewadin Casino is the U.P.'s biggest employer—an entertainment, lodging, and cultural complex that sets the standard for Native American casinos.

Pictured Rocks, fifteen miles of multicolored, multishaped cliffs rising up to 200 feet above Lake Superior, was designated as America's first National Lakeshore. Remote and pristine Isle Royale, accessible only by boat or floatplane, is the least visited National Park in the lower forty-eight, receiving fewer visitors in a year than Yellowstone gets in a day, and cherished by nature lovers for just that reason.

ABOVE: *Eagle Harbor Lighthouse sits high above Lake Superior.* © *Greg Ryan–Sally Beyer.* RIGHT: *Remote, tranquil Isle Royale beckons like a mirage on the water.* © *Bob Firth/Firth Photobank*

Opposite: *This black bear cub shares the forests of the U.P. with timber wolves, white-tailed deer, moose, and other wildlife.* © *Sharon Cummings/Dembinsky Photo Associates.* Above: *No motor vehicles are allowed at the Grand Hotel or anywhere else on Mackinac Island.* © *Layne Kennedy.* Below: *Ontonagon was home to Finnish settlers and copper miners.* © *Bob Firth/Firth Photobank*

A World of Possibilities

From the economic behemoth that is southeast Michigan, to the vestige of American wilderness that is the Upper Peninsula, Michigan's rich diversity offers something for everyone. An anonymous poem in the 13 February 1881 edition of the *Detroit Post and Tribune* summed it up:

> MY EASTERN FRIENDS WHO WISH TO FIND
> A COUNTRY THAT WILL SUIT YOUR MIND,
> WHERE COMFORTS ALL ARE NEAR AT HAND,
> HAD BETTER COME TO MICHIGAN.

LEFT: *This chick is a resident of Isle Royale National Park. The boy is just visiting.* © *Bob Firth/Firth Photobank.* BELOW: *The Ontonagon River's Bond Falls wear a winter veil of snow.* © *John P. George.* OPPOSITE: *Pictured Rocks National Lakeshore juts into Lake Superior.* © *Claudia Adams/Dembinsky Photo Associates*

A CENTURY OF PROGRESS

PART THREE

Less than two decades into statehood Michigan saw a copper and iron ore boom unequaled in the world and, at the same time, became the country's biggest logging state. Materials and infrastructure from these industries led to a third economic explosion—the automobile industry.

While the automobile shaped the history of Michigan and the world, the Great Lakes State's other natural resources ensured its prominence in a broad range of industries and helped create one of the greatest industrial complexes ever developed.

But Michigan's most valuable natural resource has always been its people. Dreamers, laborers, entrepreneurs, and artists from a hundred different ethnic groups came to farm the land, cut the trees, work the mines, and build the cars. They invented corn flakes, baby food, and carpet sweepers. They cured diseases, won Nobel Prizes, and went into space.

Michigan companies head up the Fortune 500. General Motors and Ford have long held the first two slots, with DaimlerChrysler, Kmart, Dow Chemical, Whirlpool, and Kellogg also prominent. Many other Michigan names—La-Z-Boy, Gerber, Jiffy, Baker, Hush Puppies, Simplicity—loom just as large in national name recognition.

Now, thanks to support from state government, financial institutions, industry, and major universities, Michigan is also a leader in robotics, computer technology, and medical research. Tax incentives, assistance with site location and development, academic research, employee recruitment and training, and enthusiastic marketing efforts have positioned Michigan for a new future of growth and prosperity.

Detroit's skyline glimmers across the Detroit River from Windsor, Ontario. The two cities have benefited from their proximity and helped foster a bustling trade between their two countries. © James Blank

© Corbis-Bettmann

FORD
1906/MODEL N

© Corbis-Bettmann

PACKARD
1899

© Corbis-Bettmann

DUESENBERG
1932/S.J.

CHEVROLET
1955/BEL AIR

© Corbis-Bettmann–UPI

© Corbis-Bettmann

OLDSMOBILE
1970/CUTLASS "S" HOLIDAY COUPE

SPECIAL FEATURE
MICHIGAN'S AUTOMOTIVE INDUSTRY

Perched atop the Fortune 500, General Motors has long reigned as the world's largest corporation. With Ford in Fortune's number-two slot, and newly formed DaimlerChrysler not far behind, Detroit dominates international commerce and industry. Michigan automakers produce 65 percent of the cars driven in the United States, and more than a third of all the automobiles in the world, exporting their products to more than 100 countries. Today one million people in the United States are employed in some phase of the automobile industry, which sprouted in the sheds of Michigan tinkerers and dreamers, and grew to change the face of the world.

© Gilles Mingasson

BUICK
1999/CIELO CONCEPT CAR

© General
Motors Corporation,
used with permission of
GM Media Archives

GENERAL MOTORS
1997/EV1 (ELECTRIC)

© Gilles Mingasson

FORD
1999/THUNDERBIRD

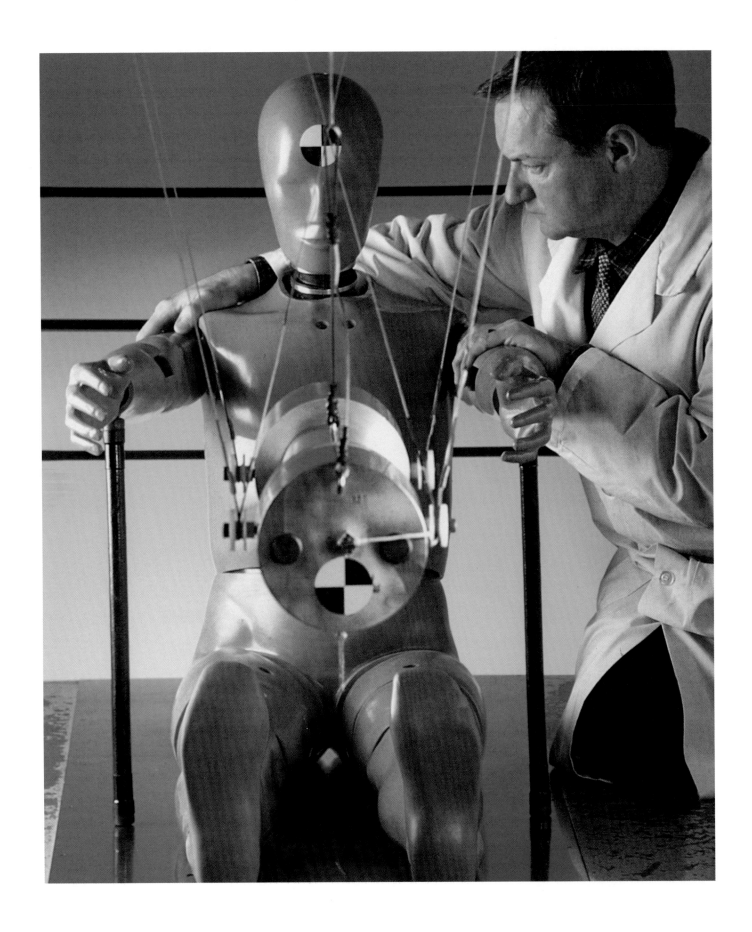

PUTTING THE WORLD ON WHEELS

CHAPTER EIGHT

HOW DID A MEDIUM-SIZED CITY IN AMERICA'S HEARTLAND BECOME THE GLOBAL CENTER OF THE TWENTIETH CENTURY'S MOST IMPORTANT INDUSTRY? THE SHORT ANSWER IS EXCELLENT LOCATION ON MAJOR SHIPPING AND RAIL LINES, A CONFLUENCE OF TALENT AND EXPERIENCE IN A VARIETY OF INDUSTRIES, AND THE PRESENCE OF DISTINCTIVE PERSONALITIES THAT COMBINED GENIUS WITH PERSEVERANCE. BUT THAT WOULD BE SKIPPING THE GOOD PARTS.

DETROIT'S PIONEERS

By 1900 southeast Michigan's lively manufacturing scene was uniquely suited to give birth to a new industry. In addition to its preeminence in stove manufacturing, Detroit led the nation in railroad car production. Flint had earned the title "Vehicle City" for the carriages, wagons, and buggies made there of fine Michigan hardwood. Bay City produced bicycles. Detroit Drydock Company made some of the world's largest marine steam engines, and Detroit's were among the busiest shipyards in the country, spurring the growth of local metalworks and paint and varnish companies.

Europe got the jump on America in the earliest development of self-propelled road vehicles, with France's auto industry predating America's by almost twenty years. But European and East Coast American auto experimenters got sidetracked with steam and battery-powered engines. What landed the automobile industry firmly and permanently in Michigan was

the determination by auto pioneers here—and particularly Ransom E. Olds—that the gasoline engine was the only way to go.

Olds built a steam-driven auto in 1886 and tested it on Lansing streets. But that same year his family started a gasoline engine business, and, by 1895, Olds was producing gasoline-driven cars for sale. The Olds Runabout was the first car that could be counted on to climb hills, which made it the country's best-selling auto from 1901 to 1907. From that time on, America's top-selling cars have always come from Michigan companies.

With the success of the Runabout, car companies sprouted in and around southeast Michigan like mushrooms, an incredible 1,100 in the first two decades of the industry. An estimated 2,500 different car brands have been manufactured in the United States. Most of them are extinct—now unfamiliar names such as the Saxon, the Flanders, the Abbott, the

OPPOSITE: *Crash test dummies have helped make safer cars. Michigan "firsts" include the first test dummy to become the government and industry standard (1972), the first child-size test dummy (1982), the first test dummy with a breakable abdomen to simulate pregnancy (1989), and the first side-impact test dummy (1989). © Richard Hirneisen.* ABOVE: *This photo was taken shortly after Henry Ford first drove his "Quadricycle" down the streets of Detroit on 4 June 1896. Courtesy, Henry Ford Museum & Greenfield Village and Ford Motor Company*

NO MORE CRANKS

history was his revolutionary application of mass production techniques. The world's first moving assembly line went into operation at the Ford Highland Park plant in 1913. Now instead of each worker building a car from the ground up, the worker stood in one place and performed one task as the cars went by on a conveyor belt. Production time for a single car dropped from twelve hours and eight minutes to one hour and thirty-three minutes. Ford bought the land for the mammoth Rouge River Complex in 1915, and by the 1920s the Dearborn plant was the world's largest manufacturing facility. It was also the world's first vertically integrated factory: iron ore was delivered by ship into one end, cars rolled off the assembly line at the other. More than 100,000 workers from all over the United States, Europe, and the Middle East came to work for Ford, who hired a crew of linguists to convey instructions to a workforce that spoke ten languages

LEFT: *Walter P. Chrysler poses with the first Plymouth in 1932.* © Baldwin H. Ward/Corbis-Bettmann. BELOW: *In 1922 William C. Durant, then president of Durant Motors, shows off his company's offering, the Star, which sold for $348.* © UPI/Corbis-Bettmann

Cartocar, the Randolph, the Earl. But the companies that did survive created many millionaires and one notable billionaire, Henry Ford.

By day the young Henry Ford was a chief engineer at what later became the Detroit Edison Company. By night he worked on a gas-powered "Quadricycle" in an old coal shed behind his home in what is now downtown Detroit. When his vehicle was ready for a test drive on 4 June 1896, it was too wide for the door. Ford broke out part of the brick wall with an ax and drove his liberated creation on a successful trial run. Seven years of fine-tuning followed. In June 1903 Ford was ready to put a car into production and formed the Ford Motor Company, which began producing the Model A. Five years later he introduced the Model T. Lightweight, durable, and affordable, the "Tin Lizzie" dominated the car market for the next nineteen years, with more than fifteen million sold around the world.

Along with making car ownership possible for the average American, Ford's most enduring contribution to

and fifteen dialects. By the late 1920s, fifty languages reputedly were spoken in south Dearborn's elementary school. The face of Michigan had changed forever.

Henry Ford became one of America's first billionaires, but he did not end up with the biggest car company. That distinction went to Flint's William C. Durant. Unlike Ford, who earned a place in the Inventors Hall of Fame for his patents on transmission mechanisms, Billy

Durant had no idea how to build a car, but he was a genius at building a business. Durant was the first to comprehend the volume of production that would be required to satisfy public demand for cars. He used profits from his hugely successful carriage firm to buy first Buick, then thirty other existing auto companies including Oldsmobile,

The moving assembly line has come a long way from its 1913 origins. ABOVE LEFT: Model T engines are lowered into place with a heavy chain. ABOVE RIGHT: Workers inspect the final product at Ford Motor Company in 1954. © Lambert/Archives Photos. LEFT: Late 1990s car bodies go through a robot welding line. © Michael Rosenfeld/Tony Stone Images

Pontiac (then called Oakland), and Cadillac. In 1908 he chartered General Motors Corporation. When his wildcat business methods got him temporarily ousted from GM, Durant appropriated the former Buick race car driver Louis Chevrolet's name and founded a new car company whose success allowed him to regain control of General Motors. In 1955 General Motors earned more than one billion dollars, the first American corporation to do so in a single year. The administrative structure developed by GM President Alfred P. Sloan Jr. in the 1920s to run the giant automaker came to be the corporate model.

By 1920 America's roads were improving, and people wanted something more from their cars than mere durability. Sloan came up with the idea of bringing out new car models every year, a radical departure from Ford, whose company produced the same car for nineteen years. Niles natives Horace and John Dodge introduced the first all-steel body, then other innovations including the sprayed-on lacquer finish and the one-piece windshield. Walter Chrysler, an ex-GM executive, founded Chrysler

Corporation, then bought Dodge in 1928. At that time the Big Three produced 75 percent of the nation's cars, a hegemony reduced by only ten percentage points today. In 1954 Hudson and Nash merged to form American Motors, which was acquired by Chrysler in 1987.

CHANGING THE WORLD

No invention had a greater impact on daily life in the twentieth century than the automobile. In an astonishingly short time, the car went from being a costly toy for the rich to a necessity for everybody. Thousands of miles of roads

COOL RUNNING

DETROIT'S PACKARD MOTOR CAR COMPANY INTRODUCED AUTOMOBILE AIR-CONDITIONING IN 1939. OTHER PACKARD INNOVATIONS INCLUDED FORCED-FEED LUBRICATION (1913), AMERICA'S FIRST TWELVE-CYLINDER CAR (1915), HYPOID GEARS (1926), AND "ECONO-DRIVE" (1938).

in hundreds of automotive suppliers also locating in Michigan. The area is home to the corporate headquarters for most of the world's largest makers of automotive modules, electronics, thermal and lighting systems, seating, brakes, wipers, and the hundreds of other parts necessary to make a car. Of the million people currently employed in the U.S. auto industry, more than half (55 percent) work for auto suppliers.

were constructed, leading to the proliferation of suburbs, a uniquely American form of urban planning. The automobile industry raised the national pay scale and, along with it, Americans' standard of living. Customs and mores changed as people became more mobile, less rooted. Cars created the family vacation and thus the tourism industry. They inspired drive-ins, fast food, and a whole new sport—speed racing. Early on the auto industry dominated the stock market and gave birth to thousands of new supply and service industries. The growth of the auto industry around Detroit inevitably resulted

Auto components, such as the car lights being examined here, account for more than half of auto industry employment. Most of the world's top suppliers are based in Michigan. © HMS Images

The strong presence of organized labor in Michigan is another offshoot of the auto industry's dominance here, and names such as Reuther and Hoffa are as much a part of Michigan history as Ford and Durant. Michigan played a crucial role in improving the lot of the working man and woman. In 1914 Henry Ford stunned the world by instituting the five-dollar day. When the average American earned pennies an hour for ten- to twelve-hour shifts, Ford increased his employees' pay and reduced the work day to eight hours because he wanted the person

A CLASSIC IS BORN

AMERICA'S FIRST TRUE PRODUCTION SPORTS CAR, THE CHEVROLET CORVETTE, DISTINGUISHED BY ITS PLASTIC-LAMINATED FIBERGLASS BODY, ROLLED OFF THE FLINT ASSEMBLY LINE IN JUNE 1953 WITH A PRICETAG OF $3,250.

the city and then beyond, eventually affecting 150,000 workers at sixty plants in fourteen states. This groundbreaking 1936–1937 strike, under Walter P. Reuther's leadership, is recognized today as the birth of the modern labor movement. The forty-four-day ordeal ended when GM recognized the UAW, and that union, headquartered in Detroit, remains a force in the state to this day.

CREATING THE FUTURE

The unions' influence on the auto industry is lessening as the number of blue-collar jobs grows at a slower rate than that of white-collar jobs. Today less than 20 percent of Michigan's 3.6 million private sector employees are unionized; a third of that 20 percent work for auto companies. Computer technology and automation in the factories, and a new philosophy of globalization in the boardrooms, are transforming the automobile industry for the twenty-first century.

Chrysler's 1998 merger with Daimler-Benz has created the world's fifth-largest-selling car manufacturer, behind General Motors, Ford, Toyota, and Volkswagen.

who made the cars to be able to afford to buy one.

But the depression of the late 1920s and early 1930s hit the auto industry and its workers hard. Car production went down by one-fifth. By 1933 half of Michigan's manufacturing workforce was out of a job.

The United Auto Workers organized in 1935 and almost immediately set its sights on industry leader General Motors. On 30 December 1936 a rumor flew through Flint's Fisher Body Plant Number One that some of its dies were being sent to other sites where unions were weaker, effectively stealing work from Flint employees. A spontaneous sit-down strike resulted, spreading first to other GM plants in

Consumer products once discarded now are recycled as new parts for Ford cars and trucks. Courtesy, Ford Motor Company

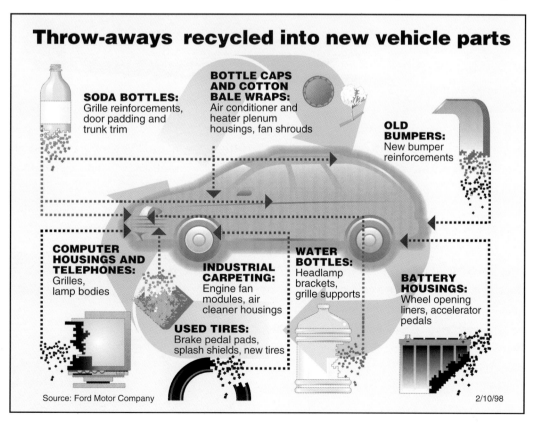

Throw-aways recycled into new vehicle parts

SODA BOTTLES: Grille reinforcements, door padding and trunk trim

BOTTLE CAPS AND COTTON BALE WRAPS: Air conditioner and heater plenum housings, fan shrouds

OLD BUMPERS: New bumper reinforcements

COMPUTER HOUSINGS AND TELEPHONES: Grilles, lamp bodies

INDUSTRIAL CARPETING: Engine fan modules, air cleaner housings

USED TIRES: Brake pedal pads, splash shields, new tires

WATER BOTTLES: Headlamp brackets, grille supports

BATTERY HOUSINGS: Wheel opening liners, accelerator pedals

Source: Ford Motor Company

2/10/98

WHEN DUTY CALLED

In terms of revenues, the new company ranks an even more impressive third. DaimlerChrysler AG maintains two headquarters, one in the Detroit suburb of Auburn Hills, the other in Stuttgart, Germany.

GM has made major investments in plants in Argentina, Brazil, China, Poland, and Thailand, while also committing to investing $21 billion in its United States operations—including Michigan—through 2003. In 1983 GM formed Saturn, the corporation's first new-car company since Chevrolet. Touted as "a different kind of car company," Saturn stresses democratic business management practices and a focus on customer satisfaction including no-haggle pricing and a money-back guarantee. Saturn's cutting-edge manufacturing facility is located in Tennessee, but the parent corporation remains firmly rooted in

Michigan. In 1998 General Motors centralized its division offices in its new world headquarters at the Renaissance Center overlooking the Detroit River.

GM, Ford, and DaimlerChrysler also are allocating significant resources toward addressing the challenges of the twenty-first century. Experimentation with alternate energy sources has resulted in a host of new vehicles that could become long-term alternatives to today's internal combustion engine cars. General Motors' EV1 is the world's first modern production electric car. The odorless, noiseless, and emission-free vehicle is currently available for lease through Saturn dealerships in several states. Ford and DaimlerChrysler are developing "hybrid electrics"—cars that combine two power sources. Ford's production electric vehicle, the Ranger electric pickup, already is available for sale throughout the United States. Ford also sells cars and trucks fueled by natural gas, propane, and ethanol. The company's natural gas vehicles are among the cleanest in the world. DaimlerChrysler's Dodge Intrepid ESX2 features a diesel-electric engine while Ford's Synergy 2010 will have a combustion engine, an electric battery, and a

FROM TOP: *In 1999 Saturn presented the SC2, the world's first three-door coupe. Courtesy, Saturn. Ford's first Mustang, the 1964 1/2, was introduced in April 1964: 100,000 sold in 100 days. Courtesy, Ford Motor Company. Ford's Synergy 2010 concept car explores futuristic technology and design ideas. Courtesy, Ford Motor Company and Wieck Photo DataBase, Inc. The 1953 Chevrolet Corvette Convertible Coupe was the first in a long line of Corvettes. © General Motors Corporation, used with permission of GM Media Archives*

LEFT: *The Jeep was the forerunner of all modern sport utility vehicles. Shown here, a new Jeep Cherokee rolls off the assembly line at DaimlerChrysler's Detroit plant. © Dennis Cox/D. E. Cox Photo Library.* BELOW: *There was only one two-seater Thunderbird made after this 1957 model until Ford unveiled a new Thunderbird concept car in 1999. Courtesy, Ford Motor Company*

flywheel. All these vehicles share the advantage of being less dependent on fossil fuels and easy on the environment.

Environmental awareness is a key feature of today's auto industry. Keep America Beautiful's 1998 "Vision for America" award went to Ford Motor Company, whose Sheldon Road plant in Plymouth uses at least 25 percent post-consumer recycled materials in all parts manufactured there. A General Motors research scientist is program manager for the National Automated Highway Systems Consortium. Made up of nine core participants including GM, Hughes Aircraft, the California Department of Transportation, and Carnegie Mellon University, the consortium believes that a future with "hands-free" driving would reduce traffic accidents and congestion, conserve energy, and make driving more relaxing and enjoyable—the way the auto pioneers meant it to be.

The year 1998 marked the U.S. auto industry's fifth fifteen million–unit year in a row. Having weathered dramatic growth and change in its first century, the Motor City is well prepared for the next. It's a safe bet that cars will continue to drive Michigan's economy into a bright future.

DON'T TRY THIS AT HOME

THE BLACK LAKE, PART OF GENERAL MOTORS' MILFORD PROVING GROUNDS, IS A PIECE OF ASPHALT THE SIZE OF FIFTY-NINE FOOTBALL FIELDS WHERE THE AUTO COMPANY PERFORMS HIGH-SPEED, STEERING, HANDLING, AND BRAKING TESTS. AT ONE TIME, CIA AND SECRET SERVICE AGENTS CAME TO THE BLACK LAKE FOR TRAINING IN EVASIVE DRIVING TECHNIQUES. ACCORDING TO GM LEGEND, THE GREAT WALL OF CHINA AND THE BLACK LAKE ARE THE ONLY MAN-MADE STRUCTURES THAT CAN BE SEEN FROM OUTER SPACE.

An engineer monitors the results of a wind tunnel test. © Michael Rosenfeld/Tony Stone Images

AUTOMOTIVE PRODUCTION
AND RESEARCH

FORD MOTOR COMPANY

Ford Motor Company will celebrate its one-hundredth anniversary in 2003 with a visionary goal for the new millennium: to be the world's leading consumer company that provides automotive products and services. Henry Ford began the twentieth century envisioning products for a society primed for personal freedom and mobility. He left a legacy of dedication to quality, value, innovation, environmental stewardship, and the betterment of society. Ford Motor Company continues that legacy as a worldwide enterprise serving the global family.

Ford is committed to quality and to caring for its customers and communities. Global production figures show that Ford is the world's largest manufacturer of trucks and second-largest manufacturer of vehicles, with approximately 350,000 employees in plants, offices, and laboratories around the world. Ford produces Aston Martin, Ford, Jaguar, Lincoln, Mazda, and Mercury vehicles and has approximately 16,000 dealers to serve its customers in more than 200 countries and territories. Through its subsidiaries, Ford produces glass, plastics, and automotive components and is the world's largest provider of automotive financing and the world's largest leasing company for cars, trucks, and equipment.

Henry Ford dreamed of providing personal mobility for the masses. He completed his first car, the Quadricycle, in 1896 in a shed behind his home in Detroit. Ford Motor Company was incorporated on 17 June 1903 and sold its first production car that year. The Model T, manufactured from 1908 through 1927, made the automobile accessible to working families. In 1913 Henry Ford revolutionized automobile manufacturing with the moving assembly line, and in 1914 he helped create the modern economy with the eight-hour, five-dollar workday. These achievements reflect Ford Motor Company's concern for the larger community.

Henry Ford put the world on wheels, and his company has had a global perspective from the start. A year after its founding, Ford Motor Company was exporting cars to distant continents.

Henry Ford is pictured with a Model T in Buffalo, New York, in 1921. The Model T automobile was introduced by Ford on 1 October 1908, and in 1921 about one million Model T's were produced. Photo from the collections of Henry Ford Museum & Greenfield Village

Within a decade, there were Ford plants in Europe. Henry Ford's world view was to create technology that benefited the customers, the business, the environment, and the larger society. He once said, "Everything can be done better than it is being done." That focus on continuous improvement has earned Ford a reputation as an innovative company. In 1927 the Ford Rouge facility in Dearborn became the world's first fully vertically integrated manufacturing operation, turning raw materials into automobiles.

In 1928 Ford became the first automobile company to make safety glass standard equipment. The Ford commitment to technology for the benefit of people has made the company a leader in automotive safety and security features over the years. In 1993 Ford put dual air bags in most cars. In 1998 Ford had more vehicles with the highest United States government front-crash-test safety rating than any other automobile manufacturer.

TAKING CARE OF THE COMMUNITY

Social responsibility is a way of life at Ford. It means that factories and offices meet or exceed the toughest environmental-management standards. It means zero tolerance for harassment or discrimination of any kind. It means encouraging minority businesses and workforce diversity. It means developing cars and trucks that are cleaner, safer, and more fuel efficient. And it means supporting charitable and cultural activities that make meaningful improvements in the quality of life.

For example, Ford of Mexico and its dealers sponsor a program to build and maintain schools. In more than seventy communities in North America, Ford Academy of Manufacturing Science introduces high school students to the technology and economics of manufacturing. These programs continue the legacy of Henry Ford, who established a school for immigrant workers in 1914 and sponsored many other educational programs.

UAW-Ford employee Roberta Lackey and 2,500 coworkers at the Ford Motor Company Atlanta Assembly Plant, in Georgia, are proud of their quality record. The plant tied for the J. D. Power and Associates 1997 Platinum Worldwide Plant Quality Award and ranked highest in the world among facilities producing vehicles for the United States market. Photo from Ford Motor Company

Taking Care of the Earth

Henry Ford was far ahead of his time in promoting fuel efficiency, recycling, and prudent use of resources. He harnessed hydroelectric power, used a strong, lightweight steel, and processed soybeans into material for automotive parts. Today more than half of Ford's research laboratory budget is devoted to environmental projects. A significant portion of the average Ford car or truck sold in the United States or Europe is recyclable. In addition, used carpet, telephones, steel drums, and tires are recycled into parts for Ford cars and trucks. Ford goes beyond the requirements of the law and is a leader in offering low-emission vehicles. It has the broadest range of alternative-fuel vehicles (AFV) of any manufacturer and is a partner in developing AFV systems for cars, trucks, and buses. Ford is developing the P2000, a lightweight prototype family vehicle that will deliver up to three times the fuel economy of the typical car of the late 1990s. The company has a drivable, fuel cell–powered P2000 research car that emits only water vapor.

Ford was the world's first automobile manufacturer to certify all its manufacturing facilities worldwide to ISO 14001, the international standard of environmental-management systems. In 1996 Keep America Beautiful gave Ford its highest award and called the company a role model. Two years later, the organization gave Ford its Vision for America award for environmental leadership. Also in 1998, Ford adopted an environmental pledge: "Ford Motor Company is dedicated to providing ingenious environmental solutions that will position us as a leader in the automotive industry of the twenty-first century. Our actions will demonstrate that we care about preserving the environment for future generations."

Taking Care of the Customer

Ford's pledge is backed with technology. The company was a pioneer in the use of supercomputing for engineering analysis and simulation, and maintains one of the largest industrial supercomputer facilities in the world. Some crash test simulation calculations that take fifteen minutes using Ford's supercomputers would take 68 million years using paper and pen. Ford is creating a single computer language for designing, engineering, and manufacturing vehicles. A leading independent technology-analysis firm described Ford's initiative as the largest and most innovative computer-based technology transformation for design and engineering in corporate history. Ford teams worldwide will have instant access to the collective knowledge of the company, present and past, further enhancing efficiency and quality.

"Quality is Job One at Ford" and always will be: Ford and its employees are committed to building the finest cars and trucks in the world. A growing number of awards from J. D. Power and Associates underscores the success of Ford teamwork and quality processes. In 1998 Ford and UAW-Ford were the recipients of the first J. D. Power Chairman's Award to jointly recognize labor and management for cooperative efforts in quality improvement.

Spirit of Ford

The public can experience the excitement of Ford's vision for the future at the company's new high-tech, interactive visitor center in Dearborn—Spirit of Ford—and experience firsthand today's and tomorrow's vehicle design, engineering, testing, and manufacturing. During a virtual manufacturing tour, a visitor has the sensation of being a vehicle on the assembly line, with sparks flying and the sounds and smells of manufacturing in the air. On the virtual test track, people feel they are banking and turning and bumping along at breathtaking speed. Spirit of Ford is a tribute to the Ford heritage of finding new ways to enrich life on our planet. "Better Ideas. Driven By You." That's the philosophy of Ford Motor Company. That's the spirit of Ford.

DAIMLERCHRYSLER

On 17 November 1998 the largest industrial company in Europe, Daimler-Benz, and one of the most innovative automotive companies in America, Chrysler Corporation, merged to form the world's largest automotive, transportation, and services company, DaimlerChrysler.

An understanding of the North American roots of this new global firm begins with Chrysler Corporation's seventy-five-year history and the life of its founder, Walter P. Chrysler.

Walter Chrysler's career in the automobile industry started in 1912, when he joined the Buick Motor Car Company. Following an illustrious career with General Motors, he retired in 1919. But his retirement soon ended, with an opportunity to aid the ailing Maxwell Motor Car Company.

On 6 June 1925, under Walter Chrysler's leadership, Maxwell Motor Car became Chrysler Corporation. By 1926 the Highland Park, Michigan-based corporation had risen from fifty-seventh to fifth place in industry sales and boasted 3,800 dealers. In 1928 the Dodge brand joined the Chrysler family and the DeSoto and Plymouth lines were established.

Chrysler became known as the "engineering" company through landmark innovations like the famous "Hemi" V-8 engine. The high-powered Hemi sport version—the legendary 426 Hemi—powered the company's famous 1960s "muscle cars."

Chrysler Corporation set sales records in 1972 and 1973. But in the mid-1970s, gasoline shortages, high interest rates, severe inflation, and weakening consumer confidence hampered the company financially. In 1978 the former president of Ford Motor Company, Lee A. Iacocca, was hired

The DaimlerChrysler Technology Center and World Headquarters, located on approximately 500 acres in Auburn Hills, Michigan, was developed at a cost of $1.1 billion. With 4.5 million square feet, it is one of the largest all-under-one-roof facilities in the world.

as president of Chrysler and later became chairman. Iacocca applied his thirty-two years of experience with Ford to rejuvenate Chrysler's operations. Despite deep cost cuts, the company was forced to apply to the federal government for aid. In late 1979 the United States Congress passed the Chrysler Corporation Loan Guarantee Act, which President Carter signed into law on 7 January 1980, providing Chrysler with $1.5 billion in federal loan guarantees.

By 1981 Chrysler was able to introduce two new cars, the Dodge Aries and the Plymouth Reliant, also known as K-Cars, which led the company to profitability in 1982. In August 1983 Chrysler paid off the loan guarantees—seven years early—at a profit to the government of $350 million.

Then, in November 1983, Chrysler created a brand new automotive market segment—the minivan—with the production of the Dodge Caravan and the Plymouth Voyager. And in 1987 the company acquired the fourth-largest United States automobile maker, American Motors Corporation. This $800 million acquisition included the world-famous Jeep® brand.

To further product excellence, in 1991 Chrysler dedicated its new 3.5 million-square-foot

Walter P. Chrysler founded Chrysler Corporation in 1925.

Auburn Hills, Michigan, technology center to support cross-functional vehicle development work. Chrysler also completely restructured its operations to simultaneously reduce development time, promote efficiency, and improve quality: It created "platform teams"—vehicle development teams composed of expert workers from each primary department. The first vehicle to be developed by a platform team was the Dodge Viper, a V-10 roadster. This was followed in 1992 by the Jeep Grand Cherokee, as well as by a new line of family sedans, including the Chrysler Concorde and the Dodge Intrepid, with innovative cab-forward design, where the wheels are moved to the outermost corners of the car, providing increased space inside for passengers and cargo.

On 16 March 1992 Robert J. Eaton, formerly of GM Europe, was named vice chairman and chief operating officer, to become chairman and chief executive officer on 1 January 1993, following the retirement of Iacocca.

Chrysler reestablished itself in the pickup-truck market in 1994 with the introduction of the Dodge Ram pickup, which increased Dodge Truck's market share from 7 percent to more than 20 percent.

In 1996 the new Chrysler World Headquarters building, a fifteen-story, one million-square-foot office complex crowned by a two-story Pentastar, the corporate logo, was added on to the Chrysler Technology Center. Chrysler could then, under one roof, design, engineer, test, build, and evaluate new vehicles and develop marketing plans for its products. These facilities helped make Chrysler one of the lowest-production-cost, highest-profit-per-vehicle manufacturers in the industry.

Daimler-Benz chairman Juergen Schrempp and Chrysler Corporation chairman Bob Eaton signed the official merger agreement forming DaimlerChrysler on 7 May 1998 in London. Six months later DaimlerChrysler began trading publicly (NYSE:DCX).

Chrysler's future changed on 12 January 1998 when Eaton met with Daimler-Benz chairman, Juergen Schrempp, to discuss a possible merger between their two companies. The historic merger was announced on 7 May 1998. Six months later, DaimlerChrysler stock began trading publicly (NYSE:DCX).

With dual headquarters in Auburn Hills and in Stuttgart, Germany, DaimlerChrysler ranks third in the automotive industry in revenues—$154 billion in 1998, and fifth in vehicle sales—more than four million units in 1998.

DaimlerChrysler's automotive brands include Mercedes-Benz, Chrysler, Jeep, Dodge, Plymouth, and Smart. It also makes commercial vehicles, manufactures aircraft and equipment, and provides financial services as well as information technology, telecommunications, and media services. The company has more than 428,000 employees worldwide and sells its products in more than 200 nations.

DaimlerChrysler is committed to the communities in which its employees live and work and supports the arts, education, and community outreach programs. In 1997 the former Chrysler Corporation distributed more than $25 million in grants to qualified nonprofit organizations. It is DaimlerChrysler's goal to continue investing today to fulfill the hopes of tomorrow.

The Dodge Viper, introduced in 1992, was the first vehicle developed by Chrysler's innovative platform team concept. Viper's exclusive 8.0-liter V-10 engine is the largest and most powerful available in an American production sports car.

GENERAL MOTORS CORPORATION

General Motors is the world's largest company and the leading automotive company. The corporation has manufacturing operations in 50 countries and a presence in more than 190 countries. General Motors (GM) brands include Buick, Cadillac, Chevrolet, GMC, Oldsmobile, Pontiac, Saturn, Holden, Isuzu, Opel, Vauxhall, and Saab.

Having purchased the Renaissance Center in downtown Detroit in 1996—and infused more than $1 billion to update facilities and technology in the surrounding area—GM has strongly reaffirmed its commitment to southeastern Michigan.

By maintaining its global headquarters in Detroit, GM also has taken a leap toward improving internal communications and facilitating a strong corporate culture. Grouped together now in such locations as the Renaissance Center and GM's Technical Center in Warren, employees find that working near each other reinforces the corporate bond.

That bond began in 1908 when General Motors was founded. The company was the brainchild of Billy Durant, an entrepreneurial businessman with a penchant for acquisitions. From 1908 to 1910 Durant acquired twenty-five automotive companies and established what would someday be the world's largest corporation. He added fourteen more companies to the GM family later in the decade.

The Renaissance Center in Detroit will serve as GM's new world headquarters, where its corporate functions and key marketing divisions can be brought together in a single, consolidated administrative campus.

When Alfred Sloan assumed the presidency of General Motors in 1923, he brought much-valued managerial skills to the organization. Concerned with the size and independence of GM's many units, he decentralized operations but kept coordinated control—a model that became standard for many large companies. This strategy ensured GM's unrivaled growth and success for nearly five decades.

Decentralization and complexity spelled challenges for General Motors in the 1970s and 1980s, but today new and exciting strategies are enabling the automotive giant to leverage its unrivaled global resources. The creation of a single global automotive organization—GM Automotive—has positioned GM to take advantage of opportunities associated with the new

Dedicated in 1956, GM's Warren Technical Center is the world's largest automotive technical center. GM will invest nearly $1 billion to upgrade the center.

millennium. GM's new organization allows the company to respond quickly to local market needs throughout the world.

General Motors has a strong history of success that can be attributed to a keen understanding of its customers. The company listens to them, anticipates their needs, and develops technologies to address their desires. General Motors uses market research clinics to gain further understanding of its customers, and such clinics play a big part in shaping new products.

By focusing on product innovation, customer service, and continual implementation of new technology, General Motors ensures continued leadership in the world's automotive industry.

Being on the forefront of technology is nothing new for General Motors. The company has introduced new, innovative ideas since its inception. Electric lights premiered on the Oakland automobile, an early GM brand, as early as 1909, and the first engine starter made its debut on the 1912 Cadillac. General Motors introduced independent front-wheel suspension with its 1934 Cadillac and unveiled the automatic transmission with the 1940 Oldsmobile.

This heritage of innovation lives on today through continuous product development. Recent areas of research and production include increased energy efficiency and alternative-technology vehicles. The EV1 electric car, the world's first mass-produced electric vehicle, became available in California and Arizona in 1996 and has been well received. Work on turbine auxiliary propulsion units promises breakthroughs in fuel choice, efficiency, and lower emission levels.

General Motors also is on the forefront of expanding into fast-growing markets around the world. GM began "thinking global" as far back as 1924, when it assembled its first vehicle abroad, in Denmark. Today GM invests heavily in emerging markets, where vast potential exists—particularly for companies who come to these markets early. To that end, GM has five new state-of-the-art manufacturing facilities under development or

The GM building on Grand Boulevard in Detroit was the company's headquarters for more than seventy years.

up and running in Argentina, Brazil, China, Poland, and Thailand. GMAC Financial Services has new operations in Poland, Thailand, and Greece, and it has set up joint ventures in Mexico and Sweden.

GM sites across the globe make use of the Internet, satellite positioning, and advanced telecommunications to allow cross-cultural employee teams to collaborate interactively and expedite projects. For instance, a GM engineering team in Japan may work on a design and, at the end of the Tokyo workday, send it electronically to a team in Russelsheim, Germany, where Opel is based. The Opel team can forward the design on to Warren, Michigan, when the German workday concludes. Employees operate on a virtual clock that runs twenty-four hours a day and revolutionizes the design and development process.

GM has a passion to fulfill its vision, with a faith in the future shared by its employees around the world. Growth in new areas of the business and of the globe is imminent. New products and services are being driven by new approaches and ideas. GM continues to dazzle the world's population with exciting cars and trucks as it has for generations.

The Hamtramck plant complex covers 465 acres of land. The plant has a workforce of approximately 4,000 people who build three different world-class cars—the Cadillac Seville, Eldorado, and DeVille.

A worker monitors the manufacture of engine blocks at a steel casting shop. © SuperStock

AUTOMOTIVE SUPPLIES

FEDERAL-MOGUL CORPORATION

FEDERAL-MOGUL CORPORATION MANUFACTURES PRECISION AUTOMOTIVE COMPONENTS AND SYSTEMS TO SERVE ITS CUSTOMERS WORLDWIDE

Since 1899 Federal-Mogul Corporation has manufactured precision products for automotive and industrial applications. Headquartered in Southfield, Michigan, today Federal-Mogul is a $7 billion automotive parts manufacturer providing innovative solutions and systems to global customers in the automotive, light truck, heavy-duty, railroad, farm, and industrial markets.

Federal-Mogul is a fast-growing company leading the drive toward consolidation in the automobile industry. It is divided into three main operating units. The Powertrain Systems group manufactures engine bearings, large bearings, and piston products, ignition products, and connection rods. The Sealing Systems group makes dynamic seals, gaskets, heat shields, and noise and vibration sealing systems and wiper products. The General Products group manufactures camshafts, chassis products, friction products, fuel system components, heat transfer products, lighting products, sintered products, and systems-protection products.

At Federal-Mogul the emphasis is on supplying systems, not just components.

Powertrain Systems is an industry leader in the consolidation of precision engine parts into a systems offering for original equipment manufacturers (OEMs). With seventy-one manufacturing locations in twenty-one countries, Powertrain Systems has the global reach to provide customers with the design engineering, component manufacturing, and delivery of systems to meet their worldwide needs.

Sealing Systems has the ability to seal an entire powertrain—including

Richard Roberts, of Federal-Mogul's Skokie, Illinois, manufacturing facility, is involved in the production of cylinder head gaskets.

engine, transmission, and axle. Federal-Mogul has strategically assembled its sealing system operations on every continent where there is significant development and production of engines, transmissions, and axles. With thirty manufacturing facilities in twelve countries, Federal-Mogul is a supplier of choice.

General Products provides customer-oriented, technically focused solutions, principally for the automotive and commercial vehicle markets. Its products are supplied from eighty manufacturing locations in seventeen countries.

These precision products are developed and manufactured for many of the world's major OEMs. A relentless customer focus reverberates throughout all these divisions. Federal-Mogul works side by side with customers to provide custom-developed solutions uniquely suited to their needs. By working closely with OEMs from the concept and development phase through design, testing, and production, Federal-Mogul ensures maximum value for its customers. The company

Dick Snell is chairman and CEO of Federal-Mogul Corporation, with world headquarters in Southfield, Michigan.

also sells its products into the aftermarket, maintaining a worldwide network of distribution points to service aftermarket customers.

With more than 300 locations across six continents in twenty-four countries, Federal-Mogul has more than 56,000 employees worldwide.

Federal-Mogul is committed to providing customers with technologically advanced, high-quality systems, as well as advanced technology in components and processes. Its expertise in engineering and in research and development ensures that its latest technologies, processes, and materials provide solutions for customers. Real-time engineering capabilities and design development help Federal-Mogul meet its customers' demands.

Federal-Mogul significantly expanded its capabilities in 1998 following its acquisition of T&N, a $3 billion global manufacturer of pistons, piston rings, gaskets, and camshafts; Fel-Pro, a $500 million North American leader in gaskets; and most recently, Cooper Automotive, a global leader in brakes and friction products, lighting, chassis parts, ignition systems, and wiper blades.

"We are building on the strengths of the people and processes of our acquisitions to maximize synergies to best

Among Federal-Mogul's expansive replacement parts offerings are oil seals and engine bearings and bushing.

serve our customers," says Dick Snell, chairman and chief executive officer of Federal-Mogul. "We have positioned ourselves as the growth company leading the consolidation of systems and modules in engine parts and sealing systems. We now have the capacity to provide engine submodules and to seal entire engines and transmissions."

To fuel its growth strategy, the company has adopted a new company purpose: People Serving Customers Through Manufacturing Mastery. This approach has three critical elements. The first element is the company's acknowledgment that the talented and dedicated people of Federal-Mogul are responsible for its success. The second element is its relentless focus on the customer. The third element, manufacturing mastery, is what distinguishes Federal-Mogul as its customer's supplier of choice. This approach is a crucial element in a comprehensive restructuring plan designed to realign Federal-Mogul's future growth with its core competencies in precision auto parts manufacturing.

Federal-Mogul has had a long-standing commitment to being a good corporate citizen. The company supports a variety of activities to promote economic, intellectual, and social progress wherever Federal-Mogul maintains major operations. Federal-Mogul has allocated funds and resources for many charitable and civic activities. Throughout its organization, employees are encouraged to be concerned, involved citizens and to become active in community activities.

"This is a very challenging time for our entire organization and our employees are enthused about our new direction," Snell says. "We are excited about the future. What's the real secret to our success? It is our dedicated employees, who have embraced a continuous improvement culture. We have fantastic employees and I'm very proud of their efforts. Our manufacturing facilities combined with our people are Federal-Mogul's best assets."

Josephine Gass of Federal-Mogul's Sumter, South Carolina, manufacturing facility, performs the final inspection, wash, and packing of pistons.

PRINCE CORPORATION · A JOHNSON CONTROLS COMPANY

PRINCE CORPORATION, A JOHNSON CONTROLS COMPANY, SUPPLIES THE LEADING AUTOMAKERS WITH FINE INTERIOR PRODUCTS SO INNOVATIVE THEY OFTEN BECOME STANDARD EQUIPMENT

Prince Corporation invented its first automotive interior product—a sun visor with a lighted vanity mirror—for the 1973 Cadillac. That first product, which has become a standard item in most cars, was the springboard for Prince's growth from fewer than 100 employees to more than 5,000 today.

Since introducing its first product, Prince has created hundreds of other interior automotive innovations, including interior trim and storage; integrated lighting and electronics solutions; and wireless communications for the use of drivers and passengers. Today Prince is a full-service automotive supplier involved in all stages of product design, engineering, and manufacturing.

Prince has received numerous industry awards from major automakers for its commitment to quality. Its customers include every major automobile manufacturer in the world.

Prince's technical operations, along with its original manufacturing sites, are based in the United States. Over the years, Prince also has established several international sales and manufacturing locations.

The tremendous growth of the company can be attributed in large measure to its corporate culture of teamwork and innovation that embraces the universal values of honesty, integrity, and individual responsibility. These building blocks for success are based on the philosophy of Edgar Prince, a talented engineer and veteran of the machine-tool industry who founded the company in 1965. Prince believed in the importance of hard work, careful business management, and producing high-quality products.

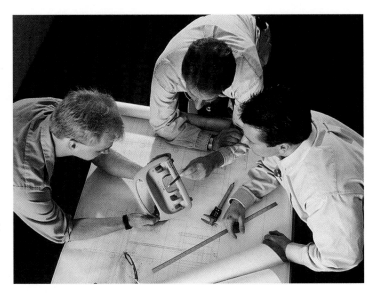

At Prince, innovation and creativity are a team effort. Designers, engineers, and technicians work together at every opportunity, across departments, to create products that "Delight the Customer!" © Prince Media Resources

Ed Prince also believed that the best way to motivate employees is to give them a sense of ownership. At Prince, open, informal communication creates a dynamic environment where people are free to share ideas.

Customer service is also a hallmark of the company's success. "The customer is the reason for our existence," says Prince CEO John Spoelhof. "Today our customers include automotive manufacturers all over the world. At Prince, we really enjoy going beyond satisfying our customers with our products and services; we call it 'delighting the customer.' Our relationships with our customers and suppliers are important to us. Helping them to be successful is an important measure of our success."

In 1996 Prince's automotive business was acquired by Johnson Controls, Inc., headquartered in Milwaukee, Wisconsin, and a global market leader in automotive systems and building controls. Prince is now part of the Johnson Controls Automotive Systems Group, Interior Systems and Trim products business unit. Through its Automotive Systems Group, it designs and produces seating and interior systems for automakers worldwide, and batteries for the

Edgar Prince (1931–1995) founded Prince Corporation in 1965.

original equipment and replacement markets. Founded in 1885, Johnson Controls operates in more than 500 locations around the world.

Elsa Prince, chair of the Prince board of directors, says, "This partnership with Johnson Controls was the perfect way to maintain the unique culture and community commitment that Ed Prince started in 1965. By joining forces with the Johnson Controls worldwide network of operations, we are continuing our global expansion. Johnson Controls provides great opportunity for our team members and promotes the continuance of the Prince tradition of trust, employee involvement, and community support."

Prince offers auto manufacturers three things: the development of exciting new product concepts that anticipate the next generation of consumer needs; the effective integration of those products into new vehicle designs; and the efficient manufacturing and delivery of those products. New product

The Edgar D. Prince Technical Campus is a 750,000-square-foot "Center of Excellence" for research, design, and engineering of automotive interior systems and trim products. © Prince Media Resources

development takes place at the Edgar D. Prince Technical Campus, a unique facility that has been designed to enhance every step in the product-development process. The 750,000-square-foot facility in Holland, Michigan, contains the personnel, development tools, laboratories, and testing and validation equipment required to take a product from concept to completion—all under one roof. It also includes a pilot plant to develop and test production equipment, so the production process can be debugged and readied for final production before moving to a manufacturing facility.

Today automakers are asking their key suppliers to take on a greater role in the development of new vehicles. One of the concepts of Prince and Johnson Controls is the vision of the "total occupant environment." Instead of building the interiors as a collection of individual systems and components, Prince intends to create a seamless, integrated environment that provides safety, comfort, convenience, and communication features.

"We strive to design, engineer, and manufacture world-class products that set the standard for quality and value," says Spoelhof. "At every level of the organization, we are committed to the success of our customers. We believe that personal integrity is the foundation of business success."

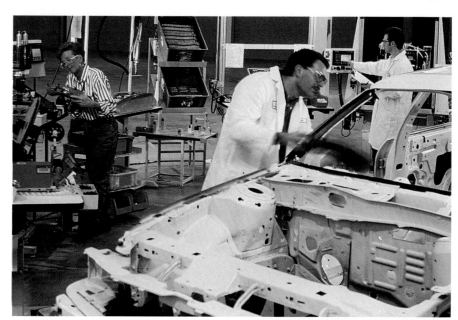

Production team members are trained and production processes are proven out in the pilot plant area before moving to the manufacturing plant. © Prince Media Resources

CREATIVE FOAM CORPORATION

One of North America's leading foam fabricators, Creative Foam Corporation designs and manufactures cellular and non-cellular foams and plastics for the automotive, material handling, and medical and leisure markets. Key ingredients in the company's success are innovative people, an abiding passion for quality, and unwavering commitment to the customer.

The Fenton, Michigan–based company started in 1969 with five factory employees, a clerk, and its founder, now chairman of the board, Peter T. Swallow. Creative Foam currently employs more than 600 people and operates three manufacturing plants and an engineering facility in Michigan and one plant in Indiana. Growing at a rate of 15 to 20 percent annually, sales are projected at $65 million for 1999.

Commenting on the thirty-year history and growth of his company, Swallow says, "I am most pleased with the excellent returns we have been able to provide both our original investors and employee stockholders. I am also pleased with the dedication of our managers, staff, and hourly workforce, and the win-win relationship we have established with our many customers. Our people have developed and implemented best-in-class production methods, quality systems, and engineering problem-solving techniques. I am truly optimistic about what the future holds for our company and our customers."

Goals set forth in Creative Foam's vision statement include the following: to be the leader in the nonintegrated fabricated and formed foam plastics industry; to provide the highest quality and the ultimate service; to be the leading innovator in product and process; to consistently deliver the highest value

Creative Foam Corporation was founded in Fenton, Michigan, where it continues to maintain corporate offices, an engineering and development center, and two manufacturing plants.

Creative Foam manufactures a wide range of coated foam products for the medical and leisure industries at its Bremen Corporation subsidiary in Indiana.

to customers; and to achieve above-normal return to shareholders. If customer satisfaction is any gauge of success, the company is well on its way to realizing these goals. Creative Foam has earned the highest ratings from General Motors, DaimlerChrysler, the Ford Motor Company, and leading tier-one suppliers. All Creative Foam production facilities have been ISO-9001, ISO-9002, or QS-9000 registered since 1996.

Creative Foam's three major divisions are the Automotive Components Team (ACT), the Special Products and Packaging Division (SPPD), and the Bremen Division. ACT develops and produces several applications in which Creative Foam is expert, including wind, dust, and water seals and acoustical absorbers and barriers (foam, nonwoven, or combinations), as well as products that are thermal insulated, vacuum formed and fusion molded. SPPD provides three-dimensional fusion-molded applications and material-handling products for OEMs and tier-one and tier-two suppliers.

Applications for Creative Foam's closed-cell materials include water or air barriers, shock absorbers, insulators, vibration dampeners, seals, and gaskets. These materials are available in a wide range of densities and polymer types, including chemically cross-linked polyethylene, metallocene polyethylene, EPDM, EVA, expanded polyethylene (non-cross-linked), irradiated cross-linked polyethylene, neoprene-blend rubber, polypropylene resilient molded bead (RMB), polyvinyl nitrile (PVN), PVC, PVN super soft, and silicone foam. Creative Foam's open-cell materials can be engineered to have very low compression-set characteristics. Available in a broad range of densities, open-cell foams include cast urethane, low-perm urethane, polyether urethane, polyester urethane, and reticulated urethane.

Creative Foam also fabricates a number of specialty products other than foam, including films, tapes, dense rubber products, dense barrier materials, and nonwoven fabrics, such as SoundZorb®. Formulated for outstanding acoustical absorption, SoundZorb provides a clean, cost-effective, odor-free, recyclable alternative to cotton shoddy. Automotive applications include acoustical absorbers for door panels, package trays, instrument panels, headliners, interior trim panels, flooring systems, and wheel wells.

Protective coatings on products for leisure use and the medical equipment industry are the specialty of Creative Foam's Bremen Division. Bremen's fabricated Cushioning Systems for the medical and health care professions, with easy-care, fully encapsulated polymer coatings, are available with or without an integrated base mounting board and have a range of applications that is almost unlimited. Bremen's medical products meet FDA 510(k) requirements and are eligible to carry the CE (Conformitée Européene) mark of conformity to European standards, for export to the European community. The Bremen Division's Sun Searcher® line of pool and spa products combines the comfort of

Creative Foam develops systems for returnable packaging and material handling made of foam and plastic for use in automotive applications.

Ensolite® foam with the convenience and durability of colorful, easy-to-clean polymer coatings. Sun Searcher's high-quality products include full-length unsinkable pool floats and pool chairs, commercial lifesaving aids, floating key chains and more.

Dedicated to satisfying customer needs from design to manufacture, Creative Foam offers complete product-development and prototyping capabilities, including CAD (computer-aided design) support. The company's manufacturing plants include tooling, fabrication, and molding facilities, while its Engineering and Development Center serves as a source of cutting-edge design solutions, complete with a certified testing laboratory. Creative Foam works with customers to provide for future as well as present needs.

Creative Foam exports products to the Americas, Europe, and the Far East. This expanding global reach has poised the company to explore establishing strategic alliances with similar companies on a global basis—the next step in satisfying the needs of its customers.

David Duthie has been with Creative Foam for eighteen years—the last seven as company president. When asked what the future holds for Creative Foam, Duthie replies, "We are a company that is young enough to be energetic but old enough to have learned from experience. We are small enough to be maneuverable but big enough to get the job done. In short, Creative Foam is well positioned in all of our key markets—automotive, material handling, medical, and sports and leisure—to help customers enter a whole new world in the twenty-first century."

Creative Foam is known in the automotive industry for its high-quality, innovative engineering solutions and for its enthusiastic employees, who are dedicated to supporting customer needs.

AMERICAN AXLE & MANUFACTURING

Truly an American success story, American Axle & Manufacturing (AAM) was formed in 1994 when Richard E. Dauch—now AAM's chairman, CEO, and president— and three investors purchased five plants that had previously comprised General Motors' driveline, propeller shaft, and forging unit. Dauch is the gifted and hardworking automotive executive credited by many industry experts with spearheading Chrysler's manufacturing renaissance during the 1980s and early 1990s. Under Dauch's experienced direction, AAM has combined an eighty-year tradition of driveline leadership with renewed corporate vision and commitment to global competitiveness. What GM spun off as unprofitable, AAM has upgraded, re-engineered, and spun into a solid, profitable business.

Headquartered in Detroit and led by a senior management team with more than 400 years of combined automotive manufacturing experience, AAM tallies annual revenues in excess of $2.5 billion and employs a workforce of approximately 11,000 associates. Product lines include rear axles, independent front axles, independent rear-drive systems (IRDS), TracRite™ differentials, propeller shafts, steering linkages, anti-roll systems, steering and suspension components, and forged and metal-formed products.

Today AAM operates eighteen facilities and offices in locations including Detroit, Rochester Hills, Oxford, Centerline, and Three Rivers, Michigan. Over the past five years, existing plants have been extensively modernized; production capacity has

American Axle & Manufacturing (AAM) established its corporate headquarters within its existing 2.3 million-square-foot manufacturing complex that straddles Detroit and Hamtramck at Holbrook Avenue and route I-75. The company repaired infrastructures, painted facilities, added greenery, and improved safety features and lighting throughout, which helped to create a safe, pleasant environment.

been expanded; and worker education, training, and skill-set development programs have been established and promoted. By 2000 the company will have spent more than $1.6 billion on development—an investment that promises to keep AAM products and customers competitive into the twenty-first century.

To its original five million square feet of plants and equipment, AAM has added a 60,000-square-foot paint and anticorrosion facility; a 15,000-square-foot prototype center where leading-edge products, processes, and systems are designed; and an 85,000-square-foot Technical Center complete with a metallurgical laboratory, product testing and validation facilities with driveline dynamometers, a noise-reduction testing facility, and an advanced manufacturing

AAM associates produce automotive propeller shafts and many other driveline systems and components at AAM's manufacturing facility in the town of Three Rivers, just south of Kalamazoo.

**AMERICAN
AXLE &
MANUFACTURING**

process-development and testing facility. With these state-of-the-art facilities, AAM can design and laboratory-validate anti-roll systems, steering linkage systems, steering or suspension components, and other products to customers' specifications.

Embracing competition on a global scale, AAM has established an Asia-Pacific sales and engineering office in Tokyo, Japan; a European business office in Ulm, Germany; and a world-class manufacturing facility in Guanajuato, Mexico, scheduled to begin operations before August 2000. The new plant will also house business offices with sales and engineering support for this emerging market, giving AAM access to vehicle manufacturers throughout Mexico and Latin America.

AAM's Scotland-based subsidiary, Albion Automotive Ltd., has a workforce of 1,000 and revenues of about $130 million for fiscal year ending 31 March 1998. Albion Automotive produces front-steerable and rear axles, driving heads, crankshafts, chassis components, and transmission parts, primarily for medium-duty trucks and buses—product lines that complement those of AAM, which are designed primarily for SUVs, light trucks, and passenger cars. AAM's other two subsidiaries, Ohio-based Colfor Manufacturing and Michigan-based MSP Industries, specialize in forgings, rounding out AAM's forged product line.

"Forging new world driveline standards" is not just a slogan at AAM, where dedication to quality means satisfying every requirement set by customers around the globe for the products and services they use. Essential to meeting this criterion are companywide policies that foster a better-educated, more flexible workforce by emphasizing teamwork, personal responsibility, continuous improvement, and recognition. These policies are overwhelmingly supported by the leaders of the United Auto Workers (UAW) and International Association of Machinists (IAM) locals that represent most of the workforce.

AAM's diverse and well-educated employee associates team up on the manufacturing floor to build excellence into each driveline system, chassis system, and forged product they produce. Associates participate in ongoing educational, training, and skill-set development to ensure continuing improvement in their individual and team efforts.

AAM's highly skilled and motivated associates can be proud of their accomplishments. In addition to achieving ISO-9001 and QS-9000 certification a full year ahead of schedule, they have produced and delivered on time, every time more than 16 million axles, 500,000 front suspensions, 11 million brake drums, 450 million forgings, 13 million propeller shafts, 11 million steering linkages, and 22 million stabilizer bars. Engineering teams at AAM have been responsible for significant breakthroughs, including a new generation of durable-metal-matrix and aluminum propeller shafts; ride-smoothing IRDS modules; and TracRite™ differentials for improved traction and handling.

AAM is already at work on the next generation of driveline systems and components, building competitive advantages into customers' vehicles. With its track record for engineering responsiveness, manufacturing capability, and on-time delivery, American Axle & Manufacturing has proven to be a production partner with a strong commitment to its own future and that of its customers.

AAM's 85,000-square-foot Technical Center in Rochester Hills was built in 1995. At this state-of-the-art facility, AAM's expert engineers from around the world perform complete design, laboratory validation, and testing all under one roof.

PROGRESSIVE TOOL & INDUSTRIES CO. (PICO)

The backbone of Michigan's industrial might can be envisioned as the companies that supply the automobile manufacturing giants, such as Ford, DaimlerChrysler, and General Motors. One of these suppliers that stands out is Progressive Tool & Industries Co.

This Southfield, Michigan–based firm, owned by the Wisne family, is a major, worldwide supplier of welding fixtures, tools, dies, special machinery, and automated manufacturing and assembly systems. Over more than half a century it

The Wisne Center in Southfield, Michigan, is the world headquarters of Progressive Tool & Industries Co. (PICO).

has built a reputation for excellence. In fact, the company has a wall full of preferred-supplier plaques received from its clients around the world.

Many of these awards are from the automobile manufacturers that Progressive Tool, commonly known as PICO, has traditionally served, such as the prestigious Platinum Pentastar Award bestowed on PICO by Chrysler in the early 1990s. This award was presented to just twenty-six of the automaker's countless suppliers worldwide. PICO also has been presented with the General Motors Targets for Excellence award and the Ford Q1 Award for Preferred Quality.

Awards come from customers outside of the automotive industry, too. Among these are the McDonnell Douglas Preferred Supplier Gold Award. Given to PICO in 1993, as one of just five given that year to the 6,000 suppliers of McDonnell Douglas, this award recognizes suppliers committed to performance values, statistical process control, service, and business standards

Tony Wisne (center) is shown here with his children (from left) Toni, Joe, Larry, and Alan.

that contribute to top quality and continuous improvement.

The McDonnell Douglas award was especially gratifying to PICO because it demonstrates the way the company's efforts toward quality and industry achievements have extended beyond the automobile manufacturing industry. PICO's reputation for excellence is well known in several non-automotive industries, including aerospace, furniture, watercraft, and telecommunications.

One characteristic that makes PICO especially valued among suppliers is that the company always strives to thoroughly understand and anticipate its customers' needs and to exceed their expectations. Moreover, PICO continually works to improve its own products, processes, and services so that it can provide innovative solutions that give its customers a competitive edge.

In addition, PICO works in partnership with its own suppliers, encouraging them to come up with new ideas that will optimize PICO's performance as well as their own.

PICO attributes much of its success to its employees. The company fosters teamwork by listening to employees, encouraging their involvement, providing them with opportunities for growth, and challenging them to find ways to improve the company's products and systems. PICO invests in its employees by providing training to advance their skills and abilities and by encouraging each employee's desire to improve.

Also contributing to its success is that throughout the company's nearly sixty-year history, the Wisne family has reinvested PICO's earnings to provide the highest-quality technology, resources, and personnel.

As a world-class, full-service supplier, PICO joins with its customers' project teams to bring about improved levels of performance, as measured by total program costs, time to market, and levels of innovation and quality applied in the manufacturing process. PICO's experience in continual

One of many automated welding systems designed and built by Progressive Tool & Industries Co. is this "Bodyside" system for a sport-utility vehicle.

improvement has enabled it to become a highly valued project team partner that can help improve a customer's projects.

PICO works with its own suppliers' decision makers in every production, design, and engineering specialty to create precision-equipment solutions and advanced systems that will meet its customers' needs today and tomorrow.

This team approach, integrating PICO's product knowledge with its expertise in system design and production technology, is used every step of the way during a customer's project, from conception to completion of the newly designed equipment on the customer's floor.

Even after a project is completed, PICO stays in constant contact with its customers and their plant personnel to ensure that the systems installed by PICO are functioning as they should.

In short, PICO's commitment to quality and excellence extends from its manufacturing floor to its customers' production facilities, and beyond. PICO is prepared to deliver its top-notch products and service to any legitimate industry anywhere in the world.

PICO®

THE MARK OF QUALITY®

NEWCOR, INC.

A MAJOR SUPPLIER

OF DIVERSIFIED

PRODUCTS TO THE

AUTOMOTIVE, HEAVY-

DUTY TRUCK, AND

AGRICULTURAL

MARKETS, NEWCOR,

INC., FORESEES A

FUTURE FILLED WITH

NEW CHALLENGES

AND SUBSTANTIAL

PROGRESS AT HOME

AND ABROAD

Headquartered in Bloomfield Hills, Michigan, Newcor, Inc., is located at the center of the automotive market. The company has a local management team that understands the idiosyncrasies of the automotive industry. Local sales and engineering support and ready access to manufacturing facilities located in the southern part of the Lower Peninsula have made Newcor an easy company with which to do business.

Newcor has production facilities in Royal Oak, Troy, Clinton Township, Corunna, Clifford, Deckerville, Livonia, and Bay City, Michigan, as well as in Iowa, Wisconsin, and Indiana. Several of Newcor's facilities were among the first in the state of Michigan to receive ISO-9001 and QS-9000 certification. Throughout the state, Newcor employs approximately 1,300 people.

As a world-class supplier to the international automotive market of precision-machined components and assemblies, rubber and plastic products, and custom machines and systems incorporating welding and forming technology, Newcor is well positioned for the future. Keith Hale, named president and CEO of Newcor in November 1998, brings renewed vision and direction to the corporate helm. He is determined to see that Newcor grows and performs well for investors without compromising the company's long-standing commitment to quality, service, and customer satisfaction. A native of England, Hale has

BELOW AND BOTTOM LEFT: *The Newcor Deco Group is a leading producer of precision-machined engine and powertrain components, including rocker arms and assemblies, transmission shafts, axle shafts, power-steering thrust plates, various engine accessory drives, and other specialized products for medium and heavy trucks and automobiles.*

launched an initiative to expand Newcor's sales operations in Europe, hoping to establish a presence in Germany, the United Kingdom, and Italy. Meanwhile, he has taken steps to consolidate operations and cut costs on the domestic front.

Newcor's exciting and challenging prospects are based on a tradition that dates back to 2 June 1933, with the formation of the National Electric Welding Machines company, located in Bay City, Michigan. In the first year of production, the company built 30 machines. Newcor's dedication to growth was already becoming evident when, in 1936, National Electric Welding Machines Company announced a major expansion, bringing additional jobs to the Bay City area. In a period of just three years, the company's production increased from 30 machines per year to more than 295 machines per year. The company operated as National Electric Welding Machines until 1969, at which time the name was changed to Newcor. Today welding machines are still a part of Newcor's product offering.

The Newcor culture and tradition manifests itself in other companies that have become part of the Newcor family over the years. The Newcor Deco Group was founded in Detroit in 1942 as the Detroit Engine Company. This small, privately owned company focused its efforts on the automotive industry by producing world-class CNC (computer numerical control)-machined components and assemblies. As a result of Deco's emphasis on technology and quality, the company expanded its horizons by producing a small engine for commercial use. Although Deco's focus has moved away from the manufacturing of these engines, many of them are still in use today, which is a tribute to the quality of their workmanship.

Deco's achievements in the marketplace required that they expand their production capabilities. In 1993 Deco opened its second facility, Deco Technologies, in Troy, Michigan. The management at Deco also recognized the need to be a participant in the international market. In response to this need, Deco International was created in 1994.

Newcor's Precision-Machined Products Group manufactures high-volume, close-tolerance products for the automotive and agricultural/off-highway vehicle industries. Major customers include DaimlerChrysler, Delphi Automotive, Detroit Diesel, Ford, General Motors, John Deere, and other leading OEMs (original equipment manufacturers) and tier-one suppliers.

THE NEWCOR FORMULA

- Dedication to the Employee
- Commitment to Excellence
- Dedication to the Customer
- Commitment to Growth

Like its sister groups, the Newcor Rubber and Plastic Group (NRPG) also has a long-standing relationship with the automotive industry. Founded in Detroit, Michigan, in 1946 as Midwest Rubber, the group has grown to five facilities including a product-design center in Bloomfield Hills.

Although headquartered in Michigan, Newcor keeps an eye on the world, and its customer list reads like a *who's who* of the international business community. In 1998 the company announced the opening of a technical office in Europe.

Today Newcor is a major supplier of diversified products to the automotive, heavy-duty truck, and agricultural markets both domestically and internationally. Newcor products and capabilities extend from welding machines and precision-machined components and assemblies through rubber and plastic components. Many of those products are pictured on these pages.

During its sixty-five-year history in Michigan, Newcor never lost sight of its dedication to the employee and to the customer while maintaining its commitment to growth and excellence. This dedication and commitment have proven to be the formula for Newcor's success.

Newcor Rubber and Plastic Group's products include transmission shift boots, steering column and gearshift lever seals, air-conditioning ducts, steering column boots, dash panel grommets, fuel filler seals, fluid-recovery systems, hose and wire brackets, speaker seals, vacuum-control systems, and attachment and restraining products.

MERITOR AUTOMOTIVE, INC.

BUILDING ON A

PROUD NINETY-YEAR

HERITAGE, MERITOR

AUTOMOTIVE, INC.,

COMBINES THE

SHARPENED FOCUS

AND FLEXIBILITY OF A

YOUNG COMPANY WITH

THE SOLID REPUTATION

AND EXPERIENCE OF

AN ESTABLISHED

INDUSTRY LEADER

Meritor's global workforce is intensely dedicated to applying innovative technologies and processes to meet the needs of its automotive and heavy truck customers wherever in the world they do business.

The history of Meritor Automotive, Inc., begins in 1909 with the founding of Timken–Detroit Axle Company, which later became a division of Wisconsin Parts Company. In 1953 Willard Rockwell, who had purchased Wisconsin Parts in 1919, merged Timken–Detroit Axle, Wisconsin Parts, and Standard Steel and Spring to form Rockwell Spring and Axle Company. Meritor was born on 1 October 1997, when Rockwell International, now an electronic controls and communications giant, completed the spin-off of its automotive businesses unit.

Concentrating its full global resources on serving automotive customers, Meritor draws on its heritage of Rockwell technology and nearly a century of experience as a leading supplier to virtually every major manufacturer of commercial trucks, trailers, off-highway vehicles, buses, light trucks, and passenger cars in North America, South America, and Europe. This exciting chapter in the company's history promises to be etched with enthusiasm, innovation, and continuous improvement on past success.

Leading Meritor Automotive is the company's chairman and CEO, Larry D. Yost.

Meritor spans the globe with more than sixty facilities in twenty-three countries, including Argentina, Australia, Belgium, Brazil, Canada, China, the Czech Republic, France, Germany, India, Ireland, Italy, Japan, Mexico, the Netherlands, Singapore, South Africa, South Korea, Spain, Sweden, Turkey, the United Kingdom, and the United States. Meritor's world headquarters are located in Troy, Michigan, and its U.S. manufacturing operations are found in Iowa, Kentucky, North Carolina, Ohio, South Carolina, Tennessee, and Wisconsin, as well as Michigan. A partner in fourteen joint ventures in nine countries, Meritor has a demonstrated ability to form alliances, adapt to regional business practices, and operate effectively abroad while maintaining high service levels throughout the company. *Automotive News* ranks Meritor as the twenty-fourth-largest automotive supplier in the world, with 18,000 employees serving more than 800 original equipment manufacturers (OEMs) worldwide.

In Meritor's first year as a publicly held company, sales were $3.8 billion, exceeding the previous year's performance by 16 percent. Net income was $147 million, an increase of 48 percent over 1997's pro forma net income. International and export business accounted for more than 50 percent of revenues.

The company's two major businesses are Light Vehicle Systems (LVS) and Heavy Vehicle Systems (HVS)—a combination that provides balance across developed and emerging markets while helping to dampen the effects of global business cycles. Meritor's HVS business is a leading supplier of drivetrain systems and components for heavy- and medium-duty commercial

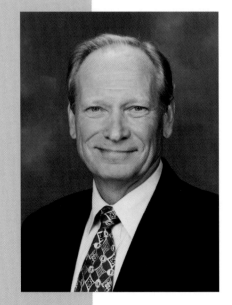

trucks, trailers, buses, off-highway commercial vehicles, and heavy-duty government vehicles. HVS products include axles, braking systems, transmissions, clutches, drivelines, air suspension systems, transfer cases, and aftermarket parts and services. Meritor's Worldwide Aftermarket business is a fast-growing global operation dedicated to servicing the heavy vehicle industry with a comprehensive offering of high-quality replacement components. Through an extensive global distribution network, Meritor can service its customers virtually anywhere in the world. Meritor's LVS business focuses on creating complete systems that are made to fit and pretested to ensure

Meritor's dedication to customer service and satisfaction is a hallmark of the company. It operates call centers that allow customers to call for assistance twenty-four-hours a day, seven days a week.

Parallelogram trailer air-suspension system was the first heavy-duty trailer component ever to win the prestigious PACE Award for technological leadership, sponsored by *Automotive News* and the accounting firm of Ernst & Young. Other Meritor innovations include the new Easy Steer Plus™ front axle; the TB Trailer Axle™ with unitized hubs; DiscPlus™ heavy-duty air disc brakes; AutoJust™ clutch; and advanced shift systems.

smooth installation, with reduced production time and costs. LVS product lines include roof systems, door systems, access-control systems, seat-adjusting systems, electric motors, suspension systems, and wheels for passenger cars, light trucks, and sport-utility vehicles.

Customers look to Meritor for the technology and service that only an industry leader can supply. Meritor's commitment to innovation does not go unnoticed. Its Highway

"Meritor is committed to being the best provider of automotive systems and technology solutions to customers who value exceptional service. We are set to unleash our full potential, combining today's enthusiasm with a well-earned reputation for unmatched service," says Larry D. Yost, chairman and chief executive officer. "Meritor is dedicated to continuous improvement as a well-managed business—one with a strong emphasis on new product development and the capabilities to quickly meet market-driven customer needs."

The company is dedicated to building a future that is even stronger than its past. It is well positioned to capitalize on current trends among OEMs in the automotive industry, such as their growing globalization, consolidation of suppliers, increased dependence on outsourcing, and emphasis on reduced production time. These trends translate to opportunities for a global manufacturer with diverse products, customers, and geographic base, as well as technological leadership and financial strength. From its unique vantage point, Meritor envisions itself as the partner of choice for customers who expect nothing short of outstanding service—a worldwide source of quality automotive systems and technological solutions.

Meritor operates one of the world's largest independent technical development and testing facilities—a 220,000-square-foot Technical Center—for automotive components and integrated systems.

HADEN, INC.

With roots dating back to the 1920s, Haden, inc., is a premier global builder of integrated automotive and industrial paint finishing and pollution control systems.

Its products include highly engineered spray booths and ovens; paint automation; pretreatment systems; chemical processing systems; wastewater treatment plants; and VOC (volatile organic compound) abatement systems. Haden's primary business focus is to provide turnkey services—from engineering through installation—supported by training and operations. Its customers are industrial makers of automobiles, heavy trucks, farm implements, aerospace components, and general industrial goods worldwide. Projects can range from making quality or productivity improvements for an existing manufacturing system to building a complete new finishing facility from a green field site.

Haden has successfully completed hundreds of projects, large and small. This broad experience has earned it a leadership role in the design, fabrication, and installation of high-quality paint finishing, industrial process, and environmental systems. Haden assures customers of the right system solution, objective selection of components, time-tested engineering, and an optimum program schedule, all at a competitive price. Its ISO-9001 certification and successful audit to QS-9000/TE evidences Haden's strict adherence to high-quality standards.

Haden is a leader in the development and application of technology to provide innovative industrial systems solutions.

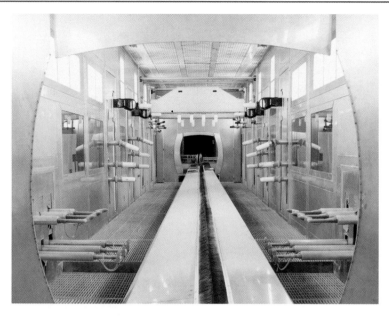

Haden's powder spray booth for the automotive industry helps to eliminate emissions from the painting process.

As a result of its expertise and leadership, Haden has developed strong relationships with major automotive manufacturers and automotive component suppliers worldwide. As a turnkey supplier, it interacts with local suppliers and subcontractors. Reflecting its community commitment, Haden received the Michigan Minority Business Development Council's award of Minority Supplier of the Year, Construction Sector, for 1997. This honor recognizes the volume of business awarded to minority suppliers.

Haden's global research and development is centered in its Auburn Hills, Michigan facility, which also houses engineering and project management services, fabrication, and training. Its operation includes more than 300 professionals and a flexible staff of skilled manufacturing and field personnel. With technology that sets an industry standard, Haden holds more than 120 United States and international patents pertaining to the paint application process.

As an affiliate of Haden MacLellan Holdings plc (HMH), based in the United Kingdom, Haden, inc., can reach throughout the industrialized world. HMH employs 5,000 people and generates annual revenues of more than $1 billion.

HADEN
international group

LAMERSON USA

Lamerson USA, located in Oak Park, Michigan, applies the genius of unique engineering and produces precision free-form design equipment. Focusing on the big picture as well as the finest detail, Lamerson USA seeks to give its clients in industry an efficient advantage from which to make crucial decisions regarding new designs.

Highly styled products, from office furniture to automobiles and recreational vehicles, pass through a critical stage in the design development process before they go into production for the mass market. Before the manufacturer invests in costly new production tools and dies, the designer's two-dimensional sketch or computer model is transformed into a three-dimensional styling-clay design model. The merits of a particular design are judged after skilled artisans have sculpted a model out of hard styling clay. Lamerson USA provides the precision tools and equipment to meet the exacting requirements of this procedure, and can offer clients a complete modeling system or a

ABOVE: *Lamerson USA is a global supplier of product design equipment and systems such as this large styling bridge with full scanning and milling capability.* LEFT: *The company was founded by U. D. "Al" Lamerson in 1956.*

basic start-up tooling package that readily adapts as technology changes.

Unique design-modeling products developed and manufactured by Lamerson USA include clay extrusion machines, modeling bridges, cast or fabricated steel floor platens, modeling platens, and currently under development, clay milling cutters.

Founded by self-made industrialist and engineering innovator U. D. "Al" Lamerson, Lamerson USA has been a global supplier of product design systems for forty-three years. Now moving aggressively into the twenty-first century, the company owned and operated by R. D. Lamerson remains dedicated to refining the industrial way of life and methodology of work. Lamerson USA is proud to contribute to the look of new-millennium products.

FROM FERTILE FIELDS

CHAPTER NINE

EVER SINCE NATIVE AMERICANS INTRODUCED FARMING TO THE SOUTHERN PART OF THE LOWER PENINSULA 2,000 YEARS AGO, AGRICULTURE HAS PLAYED A CRUCIAL ROLE IN MICHIGAN'S HISTORY AND ECONOMY. EVEN THE EARLIEST SETTLERS RECOGNIZED THE BENEFITS OF THE REGION'S LAKE-PROTECTED CLIMATE, RICH AND DIVERSE SOIL, AND ABUNDANT WATER. THE FRENCH BROUGHT PEAR TREES WHICH STILL SURVIVE IN THE GROSSE POINTE

area of Detroit 300 years after they were planted, foreshadowing Michigan's future as one of the world's leading fruit producers.

The opening of the Erie Canal in 1825 brought a flood of farmers from the eastern states and Europe, drawn by the inexpensive, fertile land. Because it required no plowing, the first crop was corn, which had been grown in southern Michigan since the time of Christ. Corn continues to occupy the major share of the state's cropland with 216 million bushels produced annually. Much of the corn is of the larger, heartier, hybrid varieties, considered agricultural miracles when developed at Michigan Agricultural College (now Michigan State University) around 1900.

But Michigan's new residents did not confine themselves to one crop for long. By the early 1830s farmers discovered how the moderating effect of Lake Michigan made the climate in the western part of the state ideal for growing fruit. The resulting fruit belt, which stretches from the Indiana border to Grand Traverse Bay, produces more than 70 percent of the nation's tart cherries, 34 percent of its Niagara grapes, 33 percent of its blueberries, and ranks Michigan among the top five producers of apples and peaches.

EXPERIMENTATION YIELDS SUCCESS

The key to Michigan's agricultural success has always been diversity. When Michigan farmers take a chance on something new, they generally make a success of it. Around 1860 Dutch farmers near Kalamazoo experimented with crossbreeding varieties of celery and came up with "ivory pascal." This new variety inspired a celery craze that swept the nation, resulting in the likes of celery cereal, celery chewing gum, and celery soda. While much of the original celery mucklands have been claimed by urban expansion, Michigan remains the number-two producer of the popular stalks once touted as "fresh as the dew from Kalamazoo."

OPPOSITE: *Picturesque dairy farms such as this one dot the Michigan countryside. But cows are big business in Michigan as well. Green Meadows Farm in Elsie has the largest family-owned, registered Holstein herd in North America. The farm's continuous milking operation circulates each of the 3,500 cows through the dairy barn three times a day. © SuperStock.* ABOVE: *Lawton grape grower William Cronenwett shows off his harvest. © Dennis Cox/D. E. Cox Photo Library*

In this 1930s photo, Dr. Henry Kellogg (left) discusses the relative merits of cultured milk with playwright George Bernard Shaw. © Archive Photos

When fire finished off the waning lumber industry in the Thumb region, Michigan Agricultural College again came to the rescue in the form of Dr. Robert Kedzie, who brought sugar beet seeds from Europe and taught Michigan farmers how to grow them. Today the Saginaw Valley area produces the fifth-largest sugar beet crop in the nation, as well as the largest crops of dry black beans, cranberry beans, and navy beans. Michigan also ranks first in the nation for pickling cucumbers, second for asparagus, third for carrots and cauliflower, and fourth for tomatoes. Michigan is an important dairy state as well,

producing three times more milk than it did in 1955 with a quarter of the number of dairy farms, thanks to cutting-edge farm technology and herd management practices.

Although its fifty-two thousand farms and 10.5 million acres of farmland represent about half of what existed at their high points early in the 1900s, Michigan ranks among the top-ten national producers for more than fifty farm commodities. The state's more than 100 commercial crops make it second only to California in variety of foods grown. Agriculture brings in $3.8 billion of revenue annually, making it Michigan's second-largest economic sector.

FIELDS OF GRAIN

With all of this bounty it is no wonder that many of America's favorite food brands come from Michigan. Battle Creek was once home to more than 100 cereal companies, and remains the Cereal Capital of the World, thanks to the presence of Kellogg, Post, and Ralston Purina's Chex. When Dr. John Harvey Kellogg assumed direction of the Battle Creek Sanitarium in 1877, he and brother Will Keith made ample use of local grains to devise new dishes to perk up their Seventh Day Adventist patients' stimulant-free, vegetarian diets. The cold cereals and coffee substitute they devised were available only to patients by catalog until one of those patients, Charles Post, decided to produce and aggressively market his own versions of the products. The huge success of Grape Nuts, Postum, and a second generation of further

Some of this farmer's corn crop will be used to make cooking oil. The rest will become feed for livestock. Michigan is one of the top ten states producing silage and grain corn. © Andrew Sacks

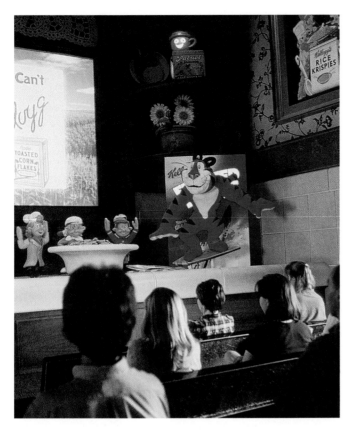

buckets of some motherless neighbor children, she decided to make a ready mix for light, flaky biscuits that "even a man could prepare." Now, nearly seventy years later, the Holmes family's Chelsea Milling Company produces 1.4 million boxes of Jiffy mixes each day. Its nineteen products represent $100 million in annual sales, and Jiffy corn muffin mix is the seventh-largest-selling dry grocery item in the country.

MORE FRUITFUL ENDEAVORS

Michigan fruits and vegetables inspired another famous success story. In 1927 the daughter-in-law of a Fremont cannery owner grew weary of straining vegetables for her baby and asked her husband if he could do it in his father's plant. This simple request made Dorothy Gerber the inventor of commercial baby food and a patron saint of harried moms the world over. Dan Gerber sold a half million cans of baby food in the first year of production, and soon the cannery had switched over to producing baby food full time. Gerber's original five products have expanded to more than 150, most made from locally grown produce. The company, still in Fremont, is by far the world's largest baby food manufacturer, with a 70 percent share of the United States market.

Other famous Michigan names on grocery shelves include Vlasic, the nation's leading distributor of pickles,

Gerber makes nearly 200 food items, plus feeding systems, pacifiers, and other baby care items. © Gerber Products Company

imitations encouraged the Kelloggs to jump on their own bandwagon. They marketed their only product which had not yet been copied—Corn Flakes—and the rest is history. Today Kellogg Company is the world's largest manufacturer of ready-to-eat cereal, with a 39 percent share of the global market. Kellogg has expanded beyond cereal to include products such as Eggo pancakes and waffles, making the company the undisputed king of the breakfast table.

Michigan's grain belt aided another unlikely entrepreneur. When Chelsea housewife Mabel White Holmes noticed the rock-hard biscuits in the lunch

THAT'S A LOT OF BABY FOOD

ALONG WITH INVENTING BABY FOOD, THE GERBERS ARE CREDITED WITH THE NATION'S FIRST MARKET SURVEY. THEY RAN AN ADVERTISEMENT IN *GOOD HOUSEKEEPING* MAGAZINE OFFERING A COUPON FOR SIX CANS OF BABY FOOD FOR A DOLLAR IF THE CONSUMER WOULD WRITE HER GROCERY STORE'S NAME ON THE ORDER FORM. DAN GERBER USED THE RESPONSES TO PERSUADE GROCERY STORES TO CARRY HIS NEW PRODUCT, RESULTING IN OVER A HALF MILLION CANS OF GERBER BABY FOOD SOLD IN THE FIRST YEAR OF OPERATION, 1927.

one of the most popular new food items to come out of Michigan in decades.

OTHER PRODUCTS

Thorn Apple Valley, based in Southfield, is a billion-dollar meat and poultry processor. Hygrade Food Products, also of Southfield, has been famous since 1957 when Tiger Stadium made Hygrade's Ball Park Frank its official hot dog. Around 1940 Detroit tinkerer and entrepreneur Harry Hoenselaar invented a machine that carved ham off the bone in one perfect, continual slice, then came up with a secret glaze recipe and founded the Honey Baked Ham Company, the largest privately held pork retailer in the country.

Michigan has made its mark on the beverage industry as well. Beer was one of Michigan's first manufactured products, thanks to the large number of German immigrants. Bernhard Stroh established one of Detroit's most successful breweries in 1850. The company survived

peppers, relishes, and sauerkraut. Once headquartered in West Bloomfield, the company is now part of New Jersey–based Campbell Foods, but retains a processing plant in Imlay City to take advantage of Michigan's bumper cucumber crop. American Spoon Foods of Petoskey has put Michigan fruit—in the form of preserves, jams, butters, and "spoon fruits"—in gourmet shops across the country. The company also took the famous local cherries and dried them, thereby creating

Wheat is among the crops that thrive in the Saginaw Valley's fertile soil. Here wheat is harvested against a lapis sky on a farm near Freeland. © Randall B. Henne/Blanchet Photographics

Prohibition by manufacturing ice cream, a product still sold in Michigan grocery stores, and in 1998 Stroh's beer was selected as the world's best-tasting lager beer in the biennial Brewing Industry International Awards competition. Hiram Walker was another Detroiter who went into the beverage business, but he opened his eponymous distillery across the river in Windsor, Ontario. Thanks to the state's bountiful grape harvest, Michigan is a leading wine producer, with eighteen licensed wineries scattered over the western part of the state.

Michigan's agricultural ascendancy is not limited to food and drink. The state's 536 commercial floriculture growers brought in $182 million in 1996, placing Michigan fourth nationally—first for sales of potted geraniums and Easter lilies, bedding impatiens, and geranium hanging baskets. Kalamazoo County produces more bedding plants than any other county in the nation.

MICHIGAN'S MOREL MUSHROOMS ARE INTERNATIONALLY FAMOUS. THE GREAT LAKES STATE IS THE ONLY PLACE IN THE WORLD WHERE ALL FIVE VARIETIES OF THE FUNGUS CAN BE FOUND IN THE WILD. NOT SURPRISINGLY, SAVVY MICHIGAN FARMERS ARE NOW WORKING TO MEET RISING DEMAND BY CULTIVATING THEM, TOO.

llama raising, agricultural tourism, and innovative products such as a twenty-six-calorie navy bean pizza. In many ways, Michigan's oldest economic sector is its most exciting. Nature's blessings, hard work, and ingenuity will keep agriculture and food in the forefront of Michigan's economic picture well into the new millennium.

AND THERE'S MORE...

Variety and innovation continue to characterize Michigan's agriculture and food sectors. Increasing consumer demand for cranberry products has prompted farmers and the state department of agriculture to develop a cranberry industry here. The nation's interest in low-fat meat products has resulted in a proliferation of ostrich, emu, and fish farms. The state currently has forty-five commercial trout operations and ranks ninth in trout production nationally. Its ninety thousand bee colonies make Michigan sixth in the nation in honey production. In 1996 the state's first soybean processing plant opened in Zeeland. At full operation the plant will purchase six to seven million bushels of Michigan soybeans annually and process nearly 600 tons of soy meal daily.

Michigan entrepreneurs are experimenting with shrimp farming,

A Dexter farmer harvests lettuce. It is not unusual to see thriving farms such as this one within an hour's drive of downtown Detroit. © Andrew Sacks

This mid-Michigan farm is one of fifty-two thousand in the state. © Randall B. Henne/Blanchet Photographics

AGRICULTURE AND FOOD PRODUCTS

MONITOR SUGAR COMPANY

While the sugar beet plant used to produce the sugar people use every day in hundreds of food items remains the same, the technology employed by Monitor Sugar Company to refine it is constantly evolving.

"Monitor Sugar continually seeks the best technology to process sugar and create a superior product for our consumer, food service, and industrial customers," says company president and CEO, Robert L. Hetzler.

Monitor Sugar's Big Chief Sugar product line includes granulated, brown, powdered, and fondant sugars to meet the needs of consumers and food processors. Granulated sugar, a leading seller in Michigan-area stores, is used by homemakers, professional chefs, and scores of industrial and institutional food preparers. Big Chief Golden Brown Sugar is a precise blend of more than 99 percent pure granulated sugar and a pre-measured amount of molasses that produces excellent color, consistency, and taste. The innovative use of wheatstarch in Big Chief Confectioners' Sugar results in a powdered sugar with taste, smoothness, and color superior to other brands containing conventional cornstarch. Satin Set is a fondant sugar that produces silky smooth glazes and icings.

The Monitor Sugar plant, in Bay City, was built in 1901, when the company was known as the "German American Farmers Cooperative Beet Sugar Company." From its very beginning and throughout its history, Monitor Sugar has been an innovator in sugar production technology. Technical advances range

Monitor Sugar Company is the exclusive processor of Big Chief Sugar products for the retail, industrial, and food service markets.

from computer-aided operational controls to environmentally friendly manufacturing technology. In 1998, as part of its $30 million capital expansion program, Monitor Sugar built a new facility for molasses desugarization. In this technology, sugar is removed from the molasses yielded during the processing of sugar beets, thereby increasing the beets' overall yield of sugar—Monitor Sugar's primary and most profitable product.

"In the future, we will continue to look for the best technology," Hetzler says. "Our goal is to remain one of the lowest-cost producers using the most highly advanced processing techniques in the sugar business."

Monitor Sugar Company fully accepts its responsibility as a corporate leader by stressing the importance of community involvement through example. The company provides financial and leadership support to a number of charitable, educational, and cultural organizations and promotes environmental awareness by protecting the local environment through safe and clean operations.

Bay City, Michigan, is the home of Monitor Sugar Company, the maker of Big Chief Sugar.

RECOGNIZING THAT ITS SUCCESS IS A DIRECT RESULT OF THE DAILY EFFORTS OF ITS EMPLOYEES, THE COCA-COLA BOTTLING COMPANY OF MICHIGAN GIVES BACK TO THE COMMUNITY BY SUPPORTING YOUTH AND EDUCATION PROGRAMS

Coca-Cola is more than just the world's best-selling soft drink; it is a quintessential American icon. The Coca-Cola Bottling Company of Michigan, a division of Coca-Cola Enterprises Inc., is responsible for distributing and marketing these popular nonalcoholic refreshments for the Michigan market.

When Dr. John Pemberton, an Atlanta pharmacist, created Coca-Cola, he didn't have a beverage in mind. He promoted the syrup as a medicine. Then a fountain operator mixed it with carbonated water, and the world's first soft drink was born.

Coca-Cola's popularity grew after 1899, when a nationwide bottling network began by granting franchise rights. Consolidation of these operations began in the late 1970s. One of the most prominent mergers resulted in the formation of Coca-Cola Enterprises Inc. in 1986. Today Coca-Cola Enterprises operates in forty-four states plus the District of Columbia, the U.S. Virgin Islands, the Netherlands, France, Belgium, the United Kingdom, and Canada.

The Coca-Cola Bottling Company of Michigan operates bottling plants in the cities of Detroit, Flint, and Grand Rapids, producing beverages for fourteen sales centers throughout the state. This extensive production, sales,

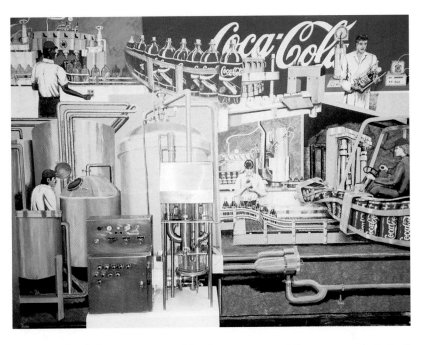

The mural in the entryway of the company's Detroit bottling facility was hand-sketched and painted by labeler operator Arnoldo Reyes.

and delivery force is responsible for marketing and distributing more than 200 products and packages—a product line that includes carbonated soft drinks, waters, juices, teas, and isotonic beverages.

Coca-Cola Bottling Company of Michigan spends a great deal of time, energy, and money supporting dozens of charitable causes. Community service and community relations programs supported by the company focus on youth and education.

"Our objective at Coca-Cola Bottling Company of Michigan is to be the premier soft-drink supplier in Michigan, and the only way to achieve that objective is by providing product, service, and programs that enhance the business of our retailers," says Don Hensen, vice president and general manager. "It is important to recognize that our success is a direct result of the daily efforts of the people who work for the Coca-Cola Bottling Company of Michigan. They give us a tremendous advantage in a very competitive business."

Education is a priority for the Coca-Cola Bottling Company of Michigan. Project Entré Coke helps prepare students for life after high school.

RICH EARTH, THICK FORESTS

CHAPTER TEN

MICHIGAN'S NATURAL RESOURCES FOSTERED A BOOM ECONOMY FROM THE EARLIEST DAYS OF ITS STATEHOOD. WITH PICKAX AND SAW, THOUSANDS OF MINERS AND LOGGERS ATTACKED THE REGION'S INDIGENOUS TREASURE TROVE, THEN MOVED WEST TO THE NEXT WILDERNESS. THANKS TO THE PEOPLE WHO STAYED TO REPAIR THE DAMAGE, MICHIGAN'S MINING AND LUMBER INDUSTRIES ARE STILL IMPORTANT AND, NOW, ENVIRONMENTALLY SOUND ECONOMIC SECTORS.

RICHES OF THE EARTH

No area of comparable size in the United States has nearly the variety of minerals that can be found in Michigan. The state has extensive deposits of iron and copper ores, natural salines, sand and gravel, petroleum, salt, stone, lime and limestone, natural gas, crude gypsum, clay and shale, peat, marl, and dolomite.

Native Americans first entered the Upper Peninsula 10,000 years ago, finding copper nuggets in the rivers and veins just a few inches below the earth's surface pure enough to be workable in their natural state. Artifacts made from this copper date back as far as 5000 B.C. French explorers in the 1600s heard tales of an enormous copper rock on the banks of the Octonagon River, but it wasn't until 1843 that the first white man—fur trader and entrepreneur Alexander Henry— saw it with his own eyes. The five-ton boulder eventually went to the Smithsonian Institution, but not before inciting America's first great mining boom. In 1845 Cliff Mine hit a copper lode that netted stockholders a 2,000 percent profit over the next twenty-five years. By 1846 more than one hundred copper mining companies had been formed, and boomtowns mushroomed along the Keweenaw Peninsula. Within a year Michigan had become the world's leading source of native copper, and was producing twelve million pounds a year by 1860.

By the early 1920s, however, less expensive open-pit mining elsewhere had begun to replace Michigan mines as major world suppliers. The Upper Peninsula's copper towns went into decline, even though only an estimated 10 percent of the region's copper had been extracted. The

OPPOSITE: *The historic Quincy Mine near Houghton boasts what is believed to be the largest steam-powered mine hoist ever made. In operation between 1920 and 1931, the hoist could haul ten tons of copper ore at thirty-six miles per hour from a depth of two miles. Though the mine is now closed, visitors still can tour the site and see the hoist in operation. © Bob Firth/Firth Photobank. ABOVE: The Republic iron mine in the Upper Peninsula's Marquette range is another remnant of Michigan's storied mining history. © Scot Stewart*

CHIP OFF THE OLD BLOCK

WHEN ALPENA BECAME "CEMENT CITY" AT THE TURN OF THE
CENTURY, HERMAN BESSER AND HIS SON JESSE INVENTED A
MACHINE THERE FOR MAKING CONCRETE BLOCKS. BESSER
COMPANY IS STILL THE WORLD'S LEADING MANUFACTURER OF
SUCH MACHINERY.

Gravel is loaded onto gravel "trains" for transport. © Ross Frid

Calumet and Hecla Mining Company, the biggest and richest of the lot, was the last to fold, closing operations in 1968. That land is now owned by Champion International, which leases it for mineral rights, logging, and recreation. A small amount of copper is still mined in the U.P. for use by the local timber industry in the production of pressure-treated lumber, but the copper glory days are long past.

Copper wasn't Michigan's only mining miracle. State surveyor William A. Burt invented a solar compass and an early version of the typewriter, but he is best remembered for the day in 1844 when his compass needle was pulled off north, leading him and his surveying party to an outcropping of iron ore. His discovery turned out to be part of a vast body of iron ore that would make the Lake Superior region the leading source of that mineral for more than a century. At its peak around 1890, Michigan's annual iron ore production reached seven million tons, making it the number-one iron-producing state. Today the miles of underground mine shafts in the U.P. are abandoned, but two open-pit mines, the Tilden and the Empire, continue to operate.

The presence of almost unlimited iron ore, accessible via the Soo Locks, resulted in a thriving steel industry in the Detroit area beginning in 1853 when Eber Brock Ward opened his Eureka Iron and Steel Company in Wyandotte. The first Bessemer steel in the United States was made at this plant, as well as the first railroad T-rails. The early generation of steel plants closed around the turn of the century, but soon Henry Ford was again making steel in Michigan, and his plant led to others, which were built along the Detroit River. Today the Great Lakes Division of the National Steel Corporation employs almost four thousand workers at its Ecorse factory. Detroit's Midwest Steel, Inc., operates in the United States, Canada, and Mexico, and Dearborn's Rouge Steel is one of the state's largest publicly held companies.

U.S. Steel is the current owner of the Michigan Limestone and Chemical Company in Rogers City, home of the world's largest limestone quarry. Limestone mined here, formed over a span of 300 million years from coral

Giant rolls of steel sheet metal dwarf a worker at Wayne Industries steel plant. © Dwight Cendrowski

Michigan is the number-two Christmas tree–producing state after Oregon. Here, a farmer tends a young tree. © Andrew Sacks

in the ancient seas that once covered Michigan, is unusually pure and therefore ideal for making steel and chemicals. The presence of more high-grade limestone near Alpena, as well as marl, shale, and clay, created a thriving portland cement industry. For nearly one hundred years Alpena boasted the largest cement factory in the world. Now owned by Lafarge Corporation, the factory remains the largest cement producer in North America.

For most of the twentieth century, mines beneath the city of Detroit produced 25 percent of the nation's salt. Saline, brine, and salt deposits—more remnants of those ancient seas—made Michigan an important center of the chemical industry. While Detroit's salt mines closed in 1983, Morton International still extracts salt brine in Michigan for chemical use.

Among Michigan's most valuable resources are oil and natural gas. The Niagaran reef's estimated one-half billion–barrel oil reserve places Michigan among the nation's top oil-producing states. The Michigan Department of Natural Resources reports 6,300 active leases on state lands under the oil and gas leasing program, and predicts steadily increasing petroleum revenues well into the next century.

GREEN GOLD

Up until the nineteenth century, thick forests covered nearly 90 percent of Michigan's thirty-seven million acres: hardwoods such as maple, oak, and walnut in the

Grinding cedar mulch in Ensign is part of Michigan's $4 billion wood and wood products industry. © Mark E. Gibson/Midwestock

south, and towering white pines in the north. "We'll never cut all this pine if we log it until hell freezes," one Maine logger remarked when he arrived in Michigan in the 1840s. He was wrong. There were already 400 sawmills in operation then, and that was just the beginning. By 1870, ten thousand lumberjacks were mowing forests at the rate of thirty-three thousand acres per year, creating scores of lumber millionaires and miles of barren, stump-strewn land. Ten years later the virgin forests were nearly gone, but by that time Michigan had produced 160 billion feet of pine—more lumber than any other logging state.

EASTERN GOLD RUSH

In 1883 Michigan chemist and geologist Julius Ropes opened the only gold mine east of the Mississippi River. He extracted more than $700,000 worth of gold and silver from his Marquette mine before labor disputes closed it four years later.

REINVENTING THE WHEEL

In the late 1800s Manistee wagonmaker Silas Overpack invented "big wheels," ten-foot-tall wagon wheels, which made it possible to haul logs over rough ground. Before Overpack's invention, logging was confined to the winter months when logs could be transported by sled. Manistee big wheels were shipped to every logging state in America for fifty years.

The lumber industry moved westward, and Michiganians began the long process of repairing the damage left behind. The Huron National Forest was established along the Au Sable River in 1909, the first of many such preserves. Then the state, its residents, and the remaining logging companies joined forces in a reforestation program that has had unprecedented success. Today eighteen million acres of the state are again forestland, 10 percent of it owned by logging companies, which now plant more trees than they cut down. Timber is once more a growth industry. According to state estimates, the timberland base has the potential to grow 1.3 billion feet annually—a 50 percent increase over current levels.

By the mid-1990s the lumber and wood products industry employed nearly 20,000 people at 350 sawmills and 250 kiln-drying companies. Michigan topped the nation in pallet firms with 220. The Michigan pulp and paper industry employs another 20,000 people at 235 facilities. Michigan paper production is up 50 percent over the 1980s, and companies such as Kimberly Clark, Mead, and Champion International are important presences in the Upper Peninsula. *National Geographic*'s glossy pages come from the Champion plant in Iron Mountain.

Michigan wood is used for furniture and in building and construction. Perhaps its most famous use is in hardwood floors. In Hermansville, a few miles west of Escanaba in the Upper Peninsula, the machinery to precision-manufacture hardwood flooring was first perfected in the 1880s by lumber mill manager George Earle. Until then, flooring was made of soft pine, but Earle developed a kiln process to remove the right amount of moisture from hardwood, then invented machinery to make tongue-and-groove hardwood sections. The Earles' IXL Company crafted floors for the main lodge at Yellowstone

The Mead Corporation produces 1.8 million tons of paper and 1.7 million tons of paperboard every year. Shown here, the Mead Paper Plant in Escanaba. © Mark E. Gibson/Midwestock

ABOVE: *Black spruce along Tamarack Bog in Hiawatha National Forest. © Rob Planck/Dembinsky Photo Associates.* RIGHT: *Burning out a safe zone downwind in Manistee National Forest. © Ross Frid*

National Park and the Mormon Temple in Salt Lake City. Flooring continues to be an important industry in the U.P., with the vast majority of the world's basketball floors produced by Robbins Floor Company of Ishpeming and Horning Flooring Company of Dollar Bay.

Christmas trees are another of Michigan's most important tree-based industries, earning growers close to $40 million each year. The state has 70,000 acres in commercial Christmas tree production, and cuts 3.5 million Christmas trees each year, selling 2.7 million out of state.

Nine Michigan institutions of higher learning offer some of the nation's most sophisticated training and education programs, as well as technical, research, and marketing resources in support of the lumber industry. Lumber and wood products currently add about $4 billion to state coffers annually, and form one of the economic sectors identified as having the most promising growth potential.

With thriving forests, untapped oil, and copper, iron, and other minerals left to spare, Michigan is as rich in resources today as it was when ten-pound copper nuggets glistened in streambeds, and squirrels could cross the state without touching the ground.

ONLY IN MICHIGAN

THE WESTERN UPPER PENINSULA GROWS VIRTUALLY THE WORLD'S SOLE SUPPLY OF BIRDS-EYE MAPLE. THE HIGHLY PRIZED WOOD IS DISTINGUISHED BY AN ABUNDANCE OF SWIRLS AND CIRCLES IN THE GRAIN, THOUGHT TO BE FORMED BY HARD WINTERS. A TEN-FOOT LOG CAN SELL FOR AS MUCH AS $7,000.

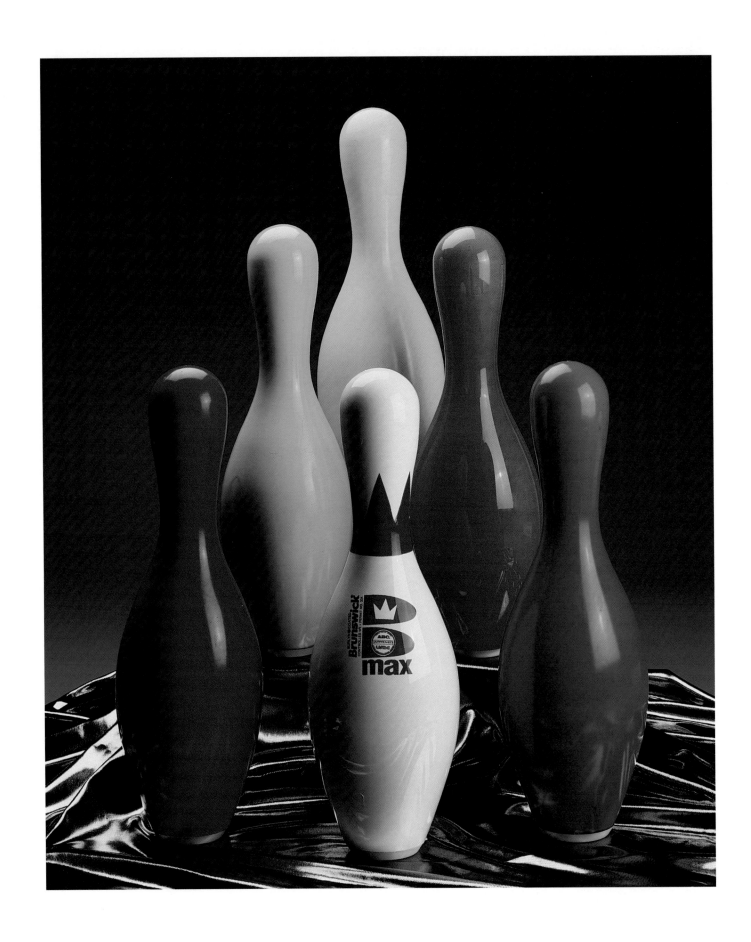

MADE IN MICHIGAN

CHAPTER ELEVEN

ALTHOUGH BILLIONS OF DOLLARS IN ANNUAL REVENUES COME FROM ITS

EARTH, MICHIGAN IS FIRST AND FOREMOST A MANUFACTURING STATE. AS

EARLY AS 1900, 25 PERCENT OF MICHIGAN WORKERS HAD FACTORY JOBS—

AND THE AUTO INDUSTRY HAD NOT YET BEEN BORN. MANUFACTURING WAS

THEN AND STILL IS CONCENTRATED IN THE SOUTHERN PART OF THE STATE,

WHERE THERE IS EASY ACCESS TO LARGE MARKETS AND READY LABOR.

Today Michigan ranks number one in the nation for new manufacturing facilities or expansions, with 1,300 projects completed in 1997 alone.

Most of the earliest Michigan factories manufactured farm equipment, with Battle Creek claiming that it made more traction engines and threshing machines than any other city in America. But the first Michigan city to gain true national fame for a manufactured product was Grand Rapids.

THE SEATING OF AMERICA

In 1837 cabinetmaker William Haldane took advantage of local hardwoods and waterpower from the Grand River to set up a small furniture-making shop. Other firms quickly followed Haldane's lead, producing high-quality cabinetry and upholstered goods until, by the turn of the century, Grand Rapids was known across the country as Furniture City. The Great Depression hit the industry hard, and

many companies went out of business or moved elsewhere. Baker, an industry leader for the finest-quality furniture, remains headquartered in Grand Rapids, where hand-painting and decorating is performed on pieces made at Baker factories in nearby Holland and in North Carolina. Now Grand Rapids is better known as Office Furniture City. More than half of America's workers are employed in offices, and most of them sit in chairs and at workstations made in western Michigan. Steelcase, Inc., the world's leading designer and largest manufacturer of office furniture, is the Grand Rapids area's biggest employer. Other notable manufacturers include American Seating, also in Grand Rapids, Herman Miller in Zeeland, and Holland's Sligh and Haworth companies.

An even more famous Michigan furniture name is La-Z-Boy. The Monroe firm, born when two cousins invented a reclining wooden porch chair seventy years

© The Procter & Gamble Company

The Bissell family had an established crockery business in Grand Rapids before Melville Bissell's allergy to straw dust led him to invent the carpet sweeper. Courtesy, Bissell

ago, is the country's largest upholstered-furniture maker. More than 1.5 million recliners were sold in 1997—up 7 percent from the previous year, a trend that is expected to accelerate as aging baby boomers place relaxation ever higher on their agendas. Casual furniture is a Michigan specialty. The Woodard family has handcrafted wrought iron furniture in Owosso since the 1930s. Menominee's Lloyd/Flanders began producing fine wicker baby buggies in 1906. Today the company uses its innovative loom technology to make a popular patio line of all-weather wicker furniture.

HEARTH AND HOME

Furniture wasn't the only Michigan product making homes around the United States more comfortable. By the 1850s stoves began to replace fireplaces for heating and cooking, and a number of stove factories opened in cities across southern Michigan. Detroit became the leading stove-producing city in the nation, with companies such as Jewel, Garland, and Detroit Stove Works making coal stoves, gas stoves, even stoves that burned blubber for Inuit customers.

Appliances have been a mainstay of Michigan manufacturing. In 1911 Saint Joseph's Upton Machine Company introduced an electric motor–driven wringer

Herman Miller, Inc., has created innovative home and office designs since 1923. Shown here is the Zeeland headquarters showroom. © B. Lindhout

This technician in a Muskegon plant uses a computer to check the vacuum mold behind him for malfunctions. © B. Lindhout

washer. The company changed its name to Whirlpool in 1948. Now headquartered in nearby Benton Harbor, Whirlpool is the world's leading manufacturer and marketer of major home appliances. Grand Rapids crockery shop owner Melville Bissell invented another appliance that made life easier for Americans. Melville was allergic to the straw his crockery came packed in. When his wife, Anna, found it impossible to remove enough straw dust from the shop's carpeting with a broom, Melville came up with a sweeper that featured an enclosed rotating brush, which scooped up particles without scattering them. He patented his invention and, in 1876, founded the Bissell Carpet Sweeper Company in Grand Rapids. Upon her husband's death in 1889, Anna became America's first female corporate CEO, overseeing new product development, including vacuum cleaners, and expanding the business around the globe.

When it comes to cleaning up, Rich DeVos and Jay VanAndel cornered the market. Selling a multipurpose cleaner out of the basement of VanAndel's Ada home in 1959, the patriotic partners named their fledgling business Amway, because entrepreneurship is "the American way." Today Amway's 5,000-plus product line, created in the company's twenty-four research and development laboratories, has expanded from soap to satellite dishes, racking up more than $6 billion in annual global sales, making Amway the world's largest direct-sales company.

SOMETHING FOR EVERYONE

In the apparel field Michigan first made a name for itself with unmentionables. The Dr. Denton Sleeping Garment Mills opened in Centerville in 1878, about the same time that the slogan "never rip and never tear, Ypsilanti underwear" carried that city's union suits to international prominence. The Prince of Wales's silk longjohns from Hay and Todd Company's Ypsilanti

EYEFUL TOWER

THE HAY AND TODD COMPANY HAD A MURAL PAINTED ON THE SIDE OF ITS UNDERWEAR FACTORY FACING THE MICHIGAN CENTRAL RAILWAY TRACKS. THE FIFTEEN-FOOT-TALL WOMAN IN THE PAINTING WORE TIGHT-FITTING YPSILANTI UNDERWEAR AND NOTHING ELSE. SOME NINETEENTH-CENTURY TRAIN TRAVELERS OBJECTED TO THE LANDMARK, AND THE FOLLOWING ANONYMOUS LIMERICK AROSE:

A SCULPTURE OF NYMPHS AND BACCHANTES
OMITTED THE COATS AND PANTIES
A KIND-HEARTED MADAM WHO KNEW THAT SHE HAD 'EM
SUPPLIED THEM WITH WARM YPSILANTIS.

Wolverine sells twenty-six million pairs of footwear on six continents, including its newly fashionable Hush Puppies. Oceana County's Shelby Gemstones supplies the world with exquisite man-made diamonds, rubies, sapphires, and emeralds. In the Shelby factory rare earth compounds are heated to several thousand degrees Fahrenheit, seeded with natural gemstone chips, then "pulled" into crystals that are cut, polished, and set. The resulting gems often surpass their natural counterparts in clarity and color purity. People who prefer to make their clothes at home have James Shapiro to thank for low-cost, high-quality sewing patterns. In 1927, when most patterns cost a dollar, he decided to print them up and sell them for fifteen cents. He called his company Simplicity, and today the Niles facility sells patterns in more than sixty countries.

For Michigan, sports and leisure are serious—and profitable—business. Model train buffs know Chesterfield as the home of Lionel. Bowlers owe a debt to Muskegon, whose Brunswick factory makes most of the nation's bowling pins. Tun-Dra Kennels and Outfitters in Nunica is the world's top producer of dogsleds, even selling the dogs to pull them and leading customers on tours to the Iditarod.

When the Plymouth Iron Windmill Company manufactured small BB guns to give away as a sales promotion, farmers bought one windmill but kept coming back for more air rifles. The windmill firm soon became the Daisey Manufacturing Company, and Plymouth was known for seventy years as "the air rifle capital of the world."

In 1894 Algonac postmaster Chris Smith attached an engine to a rowboat, thereby creating the first powerboat and giving birth to a new industry. Smith's company, Chris-Craft Corporation, opened the waterways of America to powerboats at the same time America's roads were being opened to cars. Chris-Craft and another Algonac boat-racing legend, Gar Wood, made their town on the Saint

Underwear Factory cost him $300 at the turn of the century. Today Carhartt in Dearborn is a major manufacturer of rugged outdoor and work apparel. The nation's largest pigskin tanner is Wolverine World Wide of Rockford, the number one producer of domestic footwear and the world's leading marketer of branded comfort shoes and rugged outdoor boots. Each year

CAT LOVER'S FRIEND

LIFELONG CASSOPOLIS RESIDENT ED LOWE HELD 126 PATENTS BUT MADE HIS FORTUNE FROM JUST ONE OF THEM. IN 1947 HE USED AN ABSORBENT CLAY CALLED FULLER'S EARTH AS THE BASIS OF THE INVENTION HE CALLED KITTY LITTER. HE DIED IN 1995, FIVE YEARS AFTER SELLING HIS KITTY LITTER COMPANY TO RALSTON PURINA.

Clair River the "water speed capital of the world."

Want to saw someone in half? A visit to Colon and about $7,000 will get you the famous Buzz Saw Illusion, one of two thousand magic tricks manufactured and sold by Abbott's Magic Manufacturing Company, the world's largest maker of magic supplies. It all started when renowned magician Harry Blackstone bought a summer place in tiny Colon in the 1920s, drawing fellow magicians to the area as well. One pal, Australian Percy Abbott, fell in love with a local girl and decided to give up showbiz and settle there. He partnered with Blackstone to manufacture and market magic tricks and, although the partnership soured after eight months, Abbott continued with the business. For nearly seventy years now, Colon has been the one-stop shopping spot for the world's masters of prestidigitation.

A TRULY TALL SHIP

THE WORLD'S LARGEST MANUFACTURER OF WEATHER VANES IS WHITEHALL METAL STUDIOS OF MONTAGUE. APPROPRIATELY ENOUGH, THE COMPANY ALSO LAYS CLAIM TO THE WORLD'S LARGEST WEATHER VANE, FORTY-EIGHT FEET TALL AND FESTOONED WITH A FOURTEEN-FOOT REPLICA OF A GREAT LAKES SCHOONER.

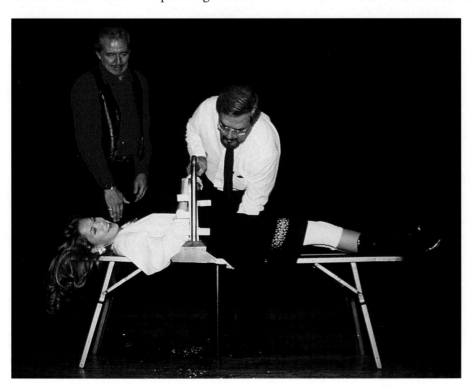

There's no denying the commanding presence of the auto industry here, but Michigan is no one-product state and never has been. For more than a century, "Made in Michigan" has meant quality, innovation, and craftsmanship, with Michigan products finding an important place in Americans' homes as well as their garages.

Magician Harry Blackstone Jr. saws a willing victim in half. The world's largest maker of magic tricks and accessories is Abbott's Magic Manufacturing Company in Colon. © Fotos International/Martha Noble/Archive Photos

Furniture is made at Westinghouse in Grand Rapids. © B. Lindhout

MANUFACTURING, DISTRIBUTION AND WAREHOUSING

KASLE STEEL CORPORATION

Steel is certainly one of the foundations of Michigan's manufacturing strengths. For more than seventy-five years, Kasle Steel Corporation, a Michigan-based company that processes steel, has been the company that many of the state's steel and automotive manufacturers have turned to for their needs. Roger Kasle, owner and president of Kasle Steel, believes his company's success and that of his customers are one and the same.

"Although we are a processing manufacturer," Kasle says, "we are truly in the service business. Without giving our customers exactly what they want, we would not be as successful as we have

Dearborn Processing is Kasle Steel's fully integrated steel-processing facility in Dearborn, Michigan, which offers efficient customer service with pickling, slitting, and blanking under one roof.

Kasle Steel Corporation's Auto Blankers in Flint, Michigan, is a leader in the production and supply of high-quality configured and nonconfigured blanks for the automotive industry worldwide.

been. Kasle Steel has consistently provided value-added services that assist its customers in becoming more profitable."

Roger Kasle is the third generation of his family to lead the company. "My grandfather started this business in 1922 by selling scrap steel; my father built it into a major service center operation, serving the automotive industry; and now I am responsible for taking it into the future," says Kasle. He is making his mark by following the principles that have earned Kasle the reputation it enjoys: being dedicated to customer requirements, providing value-added processing, and constantly improving the cost and quality of the products.

Kasle Steel Corporation has progressed from its simple start as a scrap-steel warehouse to a major supplier of processed flat-rolled sheet steel for the automotive industry, with facilities in Dearborn, Flint, and Woodhaven, Michigan, and in Windsor, Ontario, Canada. These facilities now process nearly one million tons of steel annually.

In addition, Kasle has recently formed a joint venture—the RSDC of Michigan, LLC—with Itochu International, a Japanese trading company, which has constructed one of the largest steel processing and distribution centers in North America in Holt, Michigan. This facility, encompassing 650,000 square feet, will store and process 1.2 million metric tons of steel annually.

In announcing the joint venture, Governor John Engler said: "There are few places in the world where a joint venture of this magnitude, with the ramifications that this one holds, can take place. The state of Michigan is unique in having strong companies like Kasle that are dedicated to research and development, have a business-friendly environment, and, at the same time, have international stature such that it can attract

Three generations of Kasle Steel, "the founder, the educator, and the future," include (from top to bottom) Abe Kasle, chairman and president from 1939 to 1965; Leonard Kasle, chairman and president from 1965 to 1990; and Roger Kasle, chairman and president since 1990.

a major firm like Itochu as a partner."

In 1998 Kasle Steel qualified as a QS-9000 supplier. The quality of its products and services is recognized throughout the industry. Currently the company employs approximately 550 people at its sites in Michigan and in Ontario, Canada.

As Kasle Steel Corporation enters the new millennium, the company views its future as strong and progressive. Using the current strength in the automotive industry, the company is building upon its unique position to continue to serve the needs of its customers through its value-added processing and distribution capabilities. Roger Kasle is committed to this tradition of excellence, which has been Kasle Steel's trademark for close to a century and which continues to set the tone for a dynamic and exciting future.

LEFT: *Shown under construction and currently in operation, the new Holt, Michigan, facility of the RSDC of Michigan—a joint venture of Kasle Steel Corporation and the Japanese trading company Itochu International—is one of North America's largest steel processing and distribution centers.* INSET: *Kasle Steel's Quality Coil Processing in Woodhaven, Michigan, is a modern full-service blanking and slitting steel-processing center.*

JERVIS B. WEBB COMPANY

A PIONEER OF

THE AUTOMATED

CONVEYORS

THAT CONVINCED

HENRY FORD TO USE

ASSEMBLY LINES, THE

JERVIS B. WEBB

COMPANY DESIGNS

AND MANUFACTURES

HIGH-VOLUME, COST-

EFFICIENT SYSTEMS TO

MOVE, MANAGE, AND

CONTROL MATERIALS

WORLDWIDE

Jervis B. Webb Company, the fourth-largest material-handling company in the world, is recognized as a leader in the design and construction of high-performance automated material-handling systems. This privately held corporation has wholly owned facilities and joint venture partners operating around the globe, with annual sales that exceed $400 million. The Farmington Hills, Michigan, company remains a family-owned business, headed by George H. Webb, who serves as chairman and chief executive officer.

The foundation of the Jervis B. Webb Company, incorporated in 1919, was Webb's rivetless conveyor chain, which was designed to increase production capacities for manufacturers in many industries. The conveyor chain was first used at the Studebaker automobile plant in Detroit to transport automobile bodies to the assembly department.

In 1921 Jervis Bennett Webb designed another conveyor system that combined his patented chain, skate wheels with brackets, and an overhead I-beam suspended from the plant's roof trusses. The new overhead chain conveyor followed the path of production flow and delivered its loads to workstations along the assembly line with timely and dependable regularity. This system, which was installed at the Fisher Body plant in Detroit, was one of the first automated assembly lines to clearly demonstrate that conveyors cause dramatic improvements in assembly processes and worker throughput.

Soon after, Henry Ford became interested in the

The 225,000-square-foot world headquarters building of the Jervis B. Webb Company in Farmington Hills, Michigan, accommodates 550 full-time employees engaged in administration, engineering, sales, and support-related functions.

new concept and had the overhead chain conveyor installed for production testing at the Ford plant in Walkerville, Ontario, Canada. When it proved to be successful, Ford ordered more than thirty miles of the conveyor so the system could be placed in all of his plants in the United States.

Webb's revolutionary overhead trolley-wheel conveyor was followed by the development of new material-handling products, processes, and innovations, including the first towline conveyor, designed to increase throughput in freight depots and efficiency in large truck terminals.

Next, Webb designed and patented the first overhead power-and-free conveyor, which allowed manufacturers to stop products on the conveyor at various workstations without stopping the entire production line. Loads are carried on a lower (free) track and are moved along when engaged by the continuously moving (power) track mounted above. Webb also designed and marketed no-impact accumulating roller conveyors, which reduce damage to products packed in cartons or on pallets.

At Jervis B. Webb, the design of software for material control and management is provided in-house by Ann Arbor Computer, a Webb division since 1965. The engineers at Webb Ann

The I-Beam conveyor, the Jervis B. Webb Company's original product line, is still widely used throughout the world as a reliable means of continuous material transport.

Arbor designed and installed the first computer-controlled materials-handling system at General Motors in Bay City, Michigan, in 1965. At about the same time, at Chrysler's Huber Avenue Foundry in Detroit, the world's first automatic foundry was established; iron was poured into molds on Webb Dog Magic® overhead power-and-free conveyors.

In 1959 the Triax company of Cleveland, Ohio, designed the first automated storage-and-retrieval system (AS/RS). This new system created the automated warehousing concept and pioneered high-density storage-and-retrieval systems. AS/RS dramatically improves inventory management and control of pallet loads and unit loads for automotive, newspaper, warehousing, and assembly operations. Jervis B. Webb acquired the company in 1977 and formed the Webb-Triax division.

The Jervis B. Webb Company also is a pioneer and leading manufacturer of automatic guided vehicles—driverless conveyances that proceed along electronically guided paths and automatically load, unload, and transport products that weigh from 10 to 250,000 pounds. The Automated Electrified Monorail (AEM) is a clean, quiet, self-powered, high-speed conveyor that is typically used in light-duty or sanitary environments. AEM applications include assembling automobile parts, motorcycles, and aircraft engines, and carrying spare parts to waiting airplanes.

Based on its original technology for the overhead power-and-free conveyor, Jervis B. Webb created the inverted power-and-free conveyor, a chain conveyor that accommodates a robotic interface and provides ergonomic comfort for assembly line workers. Space-saving, cost-saving inverted power-and-free conveyor systems are a leading choice for high-volume automated paint systems and clean-room environments.

Jervis B. Webb also manufactures a line of bucket elevators, apron conveyors, and screw conveyor systems that handle cement,

The patented Dog Magic®, Wide Wing™ inverted power-and-free conveyor system is a new conveyor-technology leader. This reliable conveyor system is an ideal choice for general transport, painting, assembly, and robotic interface applications in many industries.

alumina, raw sugar, hot lime, grain, salt, ore, fruits, vegetables, vitamins, coffee, recycled paper, and other consumables. These high-volume systems also are used to transport raw materials used in generating power, processing primary metals, shipping, processing pulp and making paper, managing waste, and mining.

Today the company designs, fabricates, installs, and services many types of material-handling equipment found in industrial environments. Many modern manufacturing plants save labor and reduce handling costs through the use of Webb's integrated systems—sophisticated automated-handling systems, including storage-and-retrieval machines, roller and belt conveyors, and automatic guided vehicles, that are linked to computer controls and work as unified systems.

The company's experienced engineers use sophisticated 3-D virtual-engineering design techniques to develop material-handling systems that will provide the highest level of service to its customers and help them to reduce the time needed to take new products to the market.

As the demands of industrialization and productivity increase around the globe, the Jervis B. Webb Company's mission is to focus its resources on one endeavor—to provide high-volume, cost-efficient solutions for the movement, management, and control of materials.

Rail-guided Smart-T-Car® and heavy-duty accumulation roller conveyors are used by major beverage producers. This efficient system feeds empty cans to high-speed, beverage-filling lines at a capacity of 2,000 cans per minute.

EDW. C. LEVY CO.

The Edw. C. Levy Co. has been a part of Michigan's business landscape for much of this century. Its 1918 beginning is tied to a handshake agreement between founder Edw. C. Levy and another well-known icon of Michigan business history, legendary industrialist Henry Ford. Levy offered his services to Ford to haul and refine slag, a by-product of the Ford steel-making operations. Levy's successful processing of blast furnace and steel furnace slag soon attracted the attention of other steel mill and foundry clients and the company's core business was established.

In developing its slag-processing technology, Levy ingenuity also developed state-of-the-art equipment to make the process more efficient and economical; created new uses for slag, which was once considered a waste product; and built markets for new products, such as high-quality construction aggregates. From steel mill services, therefore, the natural direction for Levy growth was into the aggregates business, recycling technologies, construction materials, and trucking operations to transport the products. The Levy family of companies includes such Michigan names as Clawson Concrete, Ace Asphalt, Cadillac Asphalt Paving, and American Aggregates of Michigan, as well as numerous aggregate mining companies and trucking companies.

As one of the largest suppliers of quality construction materials in southeast Michigan, Levy has a presence in many Michigan landmarks, such as the headquarters of General Motors and the Renaissance Center in Detroit; Ford World Headquarters in Dearborn; terminals and major runways at Detroit Metropolitan Airport in Romulus; and the United States headquarters of DaimlerChrysler, in Auburn Hills.

Edw. C. Levy Co. metal products begin with the processing of blast furnace and steel furnace slag. Steel mill services are the foundation of the Levy family of businesses, which provide high-quality construction materials for major projects throughout southeast Michigan and beyond.

From the very beginning Edw. C. Levy recognized the importance of protecting and conserving the world's natural resources—the foundation of his company's business. He was a champion of recycling before the concept became the popular and appropriate thing to do. In fact, Levy realized that, quite apart from being good for the environment, recycling simply made good business sense.

The corporate culture that he established emphasizes respect for the environment and the wise use of natural resources. Ed Levy, Jr., who now heads the company, continues and reinforces

EDW. C. LEVY CO.

that philosophy. Levy's environmental commitment goes beyond recycling the raw materials contained in slag to reclaiming the land itself. When the company completes sand and gravel mining operations at a location, the land is recycled for use in another way, such as for attractive residential communities. One Levy company, Harvest Land, is currently developing Harvest Lake, a 950-home community on 1,000 acres of a former sand and gravel pit in Novi, Michigan.

Not surprisingly, Levy also takes pride in its greatest natural resource—its people. The warmth of Levy's corporate culture has fostered a loyal, committed, and dedicated workforce of employees who often not only spend their entire career with Levy, but also recommend the company to friends and relatives. In a day when "job-hopping" has become the norm, it's still possible to find three generations of a single family pledging their allegiance to the Levy family of businesses.

"It is part of our mission to strengthen the communities in which we work and to share our success with worthy charitable causes," says Ed Levy, Jr. "Our level of employee participation in giving back to the community through worthwhile causes such as the United Way and Junior Achievement is always near the top among companies of our size. We work hard to be good corporate citizens."

A strong community provides a stronger basis for future business, and the Edw. C. Levy Co. has positioned itself well

Because structural integrity is critical, contractors look to high-quality construction products from the Edw. C. Levy Co. In asphalt and concrete mixes and masonry units, as paver base, slurry seal or trenching backfill, Levy products offer stability, durability, and economy.

Levy products, such as road-base materials or concrete or asphalt paving are an integral part of Michigan's extensive roadway system. Graceful highway interchanges, like this one near downtown Detroit, are made strong and durable with high-quality Levy materials.

for sustained future growth. It has already exported its unique technologies beyond Michigan's borders to successful operations in Ohio, Indiana, Florida, Colorado, Arizona, and South Carolina, and beyond the nation's borders to Australia and Thailand. Levy continues to look for new ways to grow its business geographically by expanding into new markets, which will provide better balance among its companies as well as more opportunities for its employees. No matter where in the world Levy establishes operations in the years to come, however, Michigan will remain the center of the Levy universe.

By building upon its eighty-plus years of success, the Edw. C. Levy Co. is taking the lead in all of the industries in which it is involved. It has done so by embracing business principles, such as its excellent quality management system and well-developed training capabilities, that will allow it to be a prosperous and profitable international company well into the coming century.

HOLNAM INC

HOLNAM INC,

HEADQUARTERED IN

DUNDEE, MICHIGAN,

SUPPLIES MILLIONS

OF TONS OF CEMENT

ANNUALLY FOR

INDUSTRIES AND

MUNICIPALITIES,

WHILE ALSO

INVESTING DEEPLY IN

ENVIRONMENTAL

PROTECTION

Cement is the key ingredient, or "glue," in concrete used to construct buildings, bridges, streets, and sidewalks—concrete structures that touch everybody's daily lives. Holnam Inc is the largest cement manufacturer in the United States.

Headquartered in Dundee, Michigan, Holnam was formed through the March 1990 merger of Dundee Cement Company and Ideal Basic Industries. It is part of Holderbank Financière Glaris Ltd., of Switzerland, the world's largest producer of cement. The name "Holnam" is an acronym for Holderbank North America.

Holnam has a nationwide presence in the United States cement industry with fourteen manufacturing facilities and more than seventy distribution terminals. As the nation's market-share leader, Holnam has the ability to manufacture more than twelve million tons of cement and

The new million-dollar cement distribution terminal in Grandville, Michigan, with more than 2,000 metric tons of storage capacity, will enable Holnam to better serve its western Michigan customers with a wide variety of products, including blended cements, fly ash, and GranCem®, Holnam's brand of ground, granulated blast-furnace slag. Other Holnam supply points in Michigan include terminals in Detroit and Elmira and Holnam's plant in Dundee.

At the Holnam Inc corporate offices, in Dundee, Michigan, a 180-member corporate team coordinates operations with Holnam employees at the company's approximately 100 other locations.

mineral components annually. Holnam markets cement through three geographical divisions, which are further subdivided into fourteen marketing regions, each with its own office, staff, and knowledge of the market it serves.

At the Dundee, Michigan, plant—which celebrates its fortieth anniversary in 1999—limestone is mined from an on-site quarry, crushed, and then mixed with water to form a slurry. This slurry is introduced into two rotating kilns, each 460 feet long and 16.5 feet in diameter. The kilns are enclosed, brick-lined steel cylinders, which are angled slightly so that upon rotation, the raw material slowly moves down toward the low end, called the "hot" end. It is here that a flame of more than 3500 degrees Fahrenheit brings up the temperature of the raw material to more than 2400 degrees. This intense heat chemically alters the material and recombines it into a new substance in the form of small stones, called "clinker." The clinker drops out of the kiln to a grate and is transported to an area where the stones are mixed with gypsum and crushed to a consistency finer than talcum powder. The finished powder is cement, and the Dundee plant manufactures more than one million tons of it each year.

Cement that contains mineral components results in better-performing concrete. The two most widely used mineral components are fly ash and GGBFS (ground, granulated blast-furnace slag). Holnam offers both to its customers; GranCem® is its trademarked brand of GGBFS. Both fly ash and slag would usually become waste materials and end up in landfills if not put to use in this way. GranCem® cement typically replaces, pound for pound, a portion of the portland cement in concrete.

At the Dundee plant, Holnam makes HolCem. HolCem is portland cement that has been blended with GranCem®. HolCem cement is a high performance cement that can help users meet the increasing performance demands, higher standards, and specifications and environmental restraints being put on today's construction industry.

Holnam takes its environmental responsibility seriously, working closely with local, state, and federal authorities to conserve natural resources. The company also supports the efforts of its employees to be active in the community with youth organizations, schools, clubs, and churches.

As an example of its dedication to preserving the environment, Holnam received approval in 1998 to replace up to 21 percent of its fuel with Tire Derived Fuel (TDF) at its Dundee Township cement plant. Under an agreement with the Monroe County Environmental Health Department, Holnam will collect 1,000 tires a month from residents who

Holnam cement becomes concrete for Michigan's roads and highways. Here, a road construction crew ensures a smoothly finished texture for a section of route M-14 in Washtenaw County during the 1998 summer construction season.

live in the townships and villages that surround the plant and will shred and burn them.

Holnam also will construct and install a scrubber and oxidizer unit, which is expected to cost the company in excess of $25 million. This effort is the culmination of nearly five years of research that sought ways to eliminate odors and the nonsteam portion of the visible plume from the plant's main stack. The equipment also will significantly reduce emissions of sulfur, sulfur oxides, and hydrocarbons from the stack, which already are well within the plant's permit-compliance limits.

Holnam's investment in these technologies is unprecedented in the cement industry, not only because of the cost but also because this is the first time such technologies have been used together at a cement plant.

HOLNAM

The Holnam cement plant in Dundee, Michigan, built in the late 1950s and modified several times since then to improve production capacity and environmental performance, produces more than 1.1 million tons of cement per year.

LA-Z-BOY INCORPORATED

Since its founding in 1929 in Monroe, Michigan, La-Z-Boy Incorporated has grown to be the nation's largest manufacturer of upholstered furniture, the world's leading producer of reclining chairs, and the third-largest North American residential furniture manufacturer.

The La-Z-Boy legacy began back in 1928 when Edward Knabusch and Edwin Shoemaker, two cousins from Monroe, Michigan, designed an innovative porch chair that reclined, offering improved relaxation over its straight-back counterpart. In 1929 they took a customer's advice and upholstered the chair to provide year-round use. The La-Z-Boy® recliner was born. Decades of consistent

A 1949 advertisement for a recliner, "the world's most comfortable chair," includes the familiar La-Z-Boy slogan, Sit in it, that's all we ask.

ABOVE: *This is the small, simple factory in Monroe, Michigan, where La-Z-Boy® recliners were first made.*
LEFT: *On the occasion of La-Z-Boy's fiftieth anniversary, founders (from left) Knabusch and Shoemaker display their original wood-slat recliner with a 1970s recliner upholstered in the style of the day.*

growth and expansion have earned La-Z-Boy a position as one of the world's largest furniture companies with the most widely recognized name in furniture.

Shoemaker's innate mechanical genius together with Knabusch's innovative marketing skills led to the creation of what today is a furniture empire. Once called Floral City Furniture, the company has sold enough reclining chairs in its history to put one in every home in the nation and a second one in just about every home east of the Mississippi.

The qualities that made that first chair possible—a passion for innovation, responsiveness to consumers' needs, and a willingness to listen to and work with those who sell its products—have become the hallmarks of La-Z-Boy.

The company, which employs 12,500 people, has thirty-one manufacturing facilities in the United States, Canada, and Europe, and operates through eight independent divisions, each with distinct products: La-Z-Boy Residential, La-Z-Boy Business Furniture Group, Hammary Furniture Company, Kincaid Furniture Company, England/Corsair, Inc., La-Z-Boy Canada, Centurion Furniture PLC, and Sam Moore Furniture Industries. Its products are sold in more than thirty countries.

La-Z-Boy Residential serves thousands of retail residential furniture outlets in the United States and Canada through a network of distributors, including independent furniture retailers, mass merchandisers, department stores, La-Z-Boy® in-store galleries, and La-Z-Boy Furniture Galleries® stores. Its products are found in hometown furniture stores as well as in regional and national chains, such as Montgomery Ward and Sears HomeLife℠.

La-Z-Boy Incorporated makes furniture for every room in the home and beyond the home as well. It offers one of the industry's broadest lines of quality products addressing

The Dreamtime™ chair, with contemporary styling, is one of La-Z-Boy's most popular recliners.

the specific function and durability requirements of commercial settings, from business offices to health clinics and major medical centers.

"We are no longer that simple chair company producing just recliners," says Patrick H. Norton, chairman of the board. "Today we are a multidimensional company with a full range of quality products, sold through a diverse distribution system, with a firm grasp on the realities of what it will take to survive and prosper in the years ahead."

Although the company has become global in scope, it retains its strong ties to the community. La-Z-Boy has long been an active community supporter and has made many philanthropic gifts to hospitals, schools, libraries, museums, and religious programs.

"Throughout our long, distinguished history, the little company started by 'the two Eds' has remained true to its values," Norton says. "It is upon these values that we intend to fulfill our vision for growth and profitability in the twenty-first century. Our vision is to be regarded globally as the premier provider of home, office, and institutional products in all markets in which we compete. We are confident in our ability to achieve this vision as long as we maintain our commitment to providing our customers with superior quality, service, and value. This was the mission of our company's founders, and it continues to be the driving force behind the La-Z-Boy of today."

LA-Z-BOY®

The Westport™ sofa and love seat are part of the American Home Collection by La-Z-Boy®, a line of stationary furniture for the home.

NELMS TECHNOLOGIES

When it comes to manufacturing precision parts for Michigan's automotive industry, Nelms Technologies provides unequaled quality, workmanship, and services.

Nelms Technologies, a true "management company," had its birth in the mind of Edwin Nelms, a man with a lifetime of experience in the valve industry. In the mid-1980s, he set his sights on the automotive industry and settled in Detroit.

He has never looked back.

In 1989 Nelms and several like-minded business colleagues formed the partnership that is today Nelms Technologies. This organization was started as a vehicle to purchase W. A. Thomas, a venerable supplier of automotive parts. One of the first challenges for Nelms at W. A. Thomas was the development of an aluminum transmission valve for Chrysler Corporation. In a make-or-break development, W. A. Thomas was able to come through for the automaker and has maintained and expanded its business relationship ever since.

Ed Nelms, company founder and CEO of Nelms Technologies, stands in front of the company's world headquarters in Romulus, Michigan.

Founded in 1946 as a supplier of high-quality aircraft and technical instrumentation products, W. A. Thomas Company is now a diversified manufacturing firm, making products that are essential to the automotive and commercial industries. With the W. A. Thomas Company, Nelms Technologies has set standards for engineering excellence with the creation of patented products, such as hard-coated aluminum wrist pins and the quick-connect fastener. While the names of such precision components may be unfamiliar to some, automobiles simply do not run without them.

Since then, Nelms Technologies has purchased Hy-Lift, formerly Johnson Products. With its 1996 Hy-Lift acquisition (from SPX), the company is positioned to increase its presence in both automotive and nonautomotive lines. Always innovative, Hy-Lift custom designs high-volume products, such as roller rocker arms, hydraulic lifters, hydraulic lash adjusters, mechanical tappets, and integrated valve actuation systems. The company continues to engineer solutions and enhance its product line for the future.

Operating units of Nelms Technologies—W. A. Thomas and Hy-Lift LLC—have benefited from the experience, vision, and direction of Edwin Nelms and his seasoned management team. Together, they have gained a leadership position in the development of innovative products, manufacturing more than one-hundred million components annually.

In 1998 Nelms Technologies opened its world headquarters in Romulus, adjacent to Detroit Metropolitan Airport, a central location for business operation, product development, and production.

Nelms Technologies' success is due to a combination of technical competence, operational solutions, commitment to quality, customer service, and a thorough understanding of manufacturing processes, all of which make it a world-class manufacturer.

"We are organized to respond quickly to the opportunities and challenges of an increasingly global marketplace," says Edwin Nelms. "Nelms Technologies has worked to consolidate and streamline its design and production resources, concentrating them into centers of excellence for a vast range of precision products. We continue to apply the same sound principles that generate profitable returns by expanding our capabilities,

preserving quality distinction, and developing innovative manufacturing processes to reach global consumers and niche-market industries."

The keys to the future of Nelms Technologies are the cross-functional, multidisciplined teams who work there. These groups identify changes and trends in customer needs. They are skilled in building competitively advantaged products, and are experienced at using state-of-the-art systems to produce problem-solving products.

"We use our management systems and strengths in personnel and technology to aggressively seek and acquire additional resources to serve an ever-expanding and diverse customer base," says Nelms. "Our success and continued planned growth will provide an improved quality of life for our employees and a sound return to our shareholders."

The goal of Nelms Technologies is to go beyond the manufacture of commercially acceptable products. "Our products are, and will continue to be, of a distinctive quality, utility, and value that were previously economically unavailable," he says. "The commitment to innovation will play an ever-increasing role in the uniqueness required to increase market penetration and assure success in the global marketplace."

NEAR RIGHT: *W. A. Thomas's patented universal, easy-to-use quick-connect fastener was developed to combine increased strength with simplicity. The quick-connect fastener, available in sizes to accommodate any fluid connection application, is a leading-edge advance in connection technology.*

CENTER RIGHT: *Aluminum wrist pins developed and patented by W. A. Thomas are made of hard-coated aluminum and are 35 percent lighter than steel, offering increased efficiency and reliability at a significant weight reduction compared to earlier versions.*

FAR RIGHT: *Roller rocker arms custom-designed by Hy-Lift for use in single- and dual-overhead camshaft valve-train systems can be tailored for a specific application by the use of one of a variety of materials.*

HELM INCORPORATED

In a state where the automobile industry is king, Helm Incorporated plays a pivotal support role in keeping that industry's wheels rolling and its engines humming.

Helm, which is based in Highland Park, Michigan, was founded in 1943 as a book binding company and incorporated in 1946. Today it is one of the dominant distributors and retailers of glove-box manuals for automobile owners and service manuals for authorized automobile dealers.

Since 1959, when Helm began distributing automotive service manuals, its name has appeared in more than 200 million of the glove-box manuals automobile dealers provide for their new-car customers annually. With these manuals and the service manuals it distributes for authorized automobile dealers, the company accounts for more than 70 percent of the North American automotive service-publication business.

Helm Incorporated produces catalogs and other corporate-identification program components, from creation through distribution.

Each year Helm handles more than one million telephone calls and ships publications to fill more than 600,000 orders. Many of these are placed by individual consumers, as well as by Helm's corporate customers, either through Helm's on-line bookstore at www.helminc.com or by telephone to the company's state-of-the-art telecommunications center in Highland Park.

However, Helm Incorporated is more than a distributor of automotive service manuals. Helm is one of the nation's top-twenty-five producers of corporate merchandise catalogs, particularly in the areas of automobiles and the aftermarket industry. Since 1969 the company also has been offering its clients specialty marketing-support services designed to heighten their corporate brand identification and increase their revenues.

The privately held company, whose clients include such automotive giants as General Motors, Ford Motor Company, Toyota Motor Sales U.S.A., American Honda Motors, American

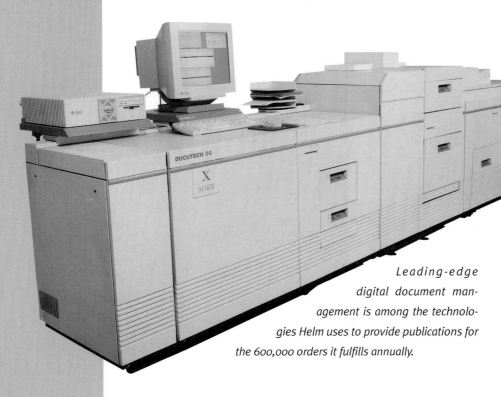

Leading-edge digital document management is among the technologies Helm uses to provide publications for the 600,000 orders it fulfills annually.

Isuzu, American Suzuki Motors, Hyundai Motors, and KIA Motors, also offers a full line of custom-designed print-to-order, print-on-demand, and bin-on-demand services. It also prints corporate documents, order forms, instruction manuals, flyers, specialty and vintage publications, and brochures.

Among the marketing-support services Helm provides are complete turnkey promotional merchandise programs offering everything from pens and apparel to signage and point-of-purchase materials.

As a result of growing Internet use, the company has developed the expertise to assist clients in the development and maintenance of Web sites and other high-technology marketing communications devices.

In the area of marketing-support services, "Our business focus is to provide our clients with value-added marketing solutions through the understanding of their business objectives," says Dennis Gusick, Helm's president.

"We have developed relationships with manufacturers such as General Motors, Ford Motor Company, and Honda with respect to both our publications services and our marketing-support services, because we understand the importance of their corporate image," adds Bob Malkiewicz, Helm's vice president of sales and marketing.

Helm Incorporated also has client relations with several automobile industry support firms and with companies outside the automotive industry. Among these are Sherwin-Williams, Johnson Controls Inc., National Automotive Parts Association (NAPA), Florists' Transworld Delivery (FTD), Aeroquip, and the motorcycle division of Honda.

Since its inception, Helm's corporate mission has been to continually meet the needs and expectations of its customers through delivery of superior service. It has accomplished that mission well.

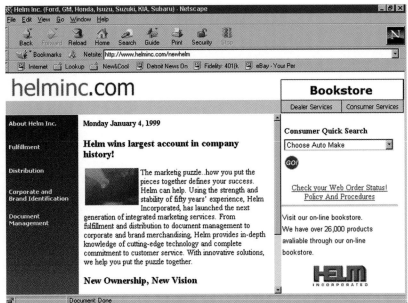

The Helm Web site (www.helminc.com) features its on-line bookstore, which enables efficient transactions with the use of the most advanced E-commerce technology.

"Our passion to serve the needs of the customer is the foundation on which we operate," Gusick says. "Our goal is excellence. We are committed to continual improvement and innovation in all aspects of our business."

Helm's strength is its employees, Gusick adds, including more than 100 plant personnel and more than 175 office and clerical staff members. Backing up the workforce are state-of-the-art facilities to help the company deliver top-quality products. Helm's Highland Park operation includes automated inventory and material-handling systems, high-speed digital printers, and sophisticated computer and telecommunication systems.

"At Helm, we stay ahead of the technological curve," Malkiewicz says. "We understand how and when to use technologies. Our strong commitment to technological superiority gives us, and, more importantly, gives our customers, a major competitive edge."

Visit the Helm Web site at www.helminc.com for additional information.

Helm Corporate Headquarters is strategically located in Highland Park, Michigan.

KURDZIEL INDUSTRIES, INC.

KURDZIEL

INDUSTRIES, INC.

IS ONE OF THE

WORLD'S LEADING

MANUFACTURERS

OF LARGE

COUNTERWEIGHT

CASTINGS FOR THE

MATERIAL-HANDLING,

CONSTRUCTION

EQUIPMENT, AND

AERIAL-LIFT

INDUSTRIES

Walter Kurdziel was typical of many of the young, determined entrepreneurs who made Michigan the industrial powerhouse that it is today. In 1937 the 26-year-old immigrant sold his family's tavern and restaurant business in Muskegon, Michigan, bought an old industrial building in the nearby town of Rothbury, and entered into the foundry business.

Despite a lack of money and virtually no experience in operating a foundry, Kurdziel persevered. Not even a fire in 1944 that destroyed his original building and put his fledgling enterprise on hold for two years could stop him from succeeding.

His perseverance and determination eventually paid off. In time Kurdziel's foundry business flourished, initially producing white-iron mill stars for larger, automotive foundries and, subsequently, counterweight castings for companies that make forklifts and other heavy-duty construction equipment vehicles.

As a result of Walter Kurdziel's work, today— six decades and three generations later—Kurdziel Industries, Inc., stands as the world's leading manufacturer of large counterweight castings (up to 70,000 pounds) for the material-handling

The Kurdziel Industries, Inc., foundry in Rothbury, Michigan, covering more than 250,000 square feet, supplies castings to the material-handling, construction equipment, and aerial working platforms industries.

KURDZIEL

(forklift), construction equipment and aerial-lift (boom-lift) industries. In fact, with an annual production of counterweights that is nearly 150,000 tons, it supplies almost 60 percent of the counterweights purchased by North American lift-truck companies and produces the majority of all cast counterweights made in North America.

"Kurdziel started out by fulfilling a crucial need of the flourishing automotive industry and developed into a company that has surpassed competition in serving the world's largest producers of construction vehicles," says Scott Pranger, vice president of sales and marketing for Kurdziel.

Users of Kurdziel's counterweights today include such forklift manufacturers as Hyster, Yale, Clark, Toyota, Nissan, and Komatsu. Heavy construction equipment makers among its clients include such firms as Caterpillar, John Deere,

Molten iron is the core of foundry operations at Kurdziel Industries.

Kobelco, and Link-Belt. Among the boom-lift manufacturers who use Kurdziel counterweights are firms such as JLG, Genie, Grove, Upright, and Condor & Snorkel.

Muskegon-based, privately owned Kurdziel Industries has expanded far beyond its birthplace in Rothbury. The main foundry still remains in the small Michigan town of 450 residents, and the company also owns and operates a casting-finishing operation and distribution center in Wauseon, Ohio, and a foundry in Sparta, Michigan, that specializes in making smaller, high-volume gray-iron products for the automotive and appliance industries. In addition, Kurdziel International Corporation was founded in 1997, with the intent of expanding Kurdziel's casting business globally. With subsidiary foundry locations in China, Kurdziel is able to support customers worldwide with a variety of casting designs.

"Thirty percent of our customers are Japanese companies," says Donald L. Huizenga, Kurdziel's president and chief executive officer. "It is in their basic business philosophy to surround their plants with suppliers. So it is necessary for us to be close to their locations to supply castings to them." Throughout its expansion and product diversification, Kurdziel Industries has continued to embrace the business philosophy of its founder, including being responsive to its customers' needs and committed to its employees and the communities in which it operates.

The company keeps a staff of engineers ready at all times to visit a client's site anywhere in the world in the event of an emergency, to help the client quickly assess problems and create solutions.

Always in the process of improving its efficiency and the quality of its products and services, the company invests heavily in and uses the

Sparta Foundry has manufactured high-quality gray-iron castings like these since 1926 for use in the automotive, appliance, utility, and various specialty industries.

latest technological advances available to ensure that its counterweight castings are always top-notch.

To help its communities environmentally, Kurdziel recently set up several million dollars worth of state-of-the-art equipment to reduce emissions from its melting process and dust created by its counterweight finishing operations.

"We take pride in our ability to succeed in today's market, while staying involved in the technological changes that are taking place," Pranger says. "Continuous investment in technology and training gives assurance that we will be able to meet the needs of our customers tomorrow, as well as today, with increased efficiency, productivity, and competitiveness."

Walter Kurdziel couldn't have said it better.

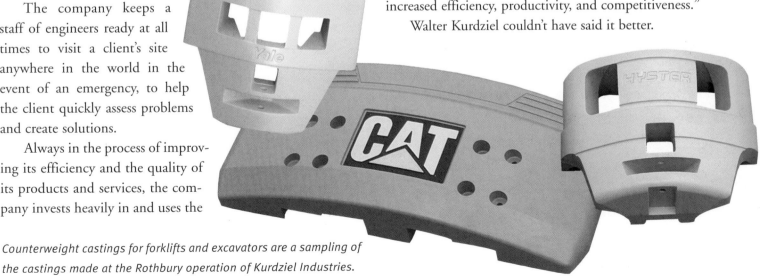

Counterweight castings for forklifts and excavators are a sampling of the castings made at the Rothbury operation of Kurdziel Industries.

EMHART FASTENING TEKNOLOGIES

A *BLACK&DECKER* COMPANY

At Emhart Fastening Teknologies the company says its motto, Creating the Future, "is about growth—it's about change, and it's about taking risks. It is not just a promise. It is who we are and what we do. We are uniquely positioned to reduce our customers' overall product assembly costs by anticipating and meeting their needs with advanced technology and market-driven solutions. In this way, Creating the Future is our business."

WORLD VISION

For a company with more than 100 years of experience in service to industry, Emhart believes the best is yet to come—the best in terms of innovation and the best in terms of solutions that add high value to its customers' assembly problems. Thousands of Emhart employees at twenty-four locations worldwide believe that their ability to Create the Future has never been greater—that Emhart has just begun to harness the power that new ideas can bring to global industry.

WORLDWIDE REACH

Over the past several years Emhart has evolved into a global leader in the design and creation of unique fastener and assembly technologies. Today the company is capable of delivering a depth and breadth of services and products through a flexible, cross-functional global organization. With this world-wide reach, Emhart has developed the local, regional, and global resources necessary to proactively respond to a wide range of industry demands.

Weldfast replaces spot-welding of brackets with advanced drawn-arc welding systems that are easier, faster, and more cost effective.

Emhart Fastening Teknologies provides Mobile Innovation Centers that tour North America and Europe to bring engineering solutions to customers. Each minitechnology center has conference areas and design, engineering, and test facilities, and also serves as a customer training unit.

Emhart's proprietary global communication network, Teknolink, contains the designs and specifications for every tool and assembly system that Emhart has created for its customers worldwide. Teknolink is the repository of Emhart's 100 years of knowledge and expertise in fastening and assembly systems. It provides the company with the where-withal to deliver global solutions in real time.

WORLDWIDE SYSTEMS SOLUTIONS

To stay competitive in today's global economy, Emhart finds it takes more than being a supplier—it takes business partners. Emhart provides technological solutions for more than 100 different industries. For each of these, Emhart has technologies designed to deliver innovative, integrated fastening system solutions for virtually any manufacturing challenge.

To do this, the company offers a total systems approach to fastening that enables simultaneous engineering to mirror customer research, design, engineering, and manufacturing processes. Its systems approach goes beyond fasteners to focus on the design of assembly systems to streamline production and improve quality.

WORLDWIDE VIEW ANALYSIS

To enable its customers to meet the challenges they face, Emhart research and development uses the joint disciplines of Application Analysis and Value Analysis. Application Analysis demonstrates the way Emhart's global technology can be applied to enhance an assembly process. Value Analysis details the costs and benefits of applying advanced Emhart technologies to a customer's needs.

Emhart has developed an application benchmark process that enables its engineers to analyze every component of a car, truck, appliance, or computer and then recommend improvements to the fastening design and process that can be achieved with assembly technology solutions—improvements that result in reduced costs for customers.

WORLDWIDE INNOVATION CENTERS

Emhart supports the design and application needs of its customers through a unique network of Innovation Centers, which are strategically located around the world. The centers are staffed by skilled application specialists and are electronically linked to share application data and new design concepts with each other and with customers. There are permanent Emhart Innovation Center locations in the United States, Japan, and Europe, as well as two mobile centers in North America and one in Europe. Each is a minitechnology center with a conference area, a design and engineering section, and a laboratory test facility. In addition, the centers serve as mobile training units where customers can be educated in the latest technologies in fastening systems. No matter which innovation center customers choose, they can be confident that the latest in technological solutions will be available.

Emhart designs flexible assembly systems that reduce the number of fasteners on components while upgrading quality and streamlining production.

Emhart's innovative electronic product library, Mentor™, provides immediate access to information on all of Emhart's products, including code numbers, line drawings with physical dimensions, and typical applications, with illustrations. A Mentor compact disk includes product catalogues, video footage, interactive search tools, and fastener "wizards" that guide users through application information and recommend fastening solutions and related assembly systems and tools.

WORLDWIDE CUSTOMER SUPPORT

As a global company, Emhart has designed its customer support to deliver products and service twenty-four hours a day, seven days a week. Every customer service program has built-in flexibility to provide custom-tailored solutions for the local, regional, and global needs of its customers.

From automotive to construction, from computer to appliance, Emhart customers represent the most productive industries worldwide. From Ford to Apple to Maytag, from DaimlerChrysler to Nokia to Toyota, from General Motors to Motorola to Honda, Emhart works with the best in the world.

Emhart Innovation Centers worldwide function as engineering facilities to identify, formulate, and deliver solutions for customers. Staffed by application specialists and electronically linked, the centers allow customers from any part of the globe to design and engineer fastening systems and assemblies on-line, with expert guidance.

EAST JORDAN IRON WORKS, INC.

East Jordan Iron Works, Inc. (EJIW), has been a part of the City of East Jordan and the Charlevoix County community, in northwest lower Michigan, since 1883. The foundry was established on the south arm of Lake Charlevoix by William E. Malpass and his father-in-law, Richard W. Round, on 8 November 1883, when East Jordan was a center of lumber operations. Railroads had not yet penetrated the region, and eleven sawmills, along with the Pine Lake Iron company, were dependent on water for transportation. Timbers were floated over the lake to the mills, and as many as fourteen lumber schooners could be seen loading simultaneously at the East Jordan docks. This activity created a demand for a foundry and machine shop operation. The East Jordan Iron Works foundry was built in 1883 by William E. Malpass. The machine shop was built two years later when his brother James, a journeyman machinist, immigrated from England.

In the 1920s the lumber mills began to close and lake shipping declined as the supply of standing timber was exhausted. East Jordan Iron Works was challenged to find new products to manufacture, and started its venture into the production of street castings, fire hydrants, and waterworks valves. In 1928 the machine shop was enlarged to accommodate this demand.

During the 1920s and 1930s, William Malpass gradually transferred management

At East Jordan Iron Works, in East Jordan, Michigan, molten iron from a cupola furnace is transferred to an electric induction holding furnace and then into a ladle on the production line, from which it is poured into molds.

functions to three of his sons, William Henry "Will" Malpass, Richard Ward "Dick" Malpass and Theodore Edward "Ted" Malpass. A third generation of management, led by Will's son, W. E. "Bill" Malpass, and Ted's son, F. Bruce Malpass, emerged in the 1940s and 1950s. The foundry converted to modern, automated molding equipment during the 1960s, and through the 1970s and into the 1980s the company continued to grow and reinvest in its facilities.

In the mid-1980s, the family-owned business began operating under the leadership of fourth-generation descendants of the Malpass family: Bill's son, Fred Malpass, and F. Bruce's sons, Tracy Malpass and Tad Malpass. A history of

The fourth generation of the Malpass family to lead East Jordan Iron Works, Inc., includes, from left, Tad, Tracy, and Fred Malpass.

family involvement, dedicated employees (many of whom also are multigenerational members of the firm), and a commitment to reinvestment has kept EJIW competitive in today's global economy.

Through the support of the community and its own dedicated employees, EJIW expanded. Today the company operates a highly automated, high-production foundry in East Jordan along with a separate machine and assembly operation for the production of fire hydrants, valves, and related products. EJIW headquarters is still in East Jordan, and a sixty-five-acre distribution center is operated in Sunfield, Michigan (near Lansing). The company also operates an additional foundry in Denham Springs, Louisiana (near Baton Rouge), and fifteen sales yards in ten states. The sales yards are located in East Jordan, Detroit, Grand Rapids, and Lansing, Michigan; Chicago, Illinois; Cleveland and Columbus, Ohio; Baltimore, Maryland; Middletown, Delaware; Atlanta, Georgia; Rockingham, North Carolina; Knoxville, Tennessee; Denham Springs, Louisiana; and Houston and San Angelo, Texas.

Through its sales yard locations and a network of product distributors, EJIW provides a full line of construction and utility castings to contractors and municipalities in more than forty states. EJIW products include many styles of manhole covers and frames, catch basins, drainage grates, tree grates, gate valves, and fire hydrants. In recent years the company has experienced a large amount of interest in its individually designed manhole covers. These covers can be custom-made for a particular city or corporation, featuring its slogan or

East Jordan Iron Works, Inc., has stood at its location on the south arm of Lake Charlevoix since its beginning in 1883.

LEFT: *Custom-designed manhole covers, featuring a customer's logo or mascot or a symbol of its popular characteristic, are produced by East Jordan Iron Works for corporations and municipalities.*

BELOW: *EJIW makes a large variety of castings for use in road building and underground and utility construction, storm sewer curb inlets, catch basins, trench and tree gratings, airport and port authority applications, and water-distribution products, such as fire hydrants and gate valves. EJIW also produces brake drums for semi-tractor and trailer applications that are used nationwide.*

motto and its logo, mascot, or popular characteristic.

EJIW also produces semi-tractor and trailer brake drums and other specialty castings.

East Jordan Iron Works is a responsible partner in the environment and is proud to be a major recycler of ferrous scrap metals, which are the primary components used in the EJIW melt operation. EJIW continues to develop ways to reduce or reuse by-products of the production process.

The company's sense of responsibility also includes its dedication to giving back to the community. EJIW and its employees are involved in a variety of school and community activities.

East Jordan Iron Works will always strive for superior quality and exceptional customer service, while continuing to reinvest in the company, its employees, and its communities, to be the leader in the production of construction castings.

DOW CORNING CORPORATION

Located in the triangle formed by Midland, Bay City, and Saginaw, Dow Corning Corporation is a global leader in silicon-based materials. Organized in 1943 as a joint venture of The Dow Chemical Company and Corning, Incorporated, Dow Corning was formed to develop the potential of new and unique materials called "silicones," which are chemical compounds based on silicon, an element refined from quartz.

Over the years, fueled by an annual research investment exceeding the industry average, Dow Corning has led silicone technology in dozens of directions and now offers more than 5,000 silicon-based products.

It is difficult to imagine the world today without Dow Corning's contributions. The central core of modern computers, the silicon chip, is created from polycrystalline silicon from Hemlock Semiconductor Corporation, a Dow Corning subsidiary. Electronic protective materials made by Dow Corning help ensure the durability and performance people have come to expect of everything from laptop computers to cellular phones, from toasters to lamps.

Innovative building-construction techniques, developed because of Dow Corning silicone adhesive/sealants, have changed architecture and the shape of modern skylines. Dow Corning silicone resins and additives enhance the durability of paints and coatings. Adhesive tapes, labels, stamps, stickers, and decals are everywhere today, made possible by Dow

The world's tallest buildings, the Petronas Towers in Kuala Lumpur, Malaysia, are testimony to the quality of silicone sealants made by Dow Corning and to the people of Dow Corning Corporation from three continents who contributed their expertise to the project. Photo courtesy of John Abols, Adamson and Associates

The Michigan Recycling Coalition has named Dow Corning Recycler of the Year an unprecedented three times. The award exemplifies the company's worldwide commitment to high environmental, health, and safety standards. © Dow Corning Corp.

Corning silicone release coatings. The aeronautics and aerospace industries rely on Dow Corning for silicon-based materials that perform even in the cold vacuum of outer space. Back on Earth, silicones from Dow Corning also find applications in the food processing and pharmaceuticals industries, in the processing of plastics, in the medical products and automotive industries, in personal care products, and more.

Thousands of businesses in dozens of industries around the world rely on Dow Corning products and expertise to make their products and processes better and more efficient. Customer success is Dow Corning's principal goal; customer satisfaction is its primary objective.

How well Dow Corning maintains its customer focus depends on how fast the corporation can change to meet the marketplace and economic demands of the future. Taking advantage of the latest technology, Dow Corning Corporation is actively managing change for the twenty-first century, creating a faster, more agile

Dow Corning technology is woven throughout the fabric of modern life. Dow Corning silicones are critical resources in dozens of industries, such as the textile industry, where silicones are used to give fabrics the softness and water repellency the market demands. © Dow Corning Corp.

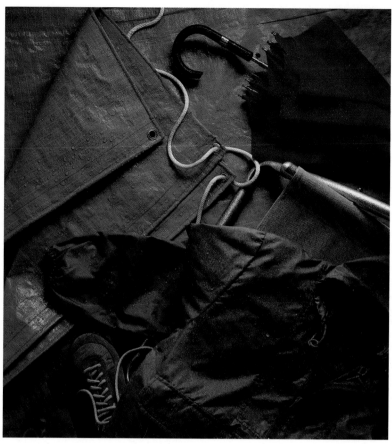

organization for the new global economy. A variety of new business operational technologies is being implemented, organizing the company around global industry businesses designed to maximize efficiency, enhance responsiveness, and more fully integrate the company's worldwide resources. All of these Dow Corning initiatives have a simple, unadorned objective: to better serve customers, whether they operate in Michigan or internationally.

Business customers are not the company's only focus. As a corporate citizen, Dow Corning is a resident of dozens of communities in Michigan and around the world. And a vital part of its corporate vision is to be a good neighbor.

As part of that imperative, Dow Corning is committed to leadership in matters of the environment, health, and safety (EHS). The company's EHS performance is measured against the Codes of Management Practices of the Responsible Care® program, an initiative of the United States chemical industry to improve the stewardship of chemical products and the environment. In addition, Dow Corning has set its own global standard.

Dow Corning is one of just a few companies that has made compliance with the demanding codes of Responsible Care an objective for all of its operations around the world. This means doing much more in some host countries than local regulations require. Nevertheless, the company's goal is worldwide code compliance by 2003. Then, when it succeeds, it will move the bar even higher.

A Midland, Michigan, company is lengthening its technological leadership, expanding its reach into new global markets and industries, and strengthening the expertise and resources that thousands of customers rely upon for their own marketplace success. That company is Dow Corning Corporation, at home in Michigan and around the world.

Headquartered in Midland, Michigan, Dow Corning Corporation is a multinational company with nearly 9,000 employees, thirty-five manufacturing sites on five continents, and research, technical support, and customer service locations around the world. © Dow Corning Corp.

MASCO CORPORATION

FOUNDED IN DETROIT

IN 1929, MASCO

CORPORATION

IS ONE OF THE

WORLD'S LEADING

MANUFACTURERS OF

FAUCETS, CABINETS,

LOCKS, AND OTHER

BRAND-NAME HOME

IMPROVEMENT AND

BUILDING PRODUCTS

Masco Corporation, composed of a family of companies with a proud tradition of growth, innovation, and market leadership, is a family where quality is a way of life. The company's past and future are tied to the belief that talented people, when provided with a creative and supportive environment, produce outstanding results.

Headquartered in Taylor, Michigan, Masco is one of the world's largest manufacturers of high-quality products for the kitchen, bath, and other rooms in the home, including kitchen and bath faucets and hand-held showering products; lock sets, and electronic locks; builders' and decorative hardware; cabinets and vanities; bath and shower products and accessories; whirlpools, steam units, spas, and hot tubs; decorative fixtures and stainless steel commercial washroom accessories; ventilating products, acoustical and thermal insulation, decorative hydronic radiators and heat convectors, and water pumps; roller shutters; and office workstations and storage units.

A prime example of the American dream come true, Masco's history began with a nineteen-year-old Armenian immigrant named Alex Manoogian, who arrived in the United States in 1920 with two suitcases, $50 in cash, and the will to succeed. In 1929 Manoogian and two partners formed the Masco Screw Products Company in Detroit. Their first major contract, a $7,000 machining job, came from the Hudson Motor Car Company. Masco went on to become a leading supplier to the automotive and transportation industries. By 1937 the company was listed on the Detroit Stock Exchange and well on its way to success.

Increased sales and experience with new technology during World War II and the Korean Conflict left Masco in a position to seize important opportunities coming its way. In 1954 the company began manufacturing parts for a product that

Alex Manoogian, the founder of Masco Corporation, shows the first single-handle faucet, made by Delta.

would revolutionize the plumbing market—the single-handle faucet. After Manoogian completely redesigned the product and acquired all rights to its manufacture, the new Delta faucet achieved overnight acceptance and launched Masco in the building products industry.

In 1958 Masco began construction of a new plant in Greensburg, Indiana, devoted exclusively to manufacturing the faucets. That same year, Richard A. Manoogian, Alex's son, joined Masco and soon embarked on a program of acquisition, diversification, and expansion made possible by the profits from faucet sales.

While growing steadily from within and through the friendly acquisition of companies that shared its commitment to excellence, Masco established its basic corporate objectives:

- focus on proprietary leadership positions;
- diversify the product base to avoid dependence on any single market;
- leverage the company's existing product development, manufacturing, and marketing skills;

Richard A. Manoogian, Alex's son, joined the company in 1958.

• manufacture only products that offer an above-average rate of return.

In 1960 Masco licensed Emco Limited, a leading manufacturer and distributor of building materials and engineered products in Canada, to market Delta faucets in that country—and the partnership still thrives today. In 1961 Masco Screw Products changed its name to Masco Corporation and, with the acquisition of Peerless Industries, Inc., began offering customers a broader line of plumbing products. In 1985 Masco expanded its presence in the building products industry with the acquisition of Merillat Industries, known as "America's Cabinetmaker." Little by little, as it acquired other manufacturers of quality home improvement and building products, Masco steadily continued to grow both at home and abroad.

MascoTech, Inc., a public company spun off from Masco Corporation in 1984, and TriMas Corporation, another member of the Masco family, merged in 1998 to form a powerful, diversified company with a broad range of leadership proprietary products for the transportation, commercial, industrial, and consumer markets.

Meanwhile Masco Corporation brought renewed focus to bear on its core home improvement and building-products businesses—with favorable results. Reported net income for 1998 was a record $476 million, an increase of 24 percent over 1997. Net sales from continuing operations also set a record at $4.35 billion for 1998. The figures offer encouragement to

Masco offers 4,000 faucet models, which are sold in fifty-three countries, at virtually every price point.

Richard Manoogian, now chairman and CEO, and Raymond F. Kennedy, president and chief operating officer, who remain committed to creating value for shareholders by maintaining leadership positions in the markets that Masco serves.

Although founder Alex Manoogian passed away in 1996, his words continue to inspire Masco's management and associates around the world: "Do not be satisfied with average performance. Strive for excellence. If you cannot give your customers a better value and a better product, do not sell the product." Fundamental insistence on quality products, good value, and outstanding service helped to shape the principles that guide Masco to this day.

Masco's broad offering of brand-name products enables its cabinet companies to offer market exclusivity for different brands and cabinet styles to home centers, kitchen and bath centers, and other retail and wholesale customers.

MASCO BRANDS AT A GLANCE

- **Faucets:** Alsons, Artistic Brass, Damixa, Delta, Mariani, Mixet, Peerless
- **Cabinets:** Alma Küchen, The Alvic Group, Fieldstone, KraftMaid, Merillat, The Moores Group, StarMark, Texwood
- **Other Kitchen and Bath Products:** American Shower & Bath, Aqua Glass, Brass Craft, Cobra, Franklin Brass, General Accessory, Horst Breuer, Hüppe, Melard, Mirolin, NewTeam, Water Control Technology, Watkins, Zenith
- **Builders' Hardware:** Baldwin, LaGard, Liberty Hardware, Safekeeper, Saflok, Weiser, Winfield
- **Other Specialty Products:** Ameri-Flow®, Ameri-Vent®, AMPCO, the Brugman Group, E. Missel, Gale Industries, Gebhardt, Gutter Helmet®, F&W, Jung Pumpen, The SKS Group, Vasco.

THE DELFIELD COMPANY

The Delfield Company, based in Mt. Pleasant, Michigan, is a major manufacturer of state-of-the-art food service equipment for restaurants, hotels, and cafeterias. Delfield custom-designed kitchens and refrigeration are found in a wide variety of facilities, from quick-service restaurants to luxury resorts. Celebrating its fiftieth anniversary in 1999, Delfield has manufactured thousands of different products from eight product lines, including Mark 7 Custom Systems, Shelleyglas® and Shelleysteel™ mobile cafeteria systems, AirTech® ventilation systems, Shelleymatic® dispensers, and a full line of reach-in refrigerators and freezers.

Founded in a small building on Detroit's east side in 1949, Delfield was established by Paul DeLorenzo and Thomas Springfield. The company name was derived from "Del" in DeLorenzo and "field" in Springfield. By 1969 a second manufacturing plant was opened in Cadillac, Michigan. Springfield sold his portion of the business to DeLorenzo, and the company was acquired by Clark Equipment. In 1971 the general offices were relocated from Detroit to a plant in Mt. Pleasant, Michigan. Later, in 1985, the Cadillac plant was closed and a new plant was opened in Covington, Tennessee.

This custom-designed application of Delfield products, which includes Shelleymatic dispensers, was created at Keystone Ski Resort, in Colorado.

The food service industry has changed significantly in fifty years, but Delfield remains unconditionally committed to high quality and customer support. Production manager Jay Rivers has worked for Delfield for twenty years and contends that today's customers are more knowledgeable and the competition is more sophisticated. Says Rivers, "We are customer-driven, employee-oriented, process-focused, and managed by facts rather than guesses. The Delfield Company is committed to continuous improvement."

Delfield is known for developing innovations of versatility and durability in equipment for the food service industry. In 1987 Delfield introduced the Shelleyglas line of mobile serving equipment, which features a wide variety of standard colors and styles to complement the decor of any serving area. Shelleyglas units offer serving counters for hot food, cold food, or a combination, which

The Delfield Company, founded in Detroit, relocated its general offices to Mt. Pleasant, Michigan, in 1971.

enable food service operators to prepare a full self-serve menu in a limited amount of space.

Two years later Delfield offered a line of self-leveling systems, called Shelleymatic, for dispensing tableware. Whatever an operator's menu requires for service—from plates and mugs to saucers and trays—the Shelleymatic product line has a dispenser to make tableware conveniently available, yet protected, and to keep the serving area neat.

In 1989 the company also debuted the high-end Specification Line® of refrigerators, freezers, and warming units, designed for the most demanding applications, and in 1992 it introduced the AirTech line of ventilation systems.

In 1994 Delfield introduced a new product line, Shelleysteel, an all-stainless-steel mobile cafeteria system that lets food service operators mix and match pieces to meet individual serving requirements.

Offering customers flexibility is one of Delfield's most important challenges. In 1998 the company introduced Mark 7 Custom Systems, a new generation of custom-fabricated equipment featuring components that can be configured to create chef's islands, back-bar equipment, cafeteria serving counters, or server's stations. The units can be lined up end to end, back to back, or even around corners or columns to meet the specific needs of an operator's food service application. The year 1998 also saw the revision of the National Sanitation Foundation (NSF) Standard 7, which includes strict government requirements for the construction and performance of commercial refrigerators and freezers. All of the Delfield salad-top units in the Mark 7 line meet or exceed NSF-7 requirements.

The Delfield Company has grown with the food service industry over the past

This boat theme for the cafeteria at Bunn Elementary School in Franklin County, North Carolina, illustrates the design possibilities available with Shelleyglas mobile cafeteria systems.

fifty years, and today it is one of the largest manufacturers of custom-made, stainless-steel food service equipment in the world, with annual sales of more than $100 million. Although there have been significant changes and technical advances in the industry, the company has always remained committed to customer satisfaction.

"When I started my career at Delfield," says Graham Tillotson, president of Delfield, "our focus was on creating the highest-quality refrigeration available for the food service industry and taking care of our customers. We have never forgotten that our customers are the primary reason for our success. Although we continue to focus on state-of-the-art technology for all of our equipment, we have developed tremendous resources in aesthetic design over the years as well. Practical innovations and design excellence will continue to drive our business in the future."

Delfield's remote reach-in refrigerator features Delfield's exclusive Delrite ABS plastic interior.

HART & COOLEY, INC.

Howard Stanley Hart was a turn-of-the-century entrepreneur, inventor, industrialist, and builder. In 1892, in partnership with Norman P. Cooley, he established the Hart & Cooley Manufacturing Company in Chicago, the first cold-rolled steel plant west of Pittsburgh. One of Hart's many inventions of the next few years was a steel heating register that proved superior to traditional heavy cast-iron models.

In 1899 the two sold their Chicago plant and organized the Hart & Cooley Company in New Britain, Connecticut. It became the first in the nation to manufacture warm-air registers from stamped steel, a product line that gained almost instant success.

The Roaring Twenties saw Hart & Cooley expand their register business to Holland, Michigan, where they formed the Federal Manufacturing Company. In 1929 they moved their Connecticut operations to Holland, merging with Federal under the name Hart & Cooley Company, Inc. Warm-air products made in Holland, Michigan, quickly found their way to customers nationwide. Despite the Great Depression, by the early 1930s the company had become the world's largest producer of warm-air registers.

During the 1950s, when forced-air heating became widespread, the company added many new products to its residential and commercial lines of registers, grilles, and diffusers. It

Hart & Cooley, Inc.'s home office is located in Holland, Michigan, where the company has taken pride in being a good corporate citizen for more than seventy years.

introduced the Metlvent gas vent for gas-fired appliances in 1959, a product that won Michigan's Achievement of the Year honors in 1962. The Metlvent all-fuel chimney system was introduced that year.

Today Hart & Cooley, Inc., is part of Falcon Building Products, which is owned by New York–based investment firm Investcorp. Hart & Cooley continues to be a major supplier to the HVAC (heating, ventilation, and air-conditioning) industry and has grown to the point that it has manufacturing locations in seven states as well as in Mexico and Canada. As the company continues its focus on growth, new businesses are added regularly to complement its product lines in the residential and commercial HVAC markets.

While Hart & Cooley began with stamped steel registers, today it has added aluminum louvers, steel vent pipes, fans, flexible duct products, and glass and aluminum window-wall systems. Howard Stanley Hart and Norman P. Cooley would be proud to see that the business they started nearly a hundred years ago is still thriving at the beginning of another new century.

Production workers in Michigan factories earn the highest average hourly wage in all fifty states, more than four dollars above the national average in 1997. © Corbis

HIGH TECH IN HIGH GEAR

CHAPTER TWELVE

FOR MICHIGAN, THE COMPUTER AGE BEGAN IN 1920 WHEN BURROUGHS ADDING MACHINE COMPANY OPENED A PLANT IN DETROIT. BURROUGHS ADDING MACHINES BECAME CALCULATORS, WHICH BECAME BOOKKEEPING MACHINES, WHICH BECAME COMPUTERS. THE PLANTS BURROUGHS SUBSEQUENTLY BUILT IN PLYMOUTH AND ANN ARBOR WERE THE BEGINNINGS OF A FLOURISHING HIGH-TECH INDUSTRY THAT HAS GROWN INTO A RESEARCH

triangle formed by East Lansing, Ann Arbor, and metropolitan Detroit.

In the early 1980s, when auto downturns led to declining populations in many Michigan cities, Ann Arbor experienced a population boom due to the proliferation of computer-related businesses there. By 1985 more than two hundred high-tech companies had located in eighteen technology parks in and around Ann Arbor, putting that city in a league with California's Silicon Valley and Boston's Route 128 corridor. The University of Michigan played the same driving role in Ann Arbor's techno-boom as Stanford and M.I.T. had in those other advanced technology centers. Professional associations such as the Ann Arbor Area Software Council facilitate networking and industry growth with the aim of establishing Michigan as an international center of technology and

software development. Today Washtenaw and Oakland Counties are among the nation's top ten high-technology growth areas.

COMPUTER MEETS CAR

This being Michigan, the auto companies naturally played an important part in the development of this new business sector. Thanks largely to them, by the mid-1980s one-third of the nation's robotics companies were located in Michigan. About the same time, the Big Three began work on the "computerized car of the future." When GM acquired Ross Perot's E.D.S. (Electronic Data Systems, which subsequently split from the automaker in 1996), the computer technology firm's Detroit branch joined with the University of Michigan to set up a Center for Machine Intelligence. The goal of the alliance was to

OPPOSITE: *Before the solid-state circuit board became a common sight, digital pioneers embarked on decades of research and experimentation. Several Michigan companies and individuals played seminal roles in that process, and Michiganians continue to be in the forefront of new ideas and technologies. © HMS Images.* ABOVE: *A team of Chrysler designers works on a prototype. Michigan is the fourth-largest center for rapid prototyping in the world. © Alan Levenson/Tony Stone Images*

Rick Snyder came back to Michigan and founded Avalon Investments to foster the growth of new technologies here. © Dwight Cendrowski

create thinking robots, a project that continues in the university's Artificial Intelligence Laboratory. The auto industry also made Michigan a global center for rapid-prototyping, a process that transforms three-dimensional computer images into model parts for use in the design of a product such as a car. If Michigan were a country it would rank as the world's fourth-largest

Computers are becoming more and more intrinsic to education. Michigan's high-tech companies help make computer technology work in both school and business environments. © HMS Images

center for this high-tech activity.

NATIONAL AND GLOBAL IMPACT

Of the hundreds of computer-related companies based in Michigan, several have earned national and international prominence. In 1973 Peter Karmanos Jr. and two partners each chipped in $3,000 and drafted a mission statement on a yellow legal pad that said simply, "We will help people do things with computers." Today their company, Compuware Corporation, with Karmanos as chairman

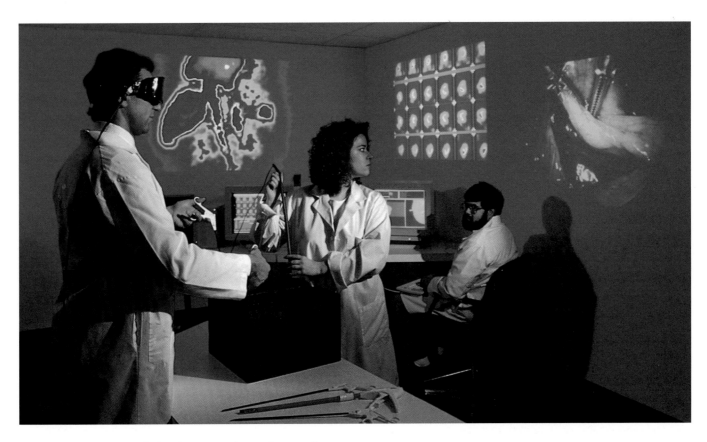

and CEO, is one of the largest independent software vendors in the world. The Farmington Hills–based firm provides software and services that help information technology professionals develop and maintain applications for large computer systems. Compuware products have been licensed by nearly eleven thousand organizations worldwide, including four out of five Fortune 500 companies. With more than a billion dollars in annual revenues,

The University of Michigan has been a key player in the development of high-technology talents and industries in the state. Shown here is the engineering campus. © Dwight Cendrowski

Physicians test a virtual reality surgery prototype. The two doctors in the foreground manipulate tools whose movements are reproduced in the simulated surgical environment. © HMS Images

Compuware is the world leader in client/server development technology and has been in the forefront of year 2000 system conversions. The company also is a leader in community involvement and service. Compuware's on-site Child Development Center is a model for progressive, family-friendly businesses. Karmanos, owner of the

BUG KILLER

AT TECHNOLOGY FORUM '98, MICHIGAN RECEIVED THE BEST PRACTICE AWARD GIVEN BY PC WEEK MAGAZINE AND THE NEW YORK–BASED TECHNOLOGY MANAGERS FORUM. BEATING OUT A DOZEN OTHER NOMINEES FOR THE HONOR, MICHIGAN WAS NAMED AS HAVING THE BEST BUSINESS PRACTICES IN DEALING WITH THE YEAR 2000 DATE CHANGE "BUG." SAID GEORGE BOERSMA, THE STATE'S CHIEF INFORMATION OFFICER, "WE'VE PUT GREAT EFFORT INTO DEVELOPING CONSISTENT, QUANTIFIABLE METHODS FOR DEALING WITH THIS ISSUE. THE STATE'S SUCCESS IS DUE TO THE UNITED SUPPORT OF OUR YEAR 2000 PLAN ACROSS STATE GOVERNMENT, AGENCY BY AGENCY."

BY THE LATE 1990S, 360 RESEARCH AND DEVELOPMENT FACILITIES FOCUSING SPECIFICALLY ON INDUSTRIAL TECHNOLOGY CALLED MICHIGAN HOME.

Carolina Hurricanes professional hockey team, provides hockey rinks and support for junior hockey teams and figure skaters across the state. The Barbara Ann Karmanos Cancer Institute, the Detroit area's largest nonprofit institution, is a leader in cancer research and treatment.

Another Farmington Hills firm helping companies get over the year 2000 computer hump is Complete Business Solutions, a worldwide information technology and computer consulting and services provider to medium and large corporations. Dearborn's National TechTeam helps market and service personal-computer-extended-warranty contracts for major manufacturers such as Hewlett-Packard, and is ranked by several financial journals among the one hundred best growth companies in the country.

One of the world's largest information archivers and distributors is UMI (University Microfilms International) of Ann Arbor. UMI provides schools and libraries in more than 160 countries with access to more than twenty thousand periodicals and seven thousand newspapers, as well as journals, dissertations, and other sources of information. Materials are available on-line and via microform (both microfilm and microfiche), paper, and CD-ROM. In 1995 the company's state-of-the-art on-line information system, ProQuest Direct, was added to the Smithsonian Institution's Permanent Research Collection on information technology innovation.

One of the oldest of the Ann Arbor–based high-tech companies is Comshare, a leading supplier of performance measurement, budgeting, and financial reporting software. Established in 1966, the company currently supplies software and technical support in forty countries.

The charming town of Ann Arbor has become a high-technology mecca for many of the field's brightest scientific and entrepreneurial minds. Here, members of the next generation of innovators board a school bus. © Dwight Cendrowski

an organization designed to run the state's technology grants and investments. Between 1996 and 1998 Michigan rose from thirty-seventh to fifteenth place nationally in the amount of venture capital available to start new businesses.

Financially, geographically, and educationally, the Great Lakes State is perfectly positioned to be the site of the next "gold rush" for a new era of high-tech entrepreneurs.

REEL IMPACT

UNIVERSITY MICROFILMS INTERNATIONAL FOUNDER EUGENE POWER OF ANN ARBOR FIRST DEVELOPED THE USE OF MICROFILM, NOW A STANDARD IN INFORMATION TECHNOLOGY.

REASON TO STAY

While the University of Michigan took a leading role in the state's technology revolution, most of Michigan's other colleges and universities rapidly joined in, developing innovative computer and advanced engineering departments. More and more Michigan graduates are ignoring the siren songs from the coasts, opting to stay in-state to fill the rapidly growing number of high-technology jobs here. Battle Creek native Rick Snyder is one notable emigrant who recognized the state's potential and chose to return. The former president and COO of Gateway 2000 established Avalon Investments in Ann Arbor to pump money into exciting new technology companies and to spread the word about Michigan as a national center for technological innovation.

Snyder joined forces with other Michigan high-tech proponents on the board of Michigan Technologies, Inc.,

Students in the computer laboratory at Powers Junior High School in Farmington Hills search the virtually limitless resources of the World Wide Web. © Dennis Cox/D. E. Cox Photo Library

Workers supervise an automotive robotics line at Autodie International in Grand Rapids. © B. Lindhout

TECHNOLOGY

COMPUWARE CORPORATION

Throughout its history Michigan has been blessed with individuals with foresight—the ability to foresee the need for something and act on it. Henry Ford had it, as did Thomas Edison. In 1973 three other men from the Great Lakes State—Peter Karmanos Jr., Thomas Thewes, and the late Allen Cutting—had it too.

Seeing a need for a service firm uniquely designed to help businesses better position themselves to succeed in their missions by mastering information technology (IT), the three men established Compuware Corporation. Over twenty-five years, they developed their Farmington Hills–based firm into one of the world's five largest independent software vendors and one of the largest professional consulting services organizations in the nation, with annual revenues of nearly $2 billion.

"Compuware offers solutions that make technology work for our clients," says Karmanos, Compuware's chairman and chief executive officer. "This allows

Peter Karmanos Jr. is chairman and chief executive officer of Compuware. Karmanos, along with Allen Cutting and Thomas Thewes, founded Compuware in 1973 using their combined income tax refunds of $9,000 as investment funding.

Compuware Corporation's world headquarters, located in Farmington Hills, Michigan, accommodates nearly 3,000 of the company's 11,000 employees.

them to concentrate on their core competencies instead of their IT problems."

Back in 1973 Compuware began with just one client. Today its productivity solutions—including mainframe and client/server computer software and consulting services ranging from business systems analysis to systems planning and software conversion—help more than 14,000 of the world's largest corporations improve quality, lower costs, and increase the speed at which their systems can be developed, implemented, and supported.

What makes Compuware stand out above the competition is that it always strives to exceed clients' expectations. The company is committed to providing its customers with high-quality products and services. Despite its phenomenal growth over the last quarter century, Compuware continues to deliver products and services that give real solutions for everyday business problems as well as an immediate and measurable return on clients' IT investments.

In recognition of its outstanding performance, Compuware was recently cited by *Business Week* magazine as one of the top-100 best-performing information technology companies in the industry.

The best measure of Compuware's success is the long-term relationships that the company has with its clients. Compuware's customers return again and again to the firm for help in improving the scope and efficiency of their systems. Ninety-seven percent of the firms that have product maintenance contracts with Compuware regularly renew those contracts when they expire. Furthermore, the list of new Compuware clients keeps growing.

Much of the credit for Compuware's success belongs to the more than 11,000 IT professionals that the company employs in its ninety-three offices in forty countries worldwide, including more than 7,000 in the firm's professional service organization.

Compuware has put together a staff of some of the most competent, motivated, and dedicated professionals in the information technology industry. The company's ability to attract and keep talented, committed people was recognized in 1999 by *Fortune* magazine, which named Compuware as one of the "100 Best Companies to Work for in America."

In Dreieich, Germany, Frank Jurgeit of Compuware activates the server-manager for the Compuware Germany facility.

"Building a world-class work environment in which individuals are respected and empowered has always been a top priority for us," Karmanos says. "Since 1973 our goal has been to create a workplace where nice people who truly liked their jobs could be productive, dedicated, and concerned for others—a place we could all be proud of. We are now recognized as an example of what a premier workplace should represent."

Like many firms in today's business climate, Compuware has undertaken major changes in recent years, including the transition in 1992 to a publicly traded corporation (NASDAQ: CPWR).

Nevertheless, Compuware remains faithful to its original mission of creating and delivering practical productivity solutions so that its clients can continue to efficiently maintain and enhance their most critical business applications. Compuware's future in today's technology age unquestionably is a bright one.

"We feel that the demand for Compuware products and services will always be high," Karmanos says, "because we make companies more efficient, more productive, and, ultimately, more competitive."

At the global network operations center of network software giant Novell, Inc., in San Jose, California, Compuware's EcoSCOPE is used to centrally monitor application performance on a worldwide network of hundreds of sites and more than 5,000 individual computers.

EDS

Everywhere you look, EDS is helping the people and businesses of Michigan use information to do extraordinary things. Whether it's eighteen-wheelers cruising route I-75 with Detroit Diesel engines that are calibrated with information from EDS laptop computers; ATMs owned by EDS banking systems that help busy people manage their finances twenty-four hours a day, seven days a week; or a Detroit Symphony Orchestra Web site that lets concertgoers buy tickets on-line and listen to sound files of actual symphony performances, EDS has an impact on the lives of virtually every citizen in the state.

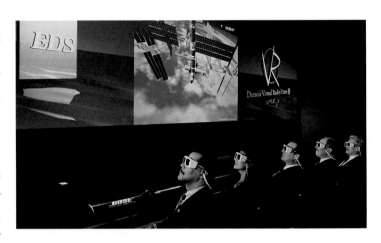

The EDS Virtual Reality Center, located in Detroit's New Center Area, is one of the world's first facilities dedicated to the commercial use of virtual reality. Simulated prototyping in an environment created by towering 3-D graphics and surround sound eliminates costly physical modeling and cuts time to market.

IN THE BUSINESS WORLD

Founded in 1962, EDS is a professional services company that shapes the way information is created, distributed, shared, enjoyed, and applied for the benefit of enterprises, governments, and individuals in fifty countries around the world. More than 118,000 EDS employees—17,000 of whom live and work in Michigan—personify the drive, range, and insight to maintain its strong position in the information technology industry.

In Michigan, the main EDS client base consists of three groups: the vehicle industry, General Motors Corp. (GM), and state and local government.

The EDS Vehicle Industry Division focuses on the global automotive and heavy truck industry, providing business consulting, process management, and technology services to original equipment manufacturers and suppliers, including Michigan-based Detroit Diesel and American Axle, and to global customers, including Saab, Volkswagen, and Mitsubishi.

Working with Michigan's Department of Natural Resources, EDS created the electronic commerce system Streamline^{SM}, making it easy for retailers to sell hunting and fishing licenses and virtually eliminating paperwork and the need to stock a variety of license tags.

EDS has served as GM's primary information technology provider since 1984, helping to create a global computing infrastructure anchored by the GM private communications network, one of the largest such networks in the world. EDS also supports GM's business objectives by developing and implementing common technical and business systems, working with GM to re-engineer GM's processes, and operating GM's centralized consumer-oriented services.

EDS state and local government agency clients purchase the desktop hardware, software, and related services they need from a catalog on the Internet, virtually eliminating red tape and delays. This "one-stop shop" for both equipment and customer care is made possible because EDS works with proven support vendors to make sure those agencies receive the consistent, well-supported products and service they need.

IN THE MARKETPLACE

In an increasingly competitive, global marketplace, smart businesses know that gathering accurate, timely data is worthwhile only if that data can be transformed into valuable information. EDS teams gold-standard technology, well-designed processes, and dynamic, intelligent people to make information work harder. Its clients represent a broad range of businesses.

For Michigan ACCESS, the EDS Automated Client Care & Eligibility Support System lets doctors' offices, hospitals, and clinics check Medicaid coverage and eligibility, helping patients receive the health care services they need and reducing the possibility of payment fraud.

The Manufacturing Enterprise Leadership Program, a six-week course, is an example of a win-win endeavor for EDS and the program's host companies. Seven hundred and fifty senior executives and middle managers in twenty-five countries have taken the course to increase their manufacturing savvy, strengthen interpersonal skills, and learn the latest business techniques. After the first three weeks, teams of participants consult with local companies to apply classroom lessons to actual business situations, at no cost to the host company.

The EDS Document Management Services group, operating under the high-quality standards of ISO-9001, is working toward a paperless business environment in which timely information is scanned, stored, and retrieved using computer technology. The result promises greater efficiency, increased accuracy, and a healthier bottom line.

The highly secure extranet Automotive Network eXchange (ANX), provided by EDS, enables consistent manufacturer-supplier communication using Internet protocol. The entire automotive trading community can conduct business electronically using ANX. Through its Vehicle Industry Division and Electronic Business Unit, EDS is one of the first ANX-certified service providers and one of the only companies to offer a comprehensive package of electronic business services.

EDS is a founding sponsor and technology provider of the JASON Project, in which students and teachers follow a scientific expedition for a year, interacting via a custom-designed curriculum, classroom broadcasts, and the Internet. This allows them to gain hands-on experience in applied technology and to witness scientific discovery as it happens.

IN THE COMMUNITY

EDS is committed to making the world in which we live and work a better place. Recently, in recognition of its ongoing corporate good citizenship in promoting education through employee volunteerism and technology grants, EDS was one of eighteen organizations and individuals to win the Points of Light Foundation President's Service Award. EDS supports numerous projects, of which the following are examples.

The EDS Software Verification and Testing Laboratory at Oakland University (OU) shows what can be accomplished when business and education work together. OU used a $200,000 gift from EDS to establish a facility to develop and test safety-critical software, which is vital in avionics, nuclear energy, medical monitoring, and vehicle brake control.

Educational Outreach has been a number one priority for EDS since 1989. EDS volunteers donate their time and talents as mentors to young people in places such as the Boys & Girls Clubs of Southeastern Michigan, Cornerstone Schools, and the Franklin Elementary School in Pontiac, Michigan. Focus: HOPE is a partnership that provides educational opportunities for local young people as well as a valuable recruiting source for skilled employees. EDS donated state-of-the-art Unigraphics® software to the Machinist Training Institute of Focus: HOPE of Detroit.

Last year alone, more than a million people's lives were touched when EDS volunteers working on 386 projects at 200 locations in 32 countries, including sites all over Michigan, gave 49,460 hours on Global Volunteer Day to make a difference in their communities. If you seek one of Michigan's most enthusiastic supporters, look to EDS.

Each year, selected Michigan teachers are awarded $1,500 for new educational tools through EDS Technology Grants. Here, EDS vice president, Doug Hoover (right), presents a check to Shannon Boardman and her class in Warren, Michigan.

RAVE COMPUTER ASSOCIATION, INC.

RECOGNIZED AS

ONE OF MICHIGAN'S

FASTEST-GROWING

PRIVATELY HELD

COMPANIES,

RAVE COMPUTER

ASSOCIATION, INC.,

IS COMMITTED TO

PROVIDING

QUALITY SERVICE

AND PRODUCTS

Rave Computer Association, Inc., is a classic American success story of three friends from Michigan who started a computer hardware business in a basement. Today that small start-up has grown to a $24 million corporation with customers throughout the United States, Canada, and Europe.

The three founders and entrepreneurs—Frederick Darter, president, Kenneth Gorinski, vice president of technical support, and Dennis Asselin, controller—have succeeded by providing customers with excellence in service, solutions, and technical support in the end-user marketplace.

Based in Sterling Heights, Michigan, Rave emerged into the market in 1988 as the largest reseller of refurbished Data General hardware. In 1992 Rave joined with Sun Microsystems®, establishing itself as an authorized reseller of Sun® remanufactured hardware. While working closely with SunService®, a division of Sun Microsystems, Rave signed a service and support agreement in March 1993. The company continued along this successful path into 1995, when it joined with SunSoft®, a software division of Sun Microsystems, to resell Sun OS and Solaris® software. Rave further solidified its relationship with Sun Microsystems by meeting the requirements to become a Sun Microelectronics OEM (original equipment manufacturer). In December 1998 Rave was selected for the Sun Microsystems Partners Program. Today Rave delivers a wide

Company founders, from left, are Frederick Darter, president; Dennis Asselin, financial controller; and Kenneth Gorinski, vice president of technical support.

array of products through its broad-based vendor partnerships to fulfill customers' critical systems requirements. Rave also sells its own brand-name integrated systems.

Rave extends its industry-specialized services, such as Rave Commercial Services, Rave Federal/Education Services, Rave Telecommunications and ISP Services, and Rave Medical Services, through its central organization. Flexible financing is available from Rave Financial Services, Inc., a full-service rental and leasing company.

Rave is in the "Michigan 100," a list of Michigan's 100 fastest-growing privately held firms, and the Detroit Future 50 Index, both compiled by the Greater Detroit Chamber of Commerce. Rave also is in the *Crain's Detroit Business* "Top 50." In 1998 Rave was approved as a UL test facility and as an ISO-9002 registered company.

"We have a total company commitment to make sure we deliver quality service and quality products to our customers," says Darter. "Any company can make these types of promises verbally—at Rave, we take the extra steps to prove our sincerity and commitment to our customers."

Headquarters for Rave Computer Association, Inc., and Rave Financial Services, Inc., is at 36960 Metro Court in Sterling Heights, Michigan. Rave has grown from nine employees, in 1988, to sixty-four today.

THE DOW CHEMICAL COMPANY

More than one hundred years ago, Herbert H. Dow founded a company with little more than his own entrepreneurial spirit and passion for scientific discovery. He was a man of determination and vision, who brought the power of chemistry to bear on improving the quality of life for people around the world. His spirit and desire to put science to work for people remain the cornerstone of The Dow Chemical Company.

The twentieth century has been revolutionized by scientific discovery—and Dow has been an integral part of that discovery process. Through their innovations, Dow scientists have brought the world safer drinking water; a more secure and dependable food supply; energy-efficient homes and automobiles; smaller, faster computers; and devices for more advanced medical techniques.

As the world begins to face the emerging challenges of the twenty-first century, the 39,000 Dow people around the world continue to develop solutions based on Dow's inherent strength in science and technology—which Dow refers to as "good thinking." This good thinking will allow Dow to continue to improve the quality of life for everyone.

Dow, a global science- and technology-based company with annual sales of more than $18 billion, provides a portfolio of chemical, plastic, and agricultural products and services for customers in 168 countries around the world. Dow has 123 manufacturing sites in 32 countries supplying more than 3,500 products.

Dow helps customers to succeed through its fourteen global businesses: Adhesives, Sealants & Coatings; Engineering Plastics; Epoxy Products and Intermediates; Fabricated Products; Polyethylene; Polystyrene; Polyurethanes; Specialty Chemicals; Emulsions Polymers; INSITE™ Technology; Chemicals; Hydrocarbons & Energy; and New Businesses. Dow is a

H. H. Dow founded The Dow Chemical Company in 1897 in Midland, Michigan. He was first attracted to mid-Michigan by the vast amount of brine underneath Midland. Brine is needed to produce bromine through electrochemistry.

global leader in many of these areas, including polyethylene resins, polystyrene resins, styrene butadiene latex, olefins, and styrene. Another Dow business, Dow AgroSciences LLC, is a global leader in the agricultural industry. In 1998 Dow made significant investments in biotechnology, a field that offers the potential to revolutionize agriculture, as well as many other industries, including performance chemicals and plastics.

Dow people around the world are guided by a set of core values and purpose. Dow places special emphasis on valuing its people, its customers, the products and services it provides, and ensuring that its conduct reflects attention to ethics, safety, health, and the environment. Dow's commitment to the environment includes a set of far-reaching, voluntary goals set in 1996 to be reached in 2005. These include reducing air and water emissions of priority compounds by 75 percent, and reducing workplace injuries and illnesses by 90 percent. Accountability for reaching these goals rests with every employee, and every business decision Dow makes takes these goals into account.

Dow will continue to discover "what good thinking can do" as it enters the new millennium. In addition, Dow will continue to work toward achieving its mission to be the most productive, best value-growth chemical company in the world.

For more than a decade, Dow employees have worked with Habitat for Humanity, sharing their time, skills, and products, like STYROFOAM™ brand insulation, with families in need.

WONDERS OF CHEMISTRY

CHAPTER THIRTEEN

MICHIGAN MAY BE BEST KNOWN FOR ITS CARS, BUT CHEMICALS AND PHAR-
MACEUTICALS ARE ALSO BIG BUSINESS IN THE GREAT LAKES STATE.
CHEMICALS AND ALLIED PRODUCTS ARE THE STATE'S THIRD-LARGEST EXPORT
CATEGORY, JUST BEHIND TRANSPORTATION PRODUCTS AND INDUSTRIAL AND
COMPUTER EQUIPMENT. WHEN IT COMES TO FAMOUS NAMES, NEARLY AS
MANY CROP UP IN THIS SECTOR AS IN THE AUTO INDUSTRY.

FORMULAS FOR SUCCESS

Henry Ford and his family used to be known in Michigan as the "Car Fords" to distinguish them from the "Glass Fords"—a separate and, at one time, even better known, industrial dynasty. In 1890 Captain John B. Ford, founder of the Pittsburgh Plate Glass Company, got the idea that rock salt deposits beneath the Detroit River might be used to make soda ash. Soda ash was needed in glass manufacturing and, up to that time, had to be imported. Ford turned out to be right, which led to his creation of the Wyandotte Chemicals Corporation, now a division of BASF. The Glass Fords' success not only made them important figures in Detroit society, but also inspired the formation of other chemical companies. By 1918 Detroit was the center of a chemical industry that shipped more than 200 million pounds of soda ash each year.

About the same time the Glass Fords were settling into Wyandotte, a twenty-three-year-old chemist from Cleveland moved up to Midland, attracted by the extensive brine deposits there. Herbert H. Dow needed those deposits to try out a new process he had developed to extract bromine from brine. Bromine was a key ingredient in most of the medicines of the day, and demand for the substance was growing as new uses for it were discovered, such as in the manufacture of photographic film. Dow incorporated the Dow Chemical Company in 1897. One hundred years later, Dow is one of the world's largest chemical firms, a global operation with annual sales of more than $18 billion. Dow has 123 manufacturing sites in 32 countries, but its headquarters remains in Midland.

Dow soon found ways to extract other components from the Michigan brines. He used chlorine, calcium,

OPPOSITE: This technician at Adco & AlliedSignal Co. in Michigan Center is checking the durability of a new sealant. Standing in front of an apparatus called a weathermometer, she observes how the product performs in hot, cold, wet, and dry environments. © Dwight Cendrowski. ABOVE: Computers perform sophisticated analysis on chemical compounds, speeding the research and development process and providing a higher level of accuracy than once was possible. © HMS Images

iodine, and lithium in a range of new products which today numbers more than 2,400, including Styrofoam, Saran Wrap, and Zip-loc bags. Herbert Dow's dictum— "I can find a hundred men to tell me an idea won't work; what I want are men who will make it work"—became the company's motto. With its progressive philosophy, Dow Chemical Company attracted innovators such as

The Dow Chemical Company continues to develop new materials and technologies. The company currently markets its products in 164 countries around the world. © The Dow Chemical Company

Many wonders have emerged from Michigan test tubes, including the drug AZT, one of the few agents found to slow the effects of AIDS, discovered by Dr. Jerome Horwitz. © HMS Images

E. O. Barstow, the "father of magnesium"; Charles J. Strosaker, the man behind the invention of Saran Wrap; Mark W. Putnam, who made Dow the nation's largest aspirin producer; latex paint inventor L. L. Ryden; and John J. Grebe, who developed secondary oil recovery, a process for extracting additional oil from wells previously thought to be exhausted.

This Ann Arbor glassblower is part of an industry that took root in Michigan when the state's natural soda ash deposits attracted John B. Ford to Detroit in 1890. Ford's one plant grew into a dynasty. © Andrew Sacks

Enlightened employee relations and active involvement in the Midland community are other hallmarks of the company. From public gardens to sports teams to symphony orchestras, Dow support has enriched the mid-Michigan area.

Midland is also home to Dow Corning Corporation, which is equally owned by Corning, Inc., and the Dow Chemical Company. Dow Corning is one of the world's largest manufacturers of silicon-based materials. Its products are used in an expanding roster including automobiles, aircraft, cosmetics, paint additives, and textiles. The company's joint venture, Hemlock Semiconductor Corporation, located in Saginaw County, is the world's leading manufacturer of polycrystalline silicon, the basic material used in computer processing chips. The company experienced controversy in the 1990s over its silicone breast implants,

A LIBERATING FACE-LIFT

WHEN THE STATUE OF LIBERTY UNDERWENT MAJOR RESTORATION IN 1986, EXPERTS FOUND ONLY ONE SEALANT THAT WOULD ADEQUATELY PROTECT THE LADY'S EIGHTY-TON COPPER SKIN—A DOW CORNING HIGH-PERFORMANCE BUILDING SEALANT FREQUENTLY USED ON SKYSCRAPERS. MIDLAND'S DOW CORNING DONATED THE SILICONE PRODUCT AND COMPANY EXPERTISE IN ITS APPLICATION.

which it stopped manufacturing in 1992. Dow Corning is a $2.6 billion company with approximately thirty manufacturing locations on five continents, including its flagship Midland plant, an advanced engineering site and its world headquarters in Bay County, medical materials and semiconductor plants in

Parke-Davis was the first firm in the nation to market an antitoxin for diphtheria. Shown here, the company's Ann Arbor headquarters. © Dwight Cendrowski

Chemical storage tanks such as these await transportation of their contents to all parts of the globe. © HMS Images

Saginaw County, and an automotive technical development center in Plymouth.

MEDICINAL MARVELS

Pharmaceuticals have figured prominently in Michigan's economic picture since 1855 when Frederick Stearns opened a drugstore in Detroit and began manufacturing

---

DYNAMIC DUO

THE FIRST DPT VACCINE, WHICH PROTECTS AGAINST DIPHTHE-RIA, WHOOPING COUGH, AND TETANUS, WAS DEVELOPED IN 1939 BY TWO MICHIGAN DEPARTMENT OF HEALTH PHYSICIANS, DR. PEARL KENDRICK AND DR. GRACE ELDERING.

---

medicines to sell in it. His became one of the largest pharmaceutical firms in the country, making him rich enough to buy Detroit's baseball team and enough talented players to win the 1887 national championship. By the time Stearns won the baseball title, the title of "nation's largest drug firm" had gone to rival Parke-Davis, also in Detroit. Parke-Davis is credited with a number of important pharmaceutical "firsts," including introducing the first pure form of adrenaline (1901) and developing the first oxidized cellulose sponge for medical and surgical use (1946). Now a division of Warner-Lambert, Parke-Davis Pharmaceutical Research is headquartered in Ann Arbor.

Michigan's other major pharmaceutical firm, Upjohn, was established in 1886, a year after a young Hastings doctor, William E. Upjohn, patented a quick-dissolving coating for pills. Since then the Upjohn Company has played an important role in the Kalamazoo community financially, culturally, and by generously supporting educational institutions there. In 1995 Upjohn merged with the European pharmaceutical firm Pharmacia to become the ninth-largest prescription drug firm in the world. Pharmacia & Upjohn's Consumer Health Division remains headquartered in Kalamazoo, and is responsible for products such as Rogaine, Cortaid, and PediaCare.

Another important Michigan name in pharmaceuticals is Troy-based R. P. Scherer Corporation, the nation's largest maker of soft gelatin capsules for the drug, vitamin, and cosmetics industries. Scherer operates nineteen facilities in twelve countries, with more than one-half billion dollars in annual revenues. One of its latest products promises to revolutionize the pill industry. Zydis, a flash-frozen and fresh-dried wafer, is a new drug delivery system that dissolves in the mouth without water. The company currently has twenty Zydis projects underway, including a quick-release form of the impotence drug Viagra.

For more than a century innovative Michigan companies have played a crucial role in the health and well-being not just of Americans but of people around the globe. These research-based, cutting-edge firms guarantee Michigan's continued position in the forefront of new developments in chemistry and medicine.

Michigan pharmaceutical firms have developed treatments for high cholesterol, diabetes, and baldness. © Corbis

Pharmaceutical research tubes await analysis. © Dwight Cendrowski

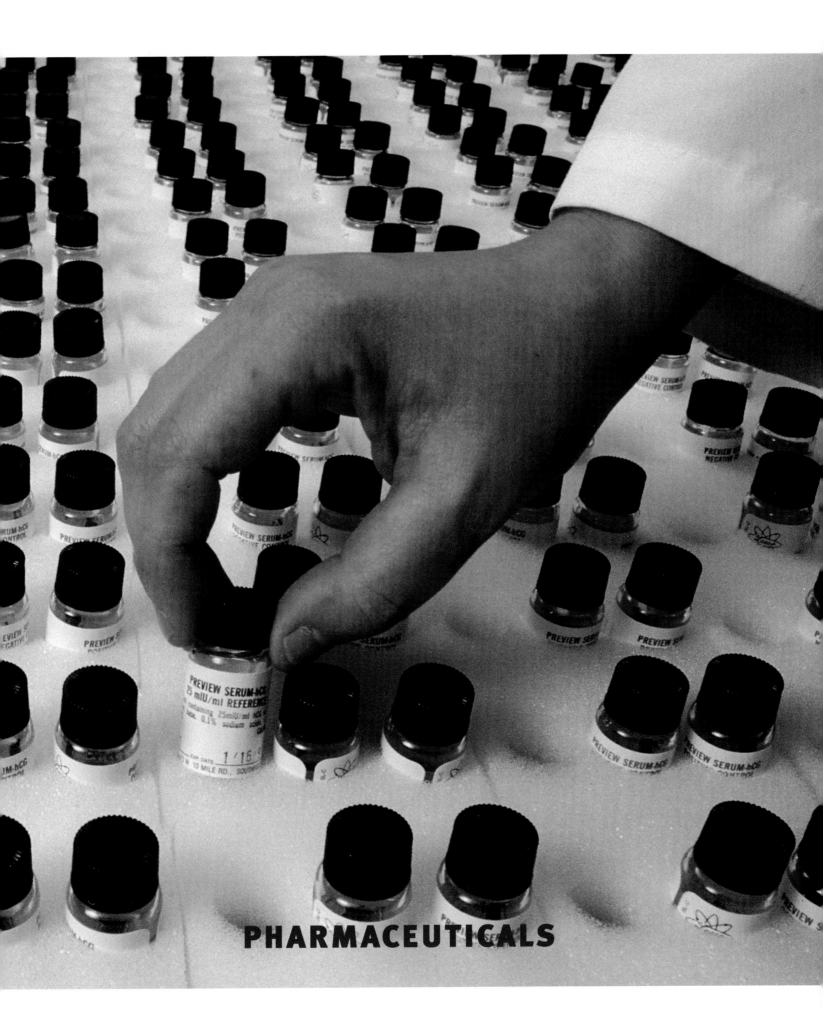

PHARMACEUTICALS

PARKE-DAVIS

By using

emerging enabling

technologies and

working with

partners,

Parke-Davis

achieves faster

growth and

breakthrough

drug development,

which, in 1998,

increased its sales

to greater than

$5 billion

Parke-Davis is focused on discovering, developing, manufacturing, and marketing high-quality pharmaceutical products. Founded in the 1870s, the Michigan-based company was among the first of the industry's pioneers to introduce the pursuit of basic research as a company policy. In 1902 Parke-Davis built the first industrial laboratory in the United States to be devoted exclusively to pharmacological research. Parke-Davis invented many of the drug-development techniques and processes that have resulted in the creation of drugs that have had a major impact on the history of medicine. Among the company's very first discoveries were treatments for diphtheria and epilepsy.

Today Parke-Davis is a division of the Warner-Lambert Company, an industry leader. The central research focus at Parke-Davis is on cardiovascular disease, diabetes, infectious diseases, disorders of the central nervous system, inflammatory diseases, and women's health care. Its Ann Arbor facility is the company's worldwide headquarters for pharmaceutical research and development activity. Today the new-product pipeline generated from this Parke-Davis facility is very attractive and is evolving into one of the best in the industry.

A decade of hard work led to the approval and launch of two new breakthrough products, Lipitor and Rezulin, in 1997. These products have been both medically and commercially successful. Lipitor (atorvastatin)

The first Parke-Davis manufacturing laboratory was located at Cass and Henry Streets in Detroit.

is a lipid-lowering agent for lowering cholesterol. Rezulin (troglitazone) is the first therapy for non-insulin-dependent diabetes. Three of the company's top sellers among its established pharmaceutical brands are the anticonvulsant Neurontin (gabapentin), the cardiovascular agent Accupril (quinapril), and the oral contraceptive Loestrin (norethindrone ethinyl estradiol).

The Parke-Davis approach to pharmaceutical research and development (R&D) is knowledge-based with the use of cross-functional teams, in order to achieve excellence in execution. The company had more than twenty-two alliances during the period from 1997 to 1998, which facilitated its rapid growth. As a result of the new drugs it has introduced using this R&D strategy, Parke-Davis sales increased from approximately $3.6 billion in 1997 to more than $5.6 billion in 1998, placing the company among the fastest-growing companies in the United States and in the pharmaceutical industry.

The financial success of the company's new products has paved the way for more research, increased staff, and a major expansion of facilities, including its manufacturing facilities in Holland, Michigan. The success of Parke-Davis benefits the community by creating new jobs as the company builds and staffs its new facilities.

Harvey C. Parke (left) and George S. Davis (right) had contrasting personalities, but they shared a common meeting ground: the insistence on high standards for their products.

"We are guided by our mission to find drugs to meet unmet medical needs," says Dr. Harvey Kaplan, vice president of scientific affairs at Parke-Davis. "The company maintains a culture in which we make decisions based on the idea of following where science leads us. Our approach encourages innovation and creativity."

The corporate culture of Parke-Davis fosters an open, highly communicative working community. The Parke-Davis knowledge-driven scientists work together in cross-functional multidisciplinary teams. "During this past decade we have built a top-flight discovery team and a superb team for drug development," says Dr. Ronnie Cresswell, former head of R&D, and now senior vice president of Warner-Lambert. "We are a highly diverse group, international in scope, and open to ideas from the widest variety of sources. We follow the best science wherever it is generated, inside or outside our company. We have a strong portfolio of early-stage lead compounds and an exciting group of drugs in later development stages. We have invested in new technologies that provide quantum leaps in efficiency in designing new drugs and screening them against disease states. And we have an extensive network of strategic alliances. They provide us with new projects, technologies, and skills. We have many ways to manage these collaborations, but they all share a Parke-Davis commitment to providing the needed scientific talent to make them successful."

The new president of R&D, Dr. Peter B. Corr, who has taken over for Dr. Cresswell, has been given the challenge of taking the R&D division to the next level and making Parke-Davis one of the best companies in the world.

"The challenge facing our R&D organization," says Corr, "is keeping our focus and our energy, while at the same time building and growing at more than 20 percent

Expansions continue at Parke-Davis in Ann Arbor, the company's worldwide headquarters for pharmaceutical research and development.

per year in terms of our infrastructure. You can get lost in the forest when you do this, so this is not the time to become diffused."

One of the key reasons the R&D arm of Parke-Davis is located in Ann Arbor is the enormous opportunity for interaction with the University of Michigan. The leadership of both the company and the university recognizes the value added by a relationship that includes shared teaching, postdoctoral students, and joint research projects. While the main focus of this working relationship is on biomedical science, the interaction also includes the schools of pharmacy, chemistry, engineering, and business. Parke-Davis also is working closely with Eastern Michigan University and Wayne State University.

Parke-Davis is the largest private taxpayer in Ann Arbor and Washtenaw County's largest private employer after Ford and General Motors. The company is in the midst of a $270 million plant expansion project that will eventually make room for about a thousand new jobs.

As supporters of the community's cultural and charitable efforts, many Parke-Davis employees serve as volunteers in local organizations. Parke-Davis also is the third-largest private giver to the University of Michigan.

The Parke-Davis research facility was located on the Detroit River until 1960, when construction was completed on a new research facility in Ann Arbor.

THE WONDERS OF CHEMISTRY

GO POWER

CHAPTER FOURTEEN

Economic success cannot be achieved or maintained without the transportation and energy infrastructure to support it, and once again Michigan's fortunate geography has endowed it with special advantages in both areas. Michigan's commercial power is directly tied to its go power—power to import the raw materials, fuel the factories, and export the goods produced. The Great Lakes State is

unique in the range and quality of its transportation options and in the richness of the energy resources that power its public utilities.

FROM HERE TO THERE

The War of 1812 inspired the first federally mandated road construction projects in Michigan, but it was the emergence of the automobile nearly 100 years later that put Michigan in the forefront of state highway development. The Michigan State Highway Department, started in 1905, oversees one of the best highway systems in the nation—nearly 10,000 miles of toll-free trunk lines, 7,000 miles of which are all-season routes with no seasonal load limits or restrictions.

Michigan roads are built for heavy traffic, in number of vehicles and in tonnage, allowing trucks to carry heavier loads than in any other state—164,000 pounds with double-axle spacing, twice the weight permitted elsewhere. Michigan's main interstate highways move

goods to every major city in the Western Hemisphere. Congress's projected "NAFTA superhighway" is already a reality in Michigan, whose international bridges and tunnels are the United States' busiest links to Canada.

Because Michigan lies at the center of the largest reservoir of fresh water in the world, it offers an unparalleled variety of shipping opportunities. It has thirty-seven deep-water ports—more than many coastal states—and all are served by the U.S. Customs offices in Detroit, Sault Sainte Marie, Saginaw, and Port Huron. An average of 168 million tons of freight travels the Great Lakes each year. The Soo Locks and the Saint Lawrence Seaway link Michigan ports with the Atlantic Ocean and European markets. In fact, via the St. Lawrence Seaway, Detroit is fewer nautical miles away from most northern European ports than are cities along the East Coast. In 1995 western Michigan ports joined the Mississippi River Barge system, thereby connecting the Great Lakes shipping system with

Opposite: *The Ambassador Bridge unites Detroit with its sister city of Windsor, Ontario. One of three bridges between Detroit and Canada, it is the world's longest international suspension bridge. © Ted and Jean Reuther/Dembinsky Photo Associates.* Above: *Despite Michigan's extensive network of roads and highways, some people still prefer the comfort of travel by rail. Shown here, passengers board an Amtrak train in Jackson. Amtrak's busy network links Michigan to both the east and west coasts. © Dwight Cendrowski*

the Mississippi River and the Gulf of Mexico. Michigan's eighty-seven recreational boating harbors serve the one million pleasure boats—more than any other state—that take advantage of the beautiful waters.

Railroads arrived in Michigan about the same time as statehood, ready to serve the timber, iron, and copper booms. At its peak in the 1920s, the state's railroad industry ran on 9,000 miles of track. Today twenty-three private rail freight companies operate on 4,000 miles of

Interstate 94 traverses southern Michigan and is part of a comprehensive national network of highways. © Dwight Cendrowski

The Soo Locks outside Sault Sainte Marie handle more tons of cargo during the eight months they are navigable than the Panama Canal handles all year. © Tom Buchkoe

Michigan mainline track, linked to Canada's rail system via a rail bridge at Sault Sainte Marie and rail tunnels in Detroit and Port Huron. Michigan's freight railroads carry hundreds of commodities essential to the state's industrial manufacturing, chemical, commercial, and

agricultural sectors, and Amtrak offers passenger rail service via Class I carrier tracks.

On 1 August 1926 Dearborn's Ford Airport opened a passenger depot, and Stout Air Services began the nation's first regularly scheduled passenger service—daily round-trips between Detroit and Grand Rapids. Stout became the first airline to carry 100,000 passengers. Stout traveled 900,000 miles over three years with a perfect safety record, and was eventually absorbed by United Airlines. Today Michigan is served by twenty-one airports, offering nonstop or one-stop flights to all major cities in the world. Detroit Metropolitan Airport, among the nation's ten busiest, is Northwest Airlines' North American hub. Metro's daily flight to Beijing is the only nonstop commercial flight offered between the United States and the People's Republic of China. The airport also has several daily nonstops to Japan, as well as to Paris, London, Frankfurt, and Amsterdam. Metro handled 15.4 million passengers in 1997, and is in the midst

An egret patrols the inlet pond near the Whiting electric generating plant on Lake Erie. Consumers Energy develops habitat areas for wildlife at all Michigan plant sites. Courtesy, Consumers Energy

YOU ARE HERE

of a $1.6 billion renovation and expansion, with a new Northwest terminal scheduled to open in 2001.

A LITERAL POWERHOUSE

Michigan residents began lighting their homes with electricity within a few short years of the invention of the incandescent bulb. In fact, Thomas Edison spent his youth in Port Huron and developed the first electrical battery there in 1861. Today the state's electric power system is among the most modern and reliable in the world. Power generating facilities here, which use a diverse mix of fuel sources including coal, nuclear energy, oil/gas and hydroelectric power, exceed present and anticipated environmental regulations. Michigan also leads the nation in electric utility deregulation. Beginning in 1997, qualifying commercial and

HENRY FORD II

ROUGE STEEL COMPANY

A freighter with a classic Michigan name passes under the Ambassador Bridge, en route to deliver steel products to customers on the East Coast and beyond.
© Dwight Cendrowski

For more than 100 years the Edison Sault Electric Company has taken advantage of the nineteen-foot drop where the Saint Mary's River connects Lake Superior with Lakes Michigan and Huron. The company's quarter-mile-long electric plant, completed in 1902, is a national historical mechanical engineering landmark. The 30,000-kilowatt plant continues to serve residents of Sault Sainte Marie and users as far away as Mackinac Island.

Consumers Energy Company, formerly named Consumers Power and still the principal subsidiary of Dearborn-based CMS Energy Corporation, is Michigan's largest utility, providing electricity and natural gas to six million of the state's 9.5 million residents in all sixty-eight Lower Peninsula counties. Wendell Wilkie, 1940 presidential candidate and president of

industrial customers could choose a power producer and pay the local utility only for the cost of transmitting that power. Further implementation of this program will permit customers to shop for the best prices and enjoy potentially unlimited capacity.

Detroit Edison is the nation's seventh-largest electric utility, serving more than two million customers in its 7,600-square-mile southeastern Michigan service area. Incorporated in 1903, Detroit Edison's power plants generate nearly fifty billion kilowatt-hours of electricity annually. The company is involved in a number of environmentally proactive projects including participation in a nationwide program to voluntarily reduce greenhouse gas emissions, exploration of renewable energy sources to produce electricity, and planting ten million trees for the new millennium.

the holding company that once owned Consumers Power, spearheaded the company's groundbreaking effort to provide electricity to the farming community. In October 1949 Consumers Power became the first utility to connect 100,000 farms, a record that has never been equaled.

Michigan's other major natural gas provider is Detroit's Michigan Consolidated Gas Company.

CYCLE PATH

THE COUNTRY'S FIRST BIKEPATH ALONG AN INTERSTATE FREEWAY WAS CONSTRUCTED BESIDE THIRTY-SEVEN MILES OF INTERSTATE 275 FROM MONROE COUNTY TO SOUTHERN OAKLAND COUNTY IN 1977.

More than 125,000 primary school students have learned how to use electricity safely through Consumers Energy's free Hazard Hamlet electric safety program. Courtesy, Consumers Energy

650 billion cubic feet. A continental hub, Michigan cycles more natural gas through storage than any other state, assuring residents a reliable supply even in the coldest winters. Fully one-fourth of the natural gas Michigan uses—225 billion cubic feet—is pumped in the state, ranking Michigan among the top ten states for gas and oil production.

INTO THE FUTURE

With its unlimited fresh water supply, abundant energy resources, and ideal location in the center of a varied transportation network, the Great Lakes State is guaranteed plenty of commercial go power for the twenty-first century.

MichCon traces its history back to the 1848 founding of the Detroit Gas Light Company, which lit the streetlamps of downtown Detroit with gas manufactured from coal. Today MichCon is one of the nation's largest natural gas distribution companies, serving 1.2 million families and businesses in 550 Michigan communities through more than 18,500 miles of pipelines.

Both Consumers Energy and MichCon take advantage of Michigan's unique geology to store gas in natural, rock-formed underground storage fields. Thanks to these geologic formations, Michigan has the most gas storage capacity in the Midwest—

Seismic exploration continues to reveal new reserves of oil and gas beneath the surface of the Upper Peninsula. Here, a technician investigates Manistee National Forest. © Ross Frid

Air traffic controllers use the naked eye as well as computers to monitor activity at Detroit Metropolitan Airport. © Andrew Sacks

TRANSPORTATION AND UTILITIES

NORTHWEST AIRLINES

The nation's oldest airline carrier with continuous name identification, Northwest Airlines began making history in 1926 with the first mail flight between Minneapolis–St. Paul and Chicago. It pioneered the Great Circle Route between the United States and Tokyo, Seoul, Shanghai, and Manila in 1947, and continues making history today as the only airline with more than fifty years of airline service from the United States to Japan.

From its hub at Wayne County's Detroit Metropolitan Airport (DTW), the airline and its partners serve 117 domestic and international destinations nonstop with more than 500 daily departures, accounting for 60 percent of the airport's local boardings. More than one million passengers flew Northwest from Detroit in 1998, taking advantage of nonstop service to such cities as Beijing, Nagoya, Osaka, Tokyo, Amsterdam, Frankfurt, London, and Paris.

The Detroit-Nagoya service, inaugurated on 2 June 1998, links the two largest automobile manufacturing centers in the world. Called the "Motown Express," the nonstop flight reduces travel time between the two destinations by several hours compared to one- and two-stop flights. Executives in the automotive industry can take advantage not only of Northwest's fast, convenient passenger service

With more than 500 daily flights offered, Northwest Airlines passengers have more than 400 destinations around the world to choose from.

between Detroit and Nagoya but also of its substantial cargo capacity for shipping parts and supplies between the two regions.

A study by Booz-Allen & Hamilton released by the airport in June 1998 shows that DTW (and Northwest, as one of its main tenants) generates $4.2 billion annually for the Detroit metropolitan area and accounts for more than 61,000 jobs. By 2000, DTW is expected to generate $5.1 billion, with related jobs increasing to 71,000.

In a 1 July 1998 *Detroit News* article, the city's mayor, Dennis Archer, expressed the benefits of Detroit being a hub for a major airline: "Since 1990 Northwest has increased domestic capacity at DTW by 42 percent and international capacity by 84 percent . . . . We in Detroit are beneficiaries of this expansion in service. We generate less than 20 percent of the traffic on all these flights but enjoy the convenience of ready access to the range of destinations and frequencies that a hub market offers."

When the airport's brand-new $1.2 billion Midfield Terminal becomes operational in 2001, Northwest will be its main tenant. Since 1997 the airline has made more than $75 million worth of improvements to its existing terminal, including a new international check-in area, a moving sidewalk between the C and D concourses and six new gates on the C concourse, and expanded curbside check-in. In addition, a new DC-10 line maintenance hangar is under way.

The positive impact of Midfield Terminal for improving conditions at overtaxed DTW is clearly shown in its figures. The terminal's two million square feet of space will house seventy-four jet gates, twenty-five commuter gates, forty-seven escalators, thirty-nine elevators, 1.5 miles of moving walkways, and an elevated train system that can be viewed from the main concourse. Both international and domestic arrivals and departures will operate out of the same building, expediting connections. Outside, the curbside drop-off area and adjacent one-and-one-half lanes of traffic will be covered.

The Midfield Terminal promises to be bright and spacious, with plenty of natural light pouring in beneath the three- to six-story arched ceilings—particularly under the thirty-seven-foot concourse ceiling, the tallest of its kind in the world. Massive areas of open space will offer unobstructed views of the specialty stores, restaurants, and train station below, and all the way to the glass wall at the terminal's far end. Visitors will walk on polished beige terrazzo flooring, past walls of beige and pewter-colored ceramic tile and stainless steel.

The regional vice president for state and local affairs, Andrea Newman, explains that Wayne County officials asked

The Northwest international departures terminal, which opened in the summer of 1997, makes check-ins for international flights more convenient than ever before.

Northwest to partner with them in building the new terminal. "This is the first partnership of its kind in the nation," she says. "It will be the county's airport, yet we're building it with no direct Wayne County taxpayers' money." The fact that two such different entities can work together successfully on such a project bodes well for the future. Newman is certain that when the terminal is complete, "many, many more people will start to have a different impression of the airport and of Detroit. They will want to pass through, want to use this airport, and perhaps want to stay," she says.

Northwest's commitment to the communities it serves is nowhere more evident than in the Detroit area, where its DTW employees number nearly 11,000. More than fifty local organizations receive Northwest Airlines financial and volunteer support, from the Detroit Children's Center and the NAACP to C. S. Mott Children's Hospital, which received $50,000 in 1998. Northwest works hard at meeting more than just transportation needs. Visit the Northwest Airlines Web site at www.nwa.com for more information.

The recently renovated Northwest Airlines international arrivals facility handles more than 100 weekly arrivals from cities all around the world.

CONSUMERS ENERGY

Michigan's future is bright with Consumers Energy.

Consumers Energy is the fourth-largest combination electric and natural gas utility in the United States and the largest utility in Michigan, providing electric and gas service to more than 6 million of the state's 9.5 million residents throughout all of the sixty-eight Lower Peninsula counties.

For more than a century, Consumers Energy has provided safe and reliable electricity and natural gas to Michigan customers. Here, an early 1930s electric line crew stands beside a company truck.

HELPING MICHIGAN GROW SINCE 1886

The company was founded in 1886 as the Jackson Electric Light Works by W. A. Foote. Foote later formed and acquired similar businesses throughout Michigan and eventually consolidated the companies into a single entity that he named Consumers Power Company.

Today the company is called Consumers Energy and is a principal subsidiary of CMS Energy, an international company that provides energy services and develops, owns, and operates a variety of energy facilities around the world. CMS Energy, with world headquarters in Dearborn, owns

Although the supply of electricity and natural gas is becoming deregulated, Consumers Energy will still deliver energy to its six million customers throughout Michigan.

$16 billion in energy assets and spans twenty-three countries on five continents.

Natural gas rates for customers of Consumers are the lowest in Michigan and among the lowest 10 percent in the nation. Michigan is a national leader in underground gas storage capacity, which allows the company to purchase commodity in the summer when it is cheaper and store it for winter use. Consumers has 25 percent of the state's total gas storage capacity, with 137 billion cubic feet. In 1998 alone, Consumers passed 360 billion cubic feet of gas through its system—enough to fill a building about 101 stories tall, 7 football fields wide and 34 miles long.

Consumers takes great pride in providing energy in a safe and reliable manner. Employees captured their sixth consecutive national safety award from the National Safety Council in 1997, extending the company's mark of winning the top safety honor eleven of the last thirteen years.

GOOD CORPORATE CITIZEN, GOOD NEIGHBOR

Besides providing electricity and natural gas that add comfort, convenience, and safety to customers' lives, Consumers Energy is committed to being a good corporate citizen and a strong contributing member through the communities it serves. Its philanthropic arm, the Consumers Energy Foundation, enhances the economic, social, and environmental progress of the communities it serves by committing more than $1 million a year to local and statewide groups for a variety of causes, including the United Way, local food banks, educational grants, environmental programs, culture, and the arts.

Consumers Energy facilities provide many recreational opportunities in Michigan, such as fishing at the Tippy hydroelectric plant on the Manistee River, above. The company operates thirteen hydroelectric plants on the Au Sable, Manistee, Muskegon, Grand, and Kalamazoo Rivers.

Consumers Energy employees make wildlife enhancement of the company's facilities a priority. In Ludington, volunteers installed bluebird boxes and planted pine and mountain ash trees. At the electric generating Karn-Weadock plant in Essexville, a nesting site for the endangered common tern was built in 1988. Deer, fox, rabbits, woodchucks, beavers, and muskrats inhabit the site, and an on-site flight pen helps injured birds recover before returning to the wild. Similar community and environmental activities are ongoing at company electric generating plants in Erie, Muskegon, Covert, and West Olive.

PREPARING A BRIGHT FUTURE

As the state's oldest and largest utility, Consumers has helped Michigan build one of the most robust economies in the United States. It is proud of its role in helping Michigan earn the honor of being the number-one state in the nation for attracting new businesses, according to *Site Selection* magazine. Now the company is devoting its experience

Consumers Energy employs 9,000 Michigan men and women. Line workers often use bucket trucks while installing new electric services. Personal protective equipment, such as a hard hat, safety glasses, rubber sleeves, and gloves, is a vital part of the job.

and knowledge to an industry transformation that will help keep Michigan a leader in the new millennium. The company's innovative Gas Customer Choice Program is one of the nation's largest deregulation pilot programs. Consumers is also introducing competition into Michigan's electricity marketplace by working closely with the Michigan Public Service Commission to form a viable plan.

As the state looks ahead to the twenty-first century and prepares for a deregulated gas and electric environment, Consumers Energy is committed to keeping Michigan's future shining bright.

For additional information visit the Consumers Energy Web site at www.consumersenergy.com.

Consumers Energy employees volunteer for a variety of causes and other community and civic activities such as the food drive in Pontiac, Michigan.

CONSUMERS ENERGY: FIRST IN ENERGY, FIRST IN MICHIGAN

Consumers Energy has set many firsts and industry standards while bringing electricity and natural gas to Michigan customers.

Here are just a few:

- 1899—Founder William Augustine Foote sends power twenty-four miles from Trowbridge Dam near Allegan to Kalamazoo, marking the first long-distance transmission of electricity.

- 1949—Consumers completes a rural electrification program, bringing power to its 100,000th Michigan farm—making Michigan the first state to reach that milestone.

- 30 August 1962—The Big Rock Point nuclear facility, near Charlevoix, becomes the world's first high-power density boiling water reactor to generate commercial electricity. The plant was retired on 29 August 1997 as the nation's longest-running nuclear plant.

- 1973—Ludington pumped-storage hydroelectric generating plant becomes the largest facility of its kind in the world, capable of serving 1.4 million people. The American Society of Civil Engineers honors the facility as the Outstanding Engineering Achievement of 1973.

- November 1987—Consumers earns Electric Light & Power's prestigious Utility of the Year honor.

- 16 March 1990—CMS Energy completes the world's first conversion from an unfinished nuclear site to a natural gas-fired cogeneration plant at the Midland Cogeneration Venture.

- 13 January 1998—Big Rock Decommissioning Project becomes the first in the world to successfully complete a special chemical decontamination process, as employees return the site to its natural condition.

- October 1998—CMS Energy receives the prestigious 100 Index of Investor-Owned Utilities Award from Edison Electric Institute for outstanding financial performance over a five-year period.

Plymouth Township power lines witness a winter dawn. © K. D. Dittlinger

MICHIGAN CONSOLIDATED GAS COMPANY

**MICHIGAN
CONSOLIDATED GAS
COMPANY, A PART
OF MICHIGAN'S LIFE
FOR 150 YEARS,
IS DEDICATED TO
BEING MICHIGAN'S
PREFERRED
PROVIDER OF
HIGH-VALUE
ENERGY SERVICES**

From lighting the streets of Detroit in the 1850s to firing the engines of Michigan's industries and heating more than a million homes and businesses statewide, Michigan Consolidated Gas Company (MichCon) prides itself on being a reliable source of energy and energy services, a dependable business partner, and a corporate citizen committed to the communities it serves.

MichCon traces its roots to the 1849 founding of the City of Detroit Gas Company, later renamed the Detroit Gas Light Company. At the time only the pale glow of moonlight or a candle in a window pierced the nighttime darkness. While gaslight had been used in some Eastern cities for decades, lack of access to capital and expertise slowed its spread west of the Allegheny Mountains. Despite these challenges Philadelphia gas engineer Lemuel H. Davis took on the task of organizing a gas company in Detroit and securing local financial involvement. Armed with a charter from the state legislature and a ten-year city gas-lighting contract, the Detroit Gas Light Company began building a gas manufacturing plant and laying distribution pipelines. Less than two years later, on 24 September 1851, gaslight first illuminated the streets of Detroit.

One of the Detroit City Gas Company's gas manufacturing plants, Station B, on Jefferson Avenue in Detroit, is depicted here. In 1872 the Mutual Gas Light Company constructed its gas plant at this site. Mutual Gas Light and Detroit Gas Light merged in 1893 to form the company that would be known as the Detroit City Gas Company, a forerunner of Michigan Consolidated Gas Company.

The same vision and dedication has characterized MichCon's 150 years of service.

In the 1890s, when competition among three Detroit gas companies threatened the survival of each, Detroit Gas Light employees became the backbone of a new consolidated entity, the Detroit City Gas Company.

In 1936, when the company brought clean-burning natural gas to southeast Michigan, 2,500 technicians fanned out, adjusting and inspecting more than three million gas burners, to ensure a safe conversion to the new fuel.

When federal legislation reshaped the nation's utility industry in the mid-1930s, Detroit City Gas, the Grand Rapids Gas Light Company, the Washtenaw Gas Company and the Muskegon Gas Company came together as Michigan Consolidated Gas to build a transmission and distribution system that spanned the state.

Providing dependable gas service has always been a labor-intensive job. Here, in the 1940s, a group of employees takes a break from renewing one of the company's massive gas-holding tanks. The telescopic gas holders, capable of storing up to 10 million cubic feet of manufactured gas, continued to be used for a number of years after the introduction of natural gas.

With natural gas demand growing in the 1940s, MichCon met the need by building its own pipeline to the gas fields of Oklahoma and Texas and developing Michigan's first gas storage field.

During the energy crisis of the late-1970s, when the nation's heavily regulated gas industry failed to respond to market signals, MichCon sought federal policy changes that paved the way for the industry's restructuring and lower prices for customers.

Today as one of the largest natural gas distribution companies in the United States, MichCon provides full-service energy solutions to 1.2 million families and businesses. Its 2,400 miles of transmission pipelines handle more than 900 billion cubic feet of gas annually.

In addition to drawing on an abundant supply of Michigan-produced natural gas, MichCon's pipelines link customers to sources across North America. In the summertime, MichCon makes use of Michigan's unique geology to store up to 130 billion cubic feet of gas in underground storage fields formed of permeable rock, assuring customers a reliable supply during the winter when demand is greatest.

More than just a natural gas distributor, MichCon is committed to providing customers with full-service energy solutions. MichCon's Home Protection PLUS program provides maintenance services for air conditioners and gas-fired home appliances. MichCon also promotes the use of natural gas as a transportation fuel by partnering with automakers and fleet owners to increase the use of natural gas vehicles and by building natural gas fueling stations to make refueling quick and convenient.

MichCon employees rely on in-truck computers and the latest in computer and communications technology to respond to emergencies and customers' service requests.

Being a good neighbor is critical, too. The MichCon Foundation donates approximately $1.5 million annually to support programs that enhance economic vitality, education, and the environment in the 550 communities it serves.

MichCon is a member of the MCN Energy Group Inc., a diversified energy holding company with markets and investments throughout North America and in Asia and approximately $4 billion in assets.

As competition expands, MichCon has dedicated itself to being Michigan's preferred provider of high-value energy services. It will meet the challenges of new market participants with a standard of excellence and the unrelenting pursuit of profitable growth. It is raising its commitment to Michigan businesses to new levels, as exemplified by its providing comprehensive energy services for such projects as the new Midfield Terminal at Wayne County's Detroit Metropolitan Airport.

In building on its 150 years of dependability and innovation, MichCon will become a greater, more valuable part of Michigan's life in the new millennium.

On 9 July 1936 Detroit City Gas introduced natural gas to the citizens of Detroit, replacing the more expensive manufactured gas. As shown here, C. W. Bennett, gas company vice president and general manager, turns the valve to set the new natural fuel flowing to Detroit customers.

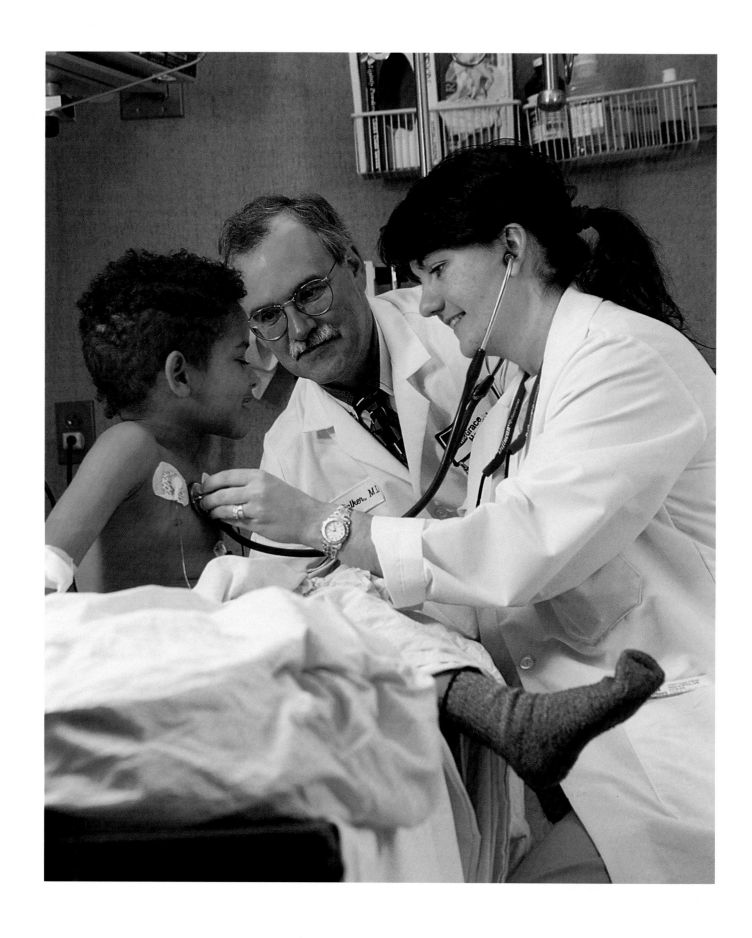

TO YOUR HEALTH

CHAPTER FIFTEEN

THERE ARE 164 COMMUNITY HOSPITALS IN MICHIGAN, INCLUDING SOME OF

THE MOST HIGHLY REGARDED MEDICAL FACILITIES IN THE NATION. NOT ONLY

ARE MICHIGAN HOSPITALS IN THE FOREFRONT OF MEDICAL TREATMENT AND

RESEARCH, THEY ALSO ARE AMONG THE STATE'S LARGEST EMPLOYERS,

PAYING CLOSE TO 200,000 FULL- AND PART-TIME WORKERS SALARIES AND

BENEFITS TOTALLING MORE THAN $6.5 BILLION ANNUALLY. EMPLOYMENT

growth in the health services sector is expected to outpace nearly every other economic sector in the state, with an anticipated 68 percent increase in the number of jobs into the first decade of the new century.

Michiganians take their health care seriously, spending about $30 billion on it annually, 13 percent of their personal income. Hospital costs account for about 40 percent of that figure, with per capita costs for hospital care in Michigan below the national average. Annual surveys by the Michigan Hospital Association indicate that health care consumers here get their money's worth. Its latest report, based on 1.3 million patient discharge records, shows that 82 percent of Michigan hospitals performed as well as or better than expected on cases measured. Such a success rate should come as no surprise. Michigan has prestigious medical schools at three of its universities, and hospitals where some of the nation's top physicians use the latest in medical

technology to treat patients as well as to perform groundbreaking research in nearly every area of health care.

UNIVERSITY OF MICHIGAN

In 1869 the nation's first university hospital opened at the University of Michigan (U-M) in a renovated faculty house. Today U-M's three-hospital system and its medical school are consistently ranked among the top twenty in the nation. Each year the medical school graduates about 185 physicians, and its research faculty receives more than $150 million in grants, making Michigan a national leader in medical research as well as patient care:

- The U-M Comprehensive Cancer Center is considered to be among the top cancer treatment facilities in the nation.
- In 1912 U-M established the nation's first department of dermatology, which today is a leading center

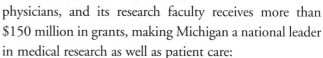

OPPOSITE: *A gentle touch can often be a crucial element in a child's health care. Here, emergency room physicians at Grace Hospital in Detroit minister to a young patient. © Richard Hirneisen.* ABOVE: *The University of Michigan's medical school is renowned for research and is awarded more than $150 million each year in research grants. It is also known for graduating superbly qualified doctors. Shown here, U-M medical school commencement ceremonies. © Larime Photographics/Dembinsky Photo Associates*

FOR FUTURE GENERATIONS

ON 12 NOVEMBER 1941 THE UNIVERSITY OF MICHIGAN OPENED THE NATION'S FIRST HEREDITY CLINIC TO RESEARCH AND COUNSEL FAMILIES ON THE EFFECTS OF INHERITED CHARACTERISTICS. U-M RESEARCHERS DISCOVERED THE GENES RESPONSIBLE FOR CYSTIC FIBROSIS, NEUROFIBROMATOSIS, AND HUNTINGTON'S DISEASE.

A researcher at Michigan State University's College of Human Medicine conducts an experiment. © Bruce A. Fox/MSU

for the study and treatment of psoriasis, skin cancer, and sun-damaged skin.

- Each year U-M surgeon Robert Bartlett is responsible for saving the lives of hundreds of newborns and adults with severe respiratory failure, thanks to the ECMO (extra-corporeal membrane oxygenation) machine he invented, now in use in 120 institutions around the world.
- The U-M Geriatric Research and Training Center is the country's first facility dedicated to research and training in geriatrics and aging.

An Oakwood Hospital doctor points out features of a fetus, visible via ultrasound, to the excited parents. © Dwight Cendrowski

- U-M is a national leader in the diagnosis and treatment of mitral valve disease.
- The university created the nation's first departmental section of thoracic surgery. U-M thoracic surgeons have performed more than 900 transhiatal esophagectomies and esophagal replacements, an operation pioneered by U-M's Mark Orringer, M.D., as a way to treat patients with cancer of the esophagus that would allow them to retain swallowing ability.

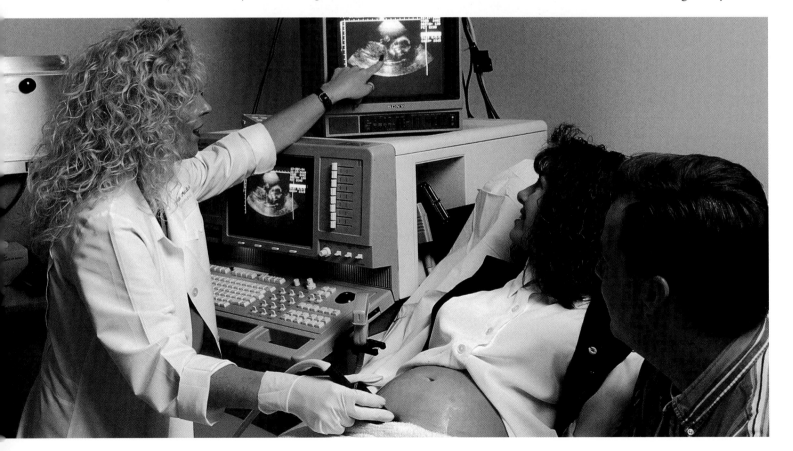

- The U-M Trauma Burn Center was one of the first in the nation and remains among the best.

DETROIT MEDICAL CENTER

The medical school at Wayne State University is affiliated with the Detroit Medical Center (DMC), one of the largest comprehensive health care systems in the United States, bringing together more than 4,000 physicians in eight hospitals. Its five institutions on the 110-acre main campus include Hutzel Hospital, whose 9,000-plus deliveries annually make it one of the busiest obstetrical services in the country; the Kresge Eye Institute, one of the Midwest's leading medical centers for the preservation of sight; and Children's Hospital, which handles 63,000 pediatric cases annually and is known for its poison control center. DMC is also a center for research in the field of emergency medicine.

MICHIGAN STATE UNIVERSITY

Michigan State University's College of Human Medicine was the result of several studies conducted around 1960, which revealed the need for a third medical school in Michigan, one focused on serving the state through direct community involvement in health care. While Michigan State University (MSU) is also actively involved in medical research, its medical school has traditionally emphasized the doctor-patient relationship and the psychosocial aspects of illness, a pioneering approach to medical education that has since been adopted by a number of American medical schools. Rather than working in a university-based hospital, MSU medical students obtain clinical training at community hospitals in Flint, Grand Rapids, Kalamazoo, Lansing, Saginaw, and the Upper Peninsula, a system which has led to an increase in physicians practicing in underserved areas.

MSU is home to the first state-supported and university-based College of Osteopathic Medicine, today one of only nineteen osteopathic medical schools in the United States. The university's School of Veterinary Medicine is recognized as one of the nation's best. In the realm of research, MSU scientist Barnett Rosenberg spearheaded the discovery of cisplatin, the most widely used cancer drug ever developed in the United States, effective in the treatment of both testicular and ovarian cancers. Technology at MSU is responsible for the world's first superconducting medical cyclotron for use in cancer treatment.

This doctor's training at Cook Institute in Grand Rapids includes practicing the technique of physical examination on a dummy patient. © HMS Images

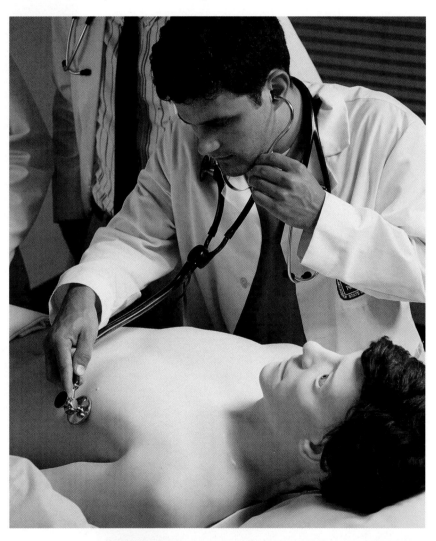

REDOUBTABLE THOMAS

ANN ARBOR–BORN MICROBIOLOGIST THOMAS WELLER WAS THE FIRST SCIENTIST TO GROW THE RUBELLA VIRUS IN A LABORATORY AND TO ISOLATE THE CHICKEN POX VIRUS. HE SHARED THE 1954 NOBEL PRIZE FOR PHYSIOLOGY AND MEDICINE FOR CULTIVATING THE POLIO VIRUS IN A LABORATORY.

OTHER CENTERS OF EXCELLENCE

Michigan is also home to two major dental schools, one at the University of Michigan, the other at the University of Detroit. The 5,500-member Michigan Dental Association, founded in 1856, is the oldest dental association in continuous existence in the United States, and counts more than 75 percent of the state's dentists as members. Michigan has long been in the forefront of the war against cavities. On 25 January 1945 Grand Rapids became the first community in the nation to fluoridate its water supply.

Top-quality medical care in Michigan is not limited to universities. Grand Rapids hospitals serve as West Michigan regional centers for treatment of cancer, diabetes, kidney disease, and burn injuries. Two of the city's hospitals are ranked among the nation's top 100, and Grand Rapids' Medical Education Program is the second-largest in the United States for cities without a medical college or university.

A legendary name in Michigan medicine is William Beaumont, the Fort Mackinac surgeon who discovered the gastronomic action of pepsin. From 1822 to 1830 Beaumont treated a gunshot patient whose wound healed with a permanent opening to his stomach, allowing Beaumont to conduct experiments and observe the stomach's response. Today William Beaumont Hospital, with branches in Royal Oak and Troy, is one of the leading hospital systems in the nation. Beaumont ranks

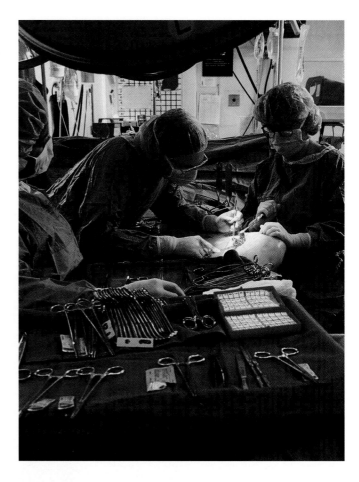

ABOVE: *Doctors remove a vein from a patient's leg in preparation for open-heart surgery at Detroit's Sinai Hospital. © Richard Hirneisen.* BELOW: *Two major dental schools call Michigan home. Here, a dentist performs a routine checkup. © Corbis*

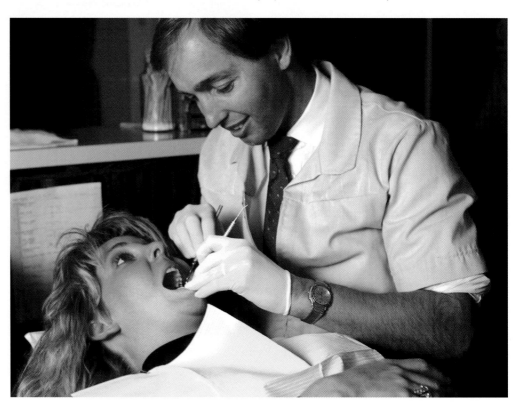

first in the state for admissions, emergency room visits, and outpatient surgeries; fourth nationally in inpatient admissions and outpatient surgeries; and seventh nationally in surgeries. Beaumont was named to *Fortune* magazine's first list of the "100 Best Companies to Work for in America."

MANAGED CARE

Managed care programs are increasingly important in Michigan's health care. Blue Cross and Blue Shield of Michigan (BCBSM) is the largest, providing health insurance coverage for almost half of Michigan's 9.5 million people and boasting $7.7 billion in annual revenues.

A 1997 survey conducted by the MEDSTAT Group of Ann Arbor, J. D. Power and Associates, and the New England Medical Center ranked Farmington Hills–based Care Choices the best health plan in southeast Michigan, outranking sixteen other health plans including Health Maintenance Organizations (HMOs), Preferred Provider Organizations (PPOs), and traditional plans.

Nearly one-quarter of Michigan's population was enrolled in an HMO in 1996. That figure is expected to rise, partly as a result of changes in Medicare and

Medicaid. For now, most Michiganians still choose their health care professionals individually from among the more than fourteen thousand physicians and nearly seven thousand dentists practicing here.

Regardless of the type of health plan one chooses, the diagnosis for now and into the future is that living in the Great Lakes State means living in a great state of health.

A radiologist prepares his patient for X rays at Harper Hospital, one of eight hospitals affiliated with Detroit Medical Center. © Dennis Cox/D. E. Cox Photo Library

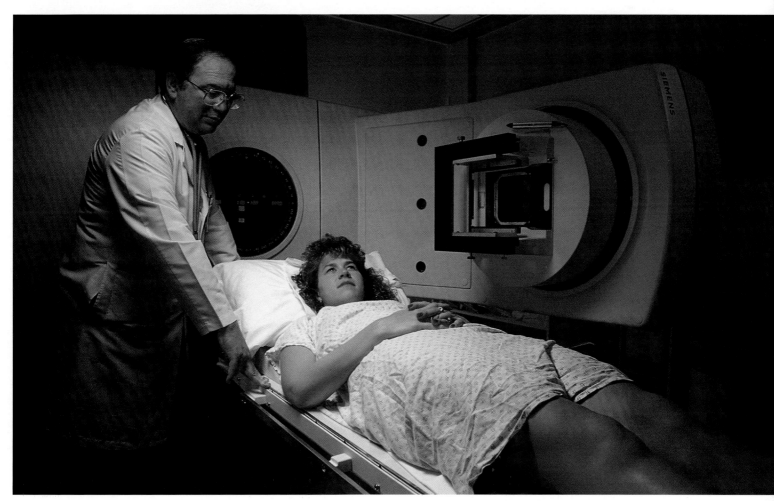

Medical teleconferencing allows doctors in different cities to confer on diagnoses. © HMS Images

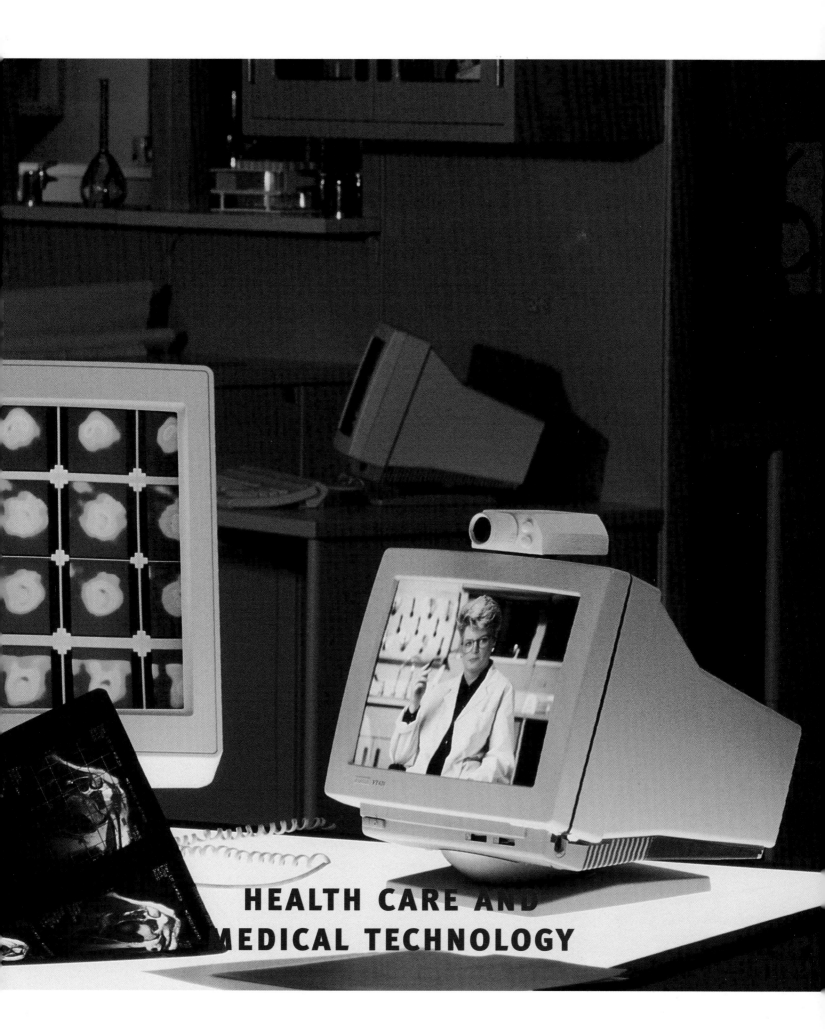

HEALTH CARE AND MEDICAL TECHNOLOGY

MERCY HEALTH SERVICES, CREATED BY THE SISTERS OF MERCY, REGIONAL COMMUNITY OF DETROIT, PROVIDES HEALTH CARE BY EMPHASIZING WELLNESS AND HELPS PEOPLE GROW BOTH IN HEALTH AND IN SPIRIT

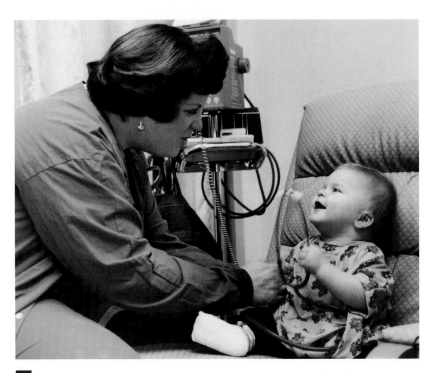

Health care with a personal touch is a hallmark of Mercy caregivers. Here, a nurse calms a little boy before his outpatient surgery.

Farmington Hills–based Mercy Health Services (MHS) is proof that the most modern of medical systems can still affirm values of mercy, human dignity, justice, service, and preferential option for the poor. The Sisters of Mercy Regional Community of Detroit religious order, which created MHS in 1976, now sponsors Michigan's largest health care network, which, as rated in *Hospitals & Health Networks* magazine, is one of the top-ten integrated health care systems in the United States.

The Sisters of Mercy's roots in Michigan began in 1908 when they purchased the Northern Hotel in Big Rapids, converted it into a hospital, and accepted thousands of patients, most of whom came with a "five-dollar insurance" ticket. This ticket entitled the disabled lumberjack (the main group served) to a home with board, medicine, doctor's fee, and special

Mercy is a caring, healing organization that has a genuine concern for the poor and a philosophy that stresses a collaborative team approach by physicians and partners.

care from the sisters. At the time this was the only hospital between Detroit and Sault Ste. Marie.

BUILDING LASTING RELATIONSHIPS

In 1827 in Dublin, Ireland, Mother Catherine McAuley opened The House of Mercy, a private care center dedicated to educating and giving care to the indigent and the underserved. It was there that Catherine McAuley established a health ministry to serve those in need. Today that mission guides MHS in building key partnerships. "Mercy Health Services is a system of relationships with our employees, physicians, patients, businesses, and entire communities," says MHS president, Judith Pelham. "We've worked hard to create ties that help others grow in health and spirit. Our values and the direction set by our sponsors, the Sisters of Mercy, Regional Community of Detroit, help make that a reality."

Today MHS delivers care through thirty-eight acute care hospitals, 200 clinics, twenty-three home health care offices, seventeen long-term care nursing facilities, and ten hospice offices. Gary Nederveld & Associates, an occupational and physical therapy company and MAS Associates, an architectural firm, also are part of MHS.

MERCY HEALTH SERVICES

A sponsored work of the Sisters of Mercy Regional Community of Detroit

MHS owns Mercy Health Plans which operates Care Choices, a health maintenance organization; Preferred Choices, a preferred provider organization; and Mercy Continuing Care, an organization that operates the system's long-term care facilities, assisted living centers, home care, and hospice.

The MHS network also sponsors hundreds of community programs for disease prevention, rehabilitation, and wellness. The network provides care for people not only when they become sick but throughout their lives.

MANAGING CHANGE

Recognizing that the increasingly complex world of health care would require strong business leadership and good organization in the decades ahead, the Sisters of Mercy organized seventeen hospitals into the Sisters of Mercy Health Corporation (SMHC) in 1976. Adopting the best management and medical features present at each facility, SMHC was able to use the strength of its organization to lower health care costs, standardize care procedures, and increase quality throughout the system.

In 1984 the Sisters of Mercy Health Corporation was restructured to become a subsidiary of MHS, transforming the organization from a system of hospitals into a system of health services with an emphasis on managed care. The managed care philosophy of caring for the individual holistically by emphasizing disease prevention and wellness parallels the founding values of Mercy Health Services.

POOLING RESOURCES

Recognizing that effective health care management requires an integrated approach, MHS is dedicated to collaboration in health care delivery. For example, MHS has established several major regional partnerships, such as the Henry Ford–

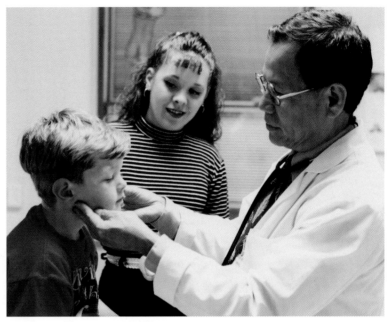

Mercy Health Services is building lasting relationships with its employees, physicians, patients, businesses and entire communities. As a result, people trust they will find compassion and top-quality health care at Mercy.

St. Joseph Mercy Health Network in Pontiac, Michigan; a management agreement with Munson Healthcare in northern Michigan; and the creation, with Catholic Health Initiatives, of the Mercy Health Network in Iowa.

Much of the growth of MHS is witnessed in its Intelligent Network, a robust and flexible structure of management that links the capabilities of each MHS facility, allowing quick and easy solutions to patients' needs. "The activities that can be difficult for an individual organization to perform are possible for a system to achieve," says Pelham. "The Intelligent Network allows us to access the best talent, resources, and practice standards."

The delivery of health care requires an organization to respond to the needs of those served with innovation, adaptation, commitment, and a willingness to take significant risk. "With our shared values to guide us and the Intelligent Network to energize us, Mercy will effectively manage change and thrive in the future," says Pelham. "In a new millennium, millions of lives will be touched by Mercy."

Visit the MHS Web site at www.mercyhealth.com for additional information.

Mercy has adapted to the evolving needs of those it serves. That has meant adding services, improving programs, and learning more about its communities' needs.

THE MEDSTAT GROUP

The MEDSTAT Group is a leading provider of health care information databases, decision-support systems, consulting, and research services for improving the quality and total value of health care. Founded in 1981 in the beautiful resort community of Petoskey, Michigan, The MEDSTAT Group now serves nearly 1,000 clients nationwide responsible for the health care of approximately 100 million Americans.

The MEDSTAT Group is a Michigan success story and takes pride in its local beginnings. In the early 1980s Ernest G. Ludy, the company founder, observed the lack of information and tools available to employers to effectively manage health care costs. His energy and enthusiasm—now common characteristics of MEDSTAT employees—prompted him to do something about this unmet need. Armed with an idea to provide these employers with better information for making decisions about health benefits, he set off for Petoskey, Michigan, to start his business, choosing this vacation paradise because he knew his vacation time would be limited while launching the company.

Soliciting seed capital from Michigan friends and colleagues, Ludy formed MEDSTAT and

The MEDSTAT Group sits at the crossroads of two exploding industries—health care and information technology.

developed the nation's first health care decision-support system—a database along with software applications to access and manipulate the data—designed to help leading-edge employers manage the cost of their health benefits. After securing several major clients, The MEDSTAT Group issued public stock in 1983 and relocated to its current headquarters in Ann Arbor, Michigan. What began with a single product focused on meeting employers' needs has now grown into a multiproduct, multimarket firm that is well-positioned to take advantage of current demographic and technological trends.

Today The MEDSTAT Group has offices in nine cities in the United States and develops products to meet the needs of clients across the entire health care spectrum, including employers, hospitals, and managed care and insurance organizations, state and federal government

Today The MEDSTAT Group is a national company with more than 750 employees in nine locations across the United States.

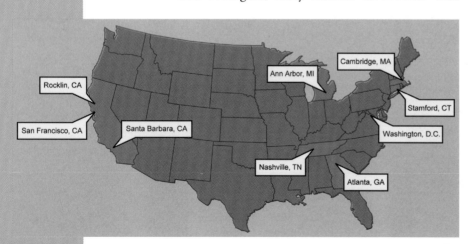

policymakers, and pharmaceutical researchers. Over the years, the company has achieved rapid growth and has been recognized by national business publications, including *Forbes* and *Business Week*, for its impressive track record in the dynamic health care information services industry.

While the challenges facing the nation's health care system have changed significantly since the company's founding, The MEDSTAT Group's prod-

ucts continue to meet its clients' needs head on.

The company's basic mission—to provide the best information products available to help clients manage the quality and cost of health care—remains as solid today as in its early days. And while inflation in health care costs continues to be a challenge industrywide, MEDSTAT's newest products focus on:

- measuring and improving the quality of health care services through scientifically tested and proven methods,
- providing greater accountability for services by all participants in the health care system, and
- empowering consumers and employers to make better health care decisions.

Challenged by leading clients to excel, The MEDSTAT Group continues to develop better methods and products for

The MEDSTAT Group is headquartered in Ann Arbor, Michigan, a university community with many amenities, including outstanding schools, friendly neighborhoods, and an array of cultural events. Photos courtesy, Ann Arbor Area Convention & Visitors Bureau. © Dean Russell

managing health care information to meet the daunting challenges presented by this fast-paced industry. The MEDSTAT Group's product offerings are as diverse as its clients' needs, but all are built around providing the following four key elements:

- MEDSTAT proprietary benchmark databases and database management services help to standardize information from multiple external sources and make the data usable by decision makers;
- methodologies are applied to data that make the information more relevant for management decision making;
- advanced analytical and decision-support software provides easy and direct access to the knowledge held within the data;
- consulting support services and client training are custom-tailored to meet the unique needs of each client.

MEDSTAT employees are provided with multiple opportunities for continuous learning, including Thomson University, a rapidly expanding internal learning forum that is offered by MEDSTAT's parent company.

The MEDSTAT Group has built long-term competitive advantage for its clients by bringing its products, services, and expertise to bear in unique ways that can best help clients answer their most pressing health care questions.

Successful execution of this strategy requires the best people and MEDSTAT has attracted some of the best talent in the industry.

Recognizing that its employees are its strongest competitive advantage, The MEDSTAT Group invests significant resources in helping them to be the best they can be. The company actively recruits both experienced and entry-level staff in a wide variety of educational disciplines, including quantitative analysis, information and computer sciences, clinical practice, and general business management. Multiple programs for continuous learning and development are offered both internally and externally. In these programs, staff members have an opportunity to discuss current industry issues and trends; participate in simulations specific to their job functions; and learn business management, communication, and problem-solving skills, all with fellow staffers or experienced teachers and lecturers. Even MEDSTAT clients are invited to participate in some of these knowledge-sharing forums, all of which include a healthy dose of fun. The MEDSTAT Group is committed to providing a happy, healthy, and productive environment for its employees, who enjoy participating in the many team-building and extracurricular cultural, athletic, and wellness opportunities sponsored by the company throughout each year.

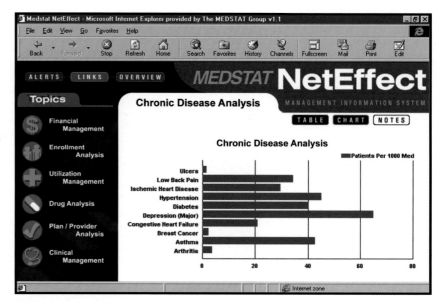

MEDSTAT products are used by clients responsible for the health care of more than 100 million Americans.

In 1994 The MEDSTAT Group became a part of The Thomson Corporation, one of the world's leading information and publishing businesses. As a result, The MEDSTAT Group has the resources necessary to expand its reach in new directions, including emerging international markets. This relationship also provides the financial depth to assure continued growth and leadership in MEDSTAT's targeted markets. Significant new investments are being made in product enhancements and new product development and ensure that the next twenty years will be as exciting and fruitful as the past twenty years have been.

The MEDSTAT Group sits at the crossroads of two exploding industries—health care and information technology—and with its committed employees and abundant resources, the company's outlook couldn't be brighter.

To learn more about The MEDSTAT Group, visit its Web site at www.medstat.com or telephone (734) 913-3000.

LEFT: MEDSTAT employees, like those in this group, represent some of the best talent in the industry with a wide variety of expertise, skills, and backgrounds.

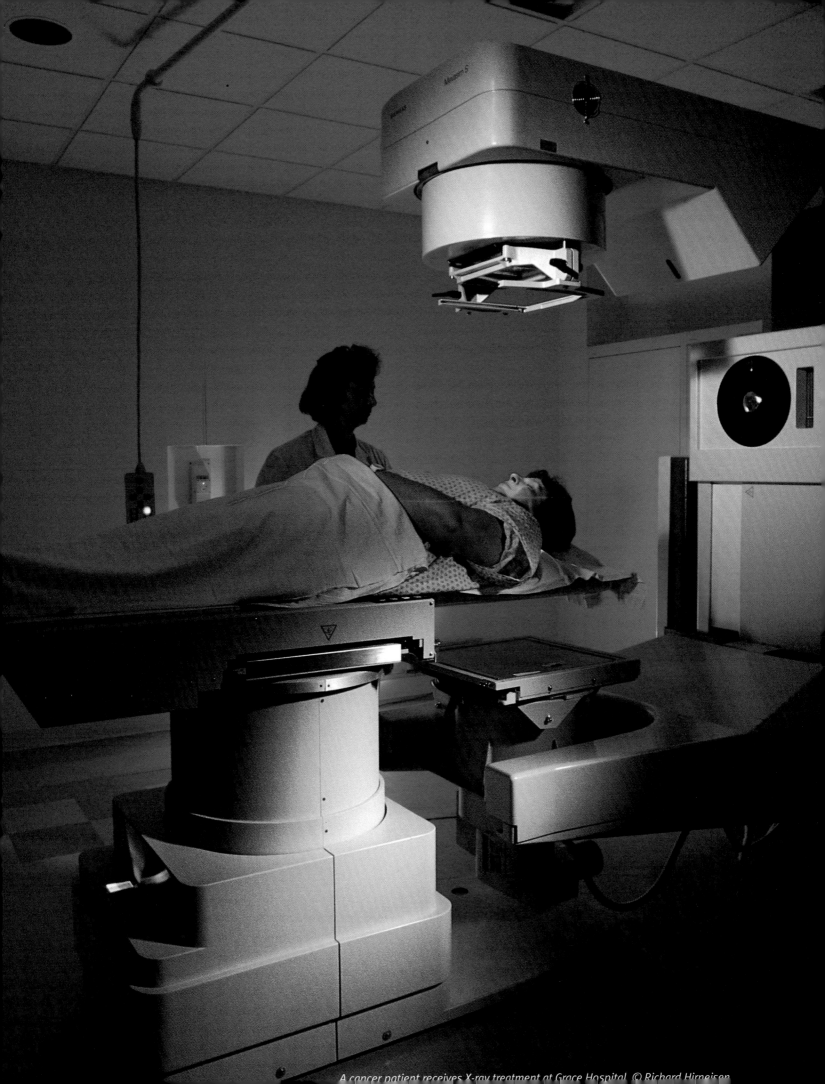

A cancer patient receives X-ray treatment at Grace Hospital. © Richard Hirneisen

HEAD OF THE CLASS

CHAPTER SIXTEEN

MICHIGAN HAS CHALKED UP AN IMPRESSIVE LIST OF "FIRSTS" IN THE FIELD OF EDUCATION. IT WAS THE FIRST STATE TO HAVE A SUPERINTENDENT OF PUBLIC INSTRUCTION, THE FIRST TO GUARANTEE EVERY CHILD A FREE HIGH SCHOOL EDUCATION, AND THE FIRST TO ESTABLISH A PUBLIC LIBRARY SYSTEM. FOUNDED IN 1817, THE UNIVERSITY OF MICHIGAN IS CONSIDERED THE "MOTHER OF STATE UNIVERSITIES," AND MICHIGAN STATE UNIVERSITY

was the first state college of agriculture and the first land-grant college (1857). Michigan schools have produced leaders in every academic field and are recognized at each level, kindergarten through postgraduate, as national leaders in quality education.

PUBLIC EDUCATION K–12

In 1994 Michigan shifted funding of K–12 education in its more than three thousand public schools away from property taxes and onto the state sales tax. Not only did this move schools to a fairer funding base, but it reinforced the state's trend of dedicating more funds per pupil and per capita than its Midwest neighbors, putting it in the forefront nationally as well.

Michigan is also a national leader in bringing the concept of continuous improvement into the classroom. The Michigan Educational Assessment Program (MEAP) tests all 1.7 million public school students on a regular basis for mastery of essential—and growing—core curricula, as well as logic and thinking skills. Each school's accreditation is linked to its students' performance on the MEAP test. Michigan students consistently score above the national average on standardized achievement tests. The establishment of Michigan Mathematics and Science Centers, which are enrichment and resource sites for students and teachers, has resulted in accelerated programming in math, science, and technology and a marked increase in the number of students taking advanced placement tests in those areas.

Michigan educators recognize that a school's impact on students is not limited to academics. More than 90 percent of all Michigan school districts teach drug and violence prevention through an award-winning comprehensive school health education program. Other educational initiatives which, in addition to core academics, are supported by the Michigan Education Association, include bilingual and multicultural

*At the world-famous Interlochen Center for the Arts, summer
students commune with nature as they perfect their bowing
technique. © Dennis Cox/D. E. Cox Photo Library*

education, environmental education, conversion to the
metric system, career education, lifesaving techniques,
and the promotion of moral and ethical values.

PRIVATE AND TECHNICAL SCHOOLS

Michigan's broad range of parochial and private schools
includes some of the nation's finest. Interlochen Arts
Academy, near Traverse City, has had
more Presidential Scholars in the Arts
than any other high school, public or
private, in the United States. In
1998, Detroit Country Day School
placed third in the nation for chemistry at the National Science
Olympiad, second in the nation at
the National Junior Science and
Humanities Symposium, third in the
nation in the Scripps Howard
Spelling Bee, and first in the state
and sixth in the nation in the
Quiz Bowl. The renowned Cranbrook Educational Community in
Bloomfield Hills consists of art
and science museums; lower, middle,
and upper schools; and a graduate
school of art.

Beginning in 1995, a selection of
industry-led trade academies opened
across the state with the objective of
preparing high school students for
high-skill, high-wage jobs. Now
numbering eight, these academies
offer a high school diploma along
with occupational and work-based

*Bicycles are a trademark of student life on
the University of Michigan campus in Ann
Arbor. © Dennis Cox/D. E. Cox Photo Library*

learning in such fields as engineering, manufacturing, construction, plastics technology, hospitality and tourism, health services, and automotive technology. Michigan's twenty-nine publicly supported community colleges also provide valuable skills training and retraining for state companies.

COLLEGES AND UNIVERSITIES

Michigan has fifteen four-year universities, sixty-six independent colleges, and twenty-nine community colleges, with more than one-half million enrolled students. The University of Michigan (U-M) is the largest of the state's institutions of higher learning, with almost 37,000 undergraduate students and more than 15,000 graduate and professional students on three campuses—Ann Arbor, Flint, and Dearborn. U-M is an academic powerhouse with many of its programs nationally rated among the top five of their kind. The school's list of "firsts" rates a volume of its own, but includes the nation's first professorship of education and the first course in forestry. In 1869 U-M became the first American university to own and operate a teaching hospital. Its 400,000 alumni could fill a who's who of American achievement. Among them are one U.S. president (Gerald R. Ford), three Supreme

Court justices, six Nobel Prize winners, and seven NASA astronauts.

With more than 40,000 students, Michigan State University (MSU) in East Lansing boasts the state's largest enrollment on a single campus. While MSU scientists were crucial to the growth and success of Michigan farming, the university has long since grown beyond its early identification as an agricultural college. MSU established the nation's first College of Communication Arts and Sciences. Its microbiology department is responsible for the eradication of brucellosis (also known as Bang's disease). MSU's College of Education is the site of the National Center for Research on Teacher Learning.

ACTION MOVIE

ON 19 JUNE 1934 ROBERT R. McMATH OF THE UNIVERSITY OF MICHIGAN MADE THE FIRST MOTION PICTURES OF THE SUN. TAKEN AT LAKE ANGELUS IN PONTIAC, THE FILMS SHOWED SUNSPOTS IN MOTION.

Detroit inner-city teenagers confer with their teacher in an arts workshop. © Dennis Cox/D. E. Cox Photo Library

Detroit's urban university, Wayne State, has top-rated medical and law schools, as well as the nation's first full-season repertory theater company at its Hilberry Theatre, and the Reuther Library of Labor and Urban Affairs, the largest archival library of its kind in the United States.

CAREER STUDIES

While academics and liberal arts are a strong suit at Michigan schools, many innovative, career-oriented programs are offered as well. Northwood University, a private, management-oriented college based in Midland, trains future generations of business leaders, entrepreneurs, and managers. This institution puts less emphasis on theory, focusing instead on preparing individuals to deal with the real everyday business world. Detroit's Center for Creative Studies ranks among the nation's leading colleges of art and design. Eastern Michigan University in Ypsilanti offers degrees in aviation administration and aviation computer technology. Golf course management is a specialty at Ferris State in Big Rapids. Paper and pulp science and

Kellogg Center is the nation's largest laboratory for hotel management students. The G. Robert Vincent Voice Library is the nation's largest academic voice library, including in its vast collection sound samples from every U.S. president since Grover Cleveland. MSU is also a national leader in Rhodes scholars and in the number of overseas academic programs offered.

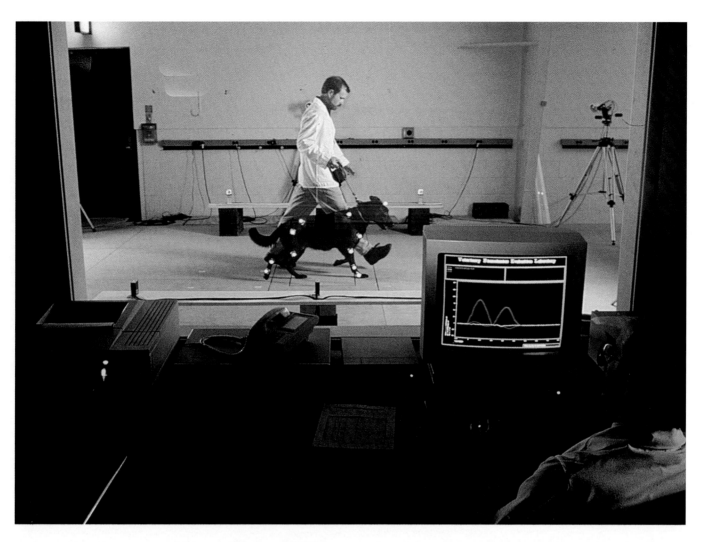

paper engineering are specialties at Western Michigan University in Kalamazoo. Upper Peninsula schools take advantage of the region's natural resources with programs in fish, game, and wildlife management at Lake Superior State in Sault Sainte Marie and mining and forestry departments at Michigan Tech in Houghton. Flint's acclaimed Kettering University (formerly GMI) has a five-year cooperative engineering program, which requires students to alternate academic terms with work-experience terms.

Michigan's small independent colleges also are nationally recognized for innovation and excellence. Kalamazoo College, for example, integrates career experience and foreign study into each student's academic program. Kalamazoo is ninth among the nation's four-year undergraduate colleges in the percentage of graduates who go on to earn doctoral degrees in all fields, outranking some Ivy League schools.

At every level Michigan schools have found a winning combination of solid academic tradition and cutting-edge innovation. When it comes to producing

In the Gait Analysis Laboratory at Michigan State University's prestigious School of Veterinary Medicine, a dog's movements are recorded by body sensors, which feed data to the computer in the foreground. © Bruce A. Fox/MSU

motivated, informed, and well-rounded graduates with skills for the twenty-first-century job market, Michigan is at the head of the class.

ON-LINE AND READY TO GO

ACCORDING TO THE PROGRESS AND FREEDOM FOUNDATION'S 1998 REPORT ON THE "DIGITAL STATE," MICHIGAN RANKS FIRST NATIONALLY IN GETTING ITS STATE INSTITUTIONS OF HIGHER LEARNING "WIRED" FOR THE TWENTY-FIRST CENTURY. THE STUDY'S RANKINGS TOOK INTO ACCOUNT AVAILABILITY OF INFORMATION AND FORM PROCESSING VIA THE INTERNET, DISTANCE LEARNING PROGRAMS OFFERED, INTERNET ACCESS FROM DORMITORIES, AND OTHER SERVICES.

University of Michigan seniors enjoy commencement. © Andrew Sacks

EDUCATION

NORTHWOOD UNIVERSITY

Northwood University's entire Midland campus was designed by the late Michigan architect-laureate Alden B. Dow, who, with his wife, Vada, his family, and others across the nation, took an early interest in "the Northwood idea" of creative, directed, and accountable education.

Dr. Arthur E. Turner took what was then a revolutionary idea for preparing students to enter the business world and on 23 March 1959 opened a two-year business college, which they named Northwood Institute, in an old mansion in Alma, Michigan, 125 miles north of Detroit.

In its first year the new institution enrolled just 100 students. But from this humble beginning evolved one of Michigan's, and one of the nation's, most respected special-purpose universities.

Today Northwood University, a private, tax-exempt, independent, coeducational, management-oriented college, consists of modern and spacious residential campuses in Midland, Michigan; Cedar Hill, Texas; and West Palm Beach, Florida. Though the university still offers two-year associate degrees in specialty business majors, the majority of students now pursue the four-year business administration degree. The university also offers two respected master's degrees in business administration through its Richard DeVos Graduate School of Management. In addition, it offers degrees to nontraditional (adult) students at more than thirty outreach locations across the United States.

Forty years ago two young men on the staff of Michigan's Alma College came up with an entirely new approach for training future generations of business leaders, entrepreneurs, and managers. Why not, they thought, set up a management-oriented educational entity that would put less emphasis on theory and more on preparing individuals to deal with the real everyday business world. Dr. R. Gary Stauffer and

Northwood's full-time enrollment has grown to more than 11,300 students, including more than 2,100 at its home campus in Midland. Campus life outside the classroom features intercollegiate athletics; a Greek system; an array of campus activities; and the EXCEL program involving all students in community and campus leadership activities, which then are reflected on graduation-time transcripts.

Dr. David E. Fry (left) has been president of Northwood University since 1982 and is past president of the American Association of Presidents of Independent Colleges and Universities. Dr. Arthur E. Turner (right) is a cofounder of the university. He and the late Dr. R. Gary Stauffer were young educators (barely thirty years old) when they pursued their vision of an innovative management curriculum closely allied to business and industry, and cofounded Northwood.

Despite its growth, Northwood adheres to its philosophy of education rooted in the principles

of the American free-enterprise system and the free-market model for economic development. Its career curricula continue to be developed and updated in response to the needs of business and industry.

As a result, students who enroll in Northwood's programs today, as in the past, are given the most up-to-date training and information relevant to what is currently transpiring in the business world. Graduates leave the institution with a solid understanding of practical, useful management skills, enabling them to immediately become productive in the business world.

"Our mission at Northwood is to prepare aspiring students of any age or station with the tools, skills, and intellectual capacities for a productive, leadership career in an economic system of free markets and private enterprise," says Dr. David E. Fry, Northwood's president and chief executive officer.

What separates Northwood from the business curricula of traditional liberal arts colleges and universities is that it offers its students more business courses in two years than are offered to students at many other institutions in four years. Those who complete their bachelor's degree at Northwood receive twice, and often three times, as many "management core" classes as usual.

Despite this emphasis on business, Northwood imbues its students with an appreciation of the arts and humanities, in keeping with its founding principles. Art classes, events, exhibitions, and the Alden B. Dow Creativity Center spark interest in creative endeavors.

"Turner and Stauffer knew instinctively, it seems, that if they succeeded in producing a world-class enterprise-management program, they could run the risk of graduating students with a single focus," Dr. Fry says. "So they undertook to energize our programs with special elements of the arts that are reflected in everything from the design of our campuses and the sponsorship of collections and a gallery to the activities of our students."

Northwood's unique balance of business and the arts, coupled with its instruction in the context of a global economy (attracting hundreds of international students to its campuses) has been a huge success. Proof of this exists in the numbers, as success in the business world is often measured. Since Northwood's inception, well beyond 100,000 students have earned degrees or completed programs offered by Northwood and have gone on to make their mark in the business world and make the world a better place in which to live.

Students and alumni find the wooded Northwood campus a welcoming place conducive to study and recreation. Campus life includes competitive sports; an EXCEL program, which rewards student participation in volunteer leadership; and myriad arts and other activities.

UNIVERSITY OF MICHIGAN–DEARBORN
SCHOOL OF MANAGEMENT

State-of-the-art facilities at UM-Dearborn School of Management are complemented by highly qualified faculty members and a rigorous curriculum, ensuring students a superlative education. © Bob Kalmbach

The School of Management at the University of Michigan–Dearborn has been a center of management education in Southeastern Michigan since 1957. The Dearborn campus is located on nearly 200 acres of the original Henry Ford Estate, the former home of Michigan's most prominent twentieth-century business leader. Initially intended to meet management education needs of Ford Motor Company, today the University of Michigan–Dearborn School of Management's

Students at the School of Management attend a seminar given by a top multinational company executive.

high-quality undergraduate, graduate, and executive programs are responsive to the education and training needs of its diverse Southeastern Michigan constituency—a key economic center in Michigan and the United States. Members of the business community are viewed as working partners, customers, and investors.

School of Management business advisory leaders, alumni, students, faculty, and staff are committed to the goal of excellence. Faculty come to the University of Michigan–Dearborn School of Management from top national and international universities, are widely published in scholarly journals, and remain connected to the business community in a variety of ways.

Today's students are being prepared to become excellent business leaders for the future of the region, guiding business and industry in the twenty-first century. More than 5,000 School of Management alumni are found in leadership positions throughout Southeastern Michigan.

The School of Management has updated its AACSB-accredited programs to address contemporary, rapidly changing business needs. The completion of a dedicated facility brought about the physical consolidation of the school's programs and served as a springboard for expanded business partnerships. New curricula have been introduced to provide high-quality management education to a diverse and talented group of graduate and undergraduate students and business leaders. These programs are recognized for innovative approaches and global perspectives.

UM–Dearborn School of Management award-winning programs prepare students for today's fast-paced business environment. © PhotoDisc

Blending theory and practice has long been the hallmark of a University of Michigan–Dearborn School of Management education, and perhaps is no more evident than in its Internship Program. From the school's inception, business internships have been an important part of management education in which students provide regional businesses with management assistance in finance, public accounting, human resources, marketing, management information systems, decision sciences, and operations management. This award-winning program has been expanded to area nonprofit organizations and entrepreneurial enterprises.

Awards are commonplace for School of Management students, whose achievements range from outstanding pass rates on the rigorous CPA examination to winning the Chancellor Medallion for exemplary scholarship at the University of Michigan–Dearborn. Most students at the School of Management are employed at least part time while they complete their degrees. In addition to their work and studies, today's business students are going beyond the profit center to become active volunteers in their communities. Some examples include accounting students annually contributing their services to assist less fortunate people with their tax returns in the regional Tax Assistance Program, participating in Habitat for Humanity projects, and working in conjunction with Junior

Since most School of Management students work at least part time while they complete their degrees, study time in between classes is important. © PhotoDisc

Achievement to provide economics lessons to local junior high school students.

Additional attributes that distinguish the School of Management from other business schools are its location in Southeastern Michigan—a top U.S. commercial and communications center; its historic association with leading industries; its academic tradition that combines scholarly excellence with continuing interaction with business leaders and current management issues; and its innovative programs to benefit underrepresented students. Consistent with its seminal benefactor, Henry Ford, innovation is an overarching characteristic of the University of Michigan–Dearborn School of Management. Change is ongoing and welcomed, presenting itself in management-development programs designed to meet emerging issues and specific needs of area businesses; initiatives to address the business of health care; leading-edge executive education; programs designed to help entrepreneurs grow their businesses; and contemporary faculty research. The School of Management at the University of Michigan–Dearborn continually searches for better ways to achieve excellence in management education. For further information contact University of Michigan–Dearborn School of Management at (313) 593-5248, or visit its Web site at www.umd.umich.edu/som.

THE UNIVERSITY OF MICHIGAN, WITH CAMPUSES AT ANN ARBOR, FLINT, AND DEARBORN, IS ACCLAIMED FOR ADVANCED RESEARCH, AN ESTEEMED FACULTY, RIGOROUS ACADEMIC STANDARDS, AND BROAD CULTURAL OFFERINGS

The University of Michigan is one of the world's premier research universities and a leader in undergraduate and graduate education. It offers rigorous academic programs, outstanding faculty, and diverse cultural and social opportunities in a stimulating research environment.

Founded in 1817, U-M has been a national model for the large public university for more than a century. Today the 52,000 students on the three U-M campuses come from every state and 115 countries. The U-M Ann Arbor campus, with 37,200 students, offers more than 5,600 undergraduate and graduate courses each term. Students can choose from 223 undergraduate majors and 608 degree programs offered by nineteen schools and colleges. Classes range in size from fewer than 10 up to 500, and the student-faculty ratio for undergraduate and graduate classes is 10:1. An average of 84 percent of undergraduate students graduate within six years. Living alumni number 400,000, more than 155,000 of whom live in Michigan.

Among the strengths of the Ann Arbor campus are its twenty-four libraries, which contain some seven million volumes; a dozen museums and galleries; several nature areas; more than 700 student clubs and organizations; and twenty-three varsity sports.

Faculty members conducting scholarly research discuss their work with students in lectures and seminars. Each year an estimated 2,000 undergraduates work in research partnerships with members of the faculty.

The Michigan Union at the University of Michigan in Ann Arbor is a model for student unions among the nation's campuses. President John F. Kennedy first proposed the idea of the Peace Corps on the steps of the Union entrance shown here, where his announcement is commemorated with a small plaque. © D. C. Goings, University of Michigan Photo Services

English professor Ted-Larry Pebworth served at the University of Michigan in Dearborn from 1971 until 1998, when he retired after forty years of teaching. © University of Michigan

University of Michigan research provides a foundation for new industries and innovative therapies. From solving the 400-year-old mathematical problem known as Kepler's Conjecture to creating cancer and influenza vaccines, the university's scholars are expanding the boundaries of knowledge in the fields of engineering, physical and life sciences, social sciences, humanities and the arts, and medicine.

The University of Michigan Health System, one of the world's largest health care complexes, registers more than one million patient visits annually. More than forty years ago, the safety and effectiveness of the Salk polio vaccine was confirmed by scientists. Today researchers are developing precision lasers for eye surgery, testing new antimicrobial agents, and providing data to policymakers on issues such as drug use among youth, health care expenditures, and the effect of technology on medical costs.

Such research strengthens the economies of the state, the region, and the nation. In fiscal 1997–1998, University of Michigan faculty and staff members announced 160 new inventions, filed 111 United States patent applications, and received 55 patents. More than a dozen new companies trace their founding to research conducted at the University of Michigan.

At the heart of the university's success is its distinguished faculty, which includes Pulitzer Prize winners, composers, novelists, poets, scientists, artists, and filmmakers. Members of the faculty advise the president of the United States and Congress on topics as diverse as global warming, Social Security, the economy, and the nation's relationship with China. They provide similar assistance to state and local governmental leaders working on issues such as transportation safety and water quality.

The faculty promotes civic responsibility through programs such as the Center for Learning through Community Service, which involves thousands of students each year, and the Arts of Citizenship program, which seeks to enrich public culture by promoting community collaborations and innovative scholarly and artistic work.

The University of Michigan campuses at Flint and at Dearborn provide high-quality educational opportunities for students of all ages living in those geographic areas.

Established originally in 1956 as a two-year senior college, U-M Flint has grown in size and mission, and now offers sixty undergraduate and master's degree programs in business

The four students in this University of Michigan, Ann Arbor, laboratory are among an estimated 2,000 undergraduates who work in research partnerships with university faculty each year. © Paul Jaronski, University of Michigan Photo Services

administration, public administration, American culture, physical therapy, anesthesia, health education, nursing, and education. More than 6,600 students are enrolled in U-M Flint's four schools. U-M Flint faculty and students work collaboratively with other public and private organizations to enhance health and education and to advance economic, cultural, and artistic interests.

The University of Michigan at Dearborn, which opened in 1959, offers undergraduate and advanced degrees in the liberal arts, sciences, engineering, management, education, and public administration. U-M Dearborn's four schools enroll more than 8,300 students in southeastern Michigan annually. U-M Dearborn responds to the needs of its area and draws strength from its many community connections, including internship and cooperative education programs. The Henry Ford Estate–Fair Lane, a National Historic Landmark, is located on the Dearborn campus.

The University of Michigan's size, complexity, and academic strength, along with its broad scholarly resources and its fine faculty, contribute to a dynamic intellectual environment for students as they encounter new people, cultures, and ideas and come away forever enriched.

The Frances Willson Thompson Library at the University of Michigan in Flint overlooks the Flint River. © T. S. Jenkins

KETTERING UNIVERSITY

Founded in 1919, Kettering University (originally known as GMI), in Flint, Michigan, is one of the nation's preeminent academic institutions for cooperative, career-based undergraduate education in engineering, applied sciences, mathematics, and business management. In addition, the university offers graduate programs in engineering, manufacturing management, and operations management. Recognized nationally for providing world-class engineering education, Kettering University attracts top students from throughout the United States and has established educational and employment exchange options in many other countries.

Kettering University emphasizes hands-on learning, which includes classroom and laboratory studies on campus and career-based work assignments offered by nearly 700 employer-partners.

The Kettering University cooperative education program offers its 2,500 students ten bachelor's degree programs that combine on-campus classroom and laboratory experience and meaningful, relevant, paid employment with nearly 700 employer-partners. At the graduate level, students can structure their academic studies around their work schedules and earn their master's degree through distance-learning options.

When they graduate, virtually all Kettering University students are either employed (often with an employer-partner) and well on their way to career success or continuing their education in leading graduate schools. Among the university's 28,000 alumni are CEOs, presidents, and many other top business executives throughout the world.

Founded in 1919, Kettering University (originally GMI) is one of the nation's preeminent universities for cooperative, career-based education in engineering, applied sciences, mathematics, and business management.

Kettering University prides itself on teaching excellence, emphasizing hands-on learning, with small classes and a 12:1 student-to-faculty ratio.

The school's employer-partners include many international Fortune 500 companies and leading-edge, high-technology businesses that provide students with a level of on-the-job training that is unequaled when compared to traditional college academic programs.

The Kettering University campus covers sixty-six acres west of downtown Flint. It features a state-of-the-art recreation center, a distinctive carillon landmark, one of the nation's top automotive history archives, a residence hall wired for the latest in information technology, and an apartment complex for upperclass students.

Kettering University is named after Charles F. Kettering (1876-1958), an American technology pioneer whose inventions include the automobile electric starter and whose beliefs about the blending of theory and practice reflect the university's cooperative education tradition. "There is no war between theory and practice," Kettering said. "The most valuable experience demands both."

Michigan ranks in the top ten states in the number of students enrolled in institutions of higher education. © Corbis

THREE KEYS TO SUCCESS

CHAPTER SEVENTEEN

THE SUCCESS OF ANY ENTERPRISE DEPENDS ON THREE KEY FACTORS: MONEY, KNOW-HOW, AND LOCATION. THE FLOURISHING DIVERSIFICATION OF MICHIGAN'S ECONOMY IN THE LAST TWO DECADES OF THE TWENTIETH CEN-TURY WAS THE RESULT OF THE READY AVAILABILITY OF ALL THREE. A STRONG FINANCIAL SECTOR ENHANCED BY AN EXCITING INFUSION OF VENTURE CAPI-TAL, SOME OF THE NATION'S TOP PROFESSIONAL FIRMS WITH THE FORESIGHT

and experience to carry out large projects, and prime real estate with low construction costs to build plans into reality—all contributed to a shift away from an auto-based economy to a broader, technology-based one with unlimited future potential.

MONEY MATTERS

Michigan has 160 commercial banks with more than 2,300 branches located throughout the state, representing combined assets of more than $117 billion, a figure that has doubled since 1986. Detroit-based Comerica is the largest financial institution head-quartered in Michigan. Formerly Detroit Bank & Trust, Comerica is the twenty-fifth-largest bank hold-ing company in the nation, with $34 billion in total assets. It is the fourteenth-largest commercial business lender and fifteenth-largest small business lender in the nation. With a $500 million commitment, Comerica is the lead lender in Detroit's Empowerment Zone, an

eighteen-square-mile area designated for intense redevel-opment. Other Michigan banks are similarly involved in the state's economic growth. Since 1853 Old Kent has been the leading financial services provider for the western part of the state. Headquartered in Grand Rapids, Old Kent is one of the top twenty-five lenders in the United States and the number-two Small Business Administration (SBA) lender in Michigan. The number-one slot is occupied by Republic Bank of Ann Arbor.

One of the most exciting new developments in Michigan's eco-nomic picture is the flood of ven-ture capital that began pouring into the state in the late 1990s. In 1997 Michigan rose from forty-fourth to thirteenth among the fifty states in the amount of venture capital under management. About a dozen venture funds are based in the state, and more than a dozen headquartered elsewhere are making deals in Michigan. With $300 million in new venture capital

OPPOSITE: Detroit's seventy-five-acre Civic Center hugs the downtown shore of the Detroit River and includes Cobo Conference/Exhibition Center, Cobo Arena, Joe Louis Arena, and, seen here from in front of the Westin Hotel, the elegant Renaissance Center. © Dennis Cox/D. E. Cox Photo Library. ABOVE: Some of the biggest business lenders in the country are based in Michigan. Here, a small business owner meets with a bank executive to discuss loan options. © Dwight Cendrowski

raised in the state in 1997, the number of deals is expected to increase each year into the new century.

The venture capital is not aimed at small businesses, an area handled very well by Michigan banks, but at companies positioning themselves for rapid growth and national or international scope. Initially, most of the state's venture capital went to firms specializing in medical technology and factory automation, inspired by a new climate of entrepreneurship at the state's major research universities. Activity continues in these fields and has expanded to software development, retail, industrial, business services, and communications companies.

Michigan-based insurance firms support the diversification trend. In its forty-year history, Southfield's Meadowbrook Insurance Group has grown to become one of the nation's leading business insurance agencies, a pioneer in "alternative risk management"—nontraditional insurance programs. Alexander Hamilton Life

The Bank of Lenawee is an independent community bank, rooted in Southeast Michigan. © Dwight Cendrowski

Insurance Company of America, headquartered in Farmington Hills, is one of the nation's largest insurers, with assets exceeding $5.4 billion and an AAA rating from Standard and Poor's.

THE PROFESSIONALS

Michigan's large professional services sector is another key to its economic success. Nearly 34,000 attorneys work in Michigan firms, many serving some of the nation's most elite business clients. Dykema Gossett is southeast Michigan's largest firm, with nearly 200 attorneys headquartered in Detroit's Renaissance Center and a client list that includes General Motors, Sears, Total Petroleum, and Champion Enterprises. Another Detroit giant—Miller, Canfield—represents Chrysler, Comerica, and the City of Detroit. But Michigan's small-practice

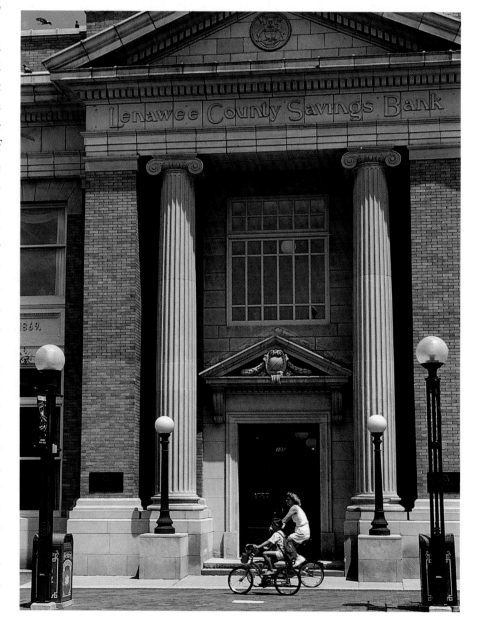

"Farm Bureau's **FARMOWNERS POLICY** covers my entire farm operation!"

Mr. Ken Wagar, well known Kalamazoo County farmer, and his 350 acre farm.

One policy cuts bookwork and saves money

"One policy covering my entire farming operation is a big convenience. Not only does the Farmowners policy cut down on my paper work, but it also makes it easier for me to be sure that I am completely covered," said Mr. Wagar. "Of course, I am also pleased with the fact that this package policy gives me _more protection_ for _less money_. It's an ideal way to protect my entire farm."

Check the many advantages of Farm Bureau's Farmowners policy for your farm. The Farmowners provides broad protection for fire, wind, theft, liability and other perils. It covers your house and contents, farm personal property, barns and outbuildings, and farm liability. It's the _new_ idea in farm protection!

GET THE _BEST_ FOR _LESS._ SEE YOUR LOCAL FARM BUREAU INSURANCE AGENT. DO IT TODAY!

FARM BUREAU INSURANCE

AUTO • FIRE • LIFE • FARM LIABILITY • HOMEOWNERS • FARMOWNERS • CARGO • INLAND MARINE

4000 North Grand River Avenue, Lansing 4, Michigan

"WORKING TOGETHER"

Farm Bureau Insurance introduced the nation's first farmowners package policy in 1960. Farm Bureau Insurance is Michigan's largest farm insurer. Courtesy, Farm Bureau Insurance

(PTA) Committee. This model program includes generous parental leave, flexible scheduling alternatives, parenting seminars, and a "buddy program," which puts together experienced and expectant staff members. PTA earned Plante & Moran a spot among *Working Mother* magazine's "100 Best Companies for Working Mothers" in 1997.

With so many nationally known consumer products manufactured here, it is not surprising that Michigan is an important center for the advertising industry. Nearly

attorneys also have made names for themselves. John Voelker, using the pen name Robert Traver, published the best-selling *Anatomy of a Murder* about a sensational Upper Peninsula trial. Voelker had been the defense attorney in a remarkably similar trial that took place in Big Bay in 1952, but would never admit that his novel, later made into an Academy Award–winning film with James Stewart, was based on actual events. Another Michigan attorney with a good deal of more recent national exposure is Geoffrey Fieger, who represented Dr. Jack Kevorkian before entering state politics.

Most of the nation's major accounting firms are represented in Michigan. One of these, Plante & Moran, LLP, headquartered in Southfield, is recognized nationally not only for its accounting and executive search services but for its innovative Parenting Tightrope Action

Southfield is home to more than 6,000 businesses and 140 of the Fortune 500. Twenty minutes from downtown Detroit and in easy reach of four major airports, Southfield bills itself as Michigan's business hub. Shown here is one of Southfield's many gleaming office structures. © Dwight Cendrowski

Construction projects currently underway in Michigan include three Detroit casinos and several new schools statewide. © Andrew Sacks

Holdings, which makes animatronic characters for Universal Studios in Florida as well as educational and product-training materials.

The employment services industry was practically invented in Michigan. In October of 1946 William Russell Kelly opened a Detroit office with two employees and the idea of providing temporary office and clerical help to local businesses. By December he had twelve customers and $828 in sales. So Kelly expanded his business, hiring people with flexible schedules, such as housewives and students. Today Kelly Services, now headquartered in Troy, is one of the world's largest companies. With more than 1,600 offices worldwide, Kelly provides the services of more than 800,000 employees annually to more than 200,000 customers, earning more than $4 billion.

every major advertising firm has an office here. J. Walter Thompson, which operates 206 offices in seventy countries, has its largest office in Detroit, with clients that include Goodyear, White Castle, Sherwin-Williams, and a division of Ford. Some of Michigan's most important agencies are homegrown. Campbell-Ewald, which counts Chevrolet, Office Max, and Continental Airlines as major clients, is headquartered in Warren. Ross Roy Communications, Chrysler's agency, is in Bloomfield Hills; and W. B. Doner, whose national clients include La-Z-Boy, Chiquita Brands, Red Roof Inns, Mazda, and Blockbuster, is in Southfield. Leading the pack among marketing services companies is Bloomfield Hills' VSI

IF YOU BUILD IT, THEY WILL COME

Michigan can lay claim to a pantheon of architects who changed the face not just of the state but of the world.

SOLD!

RALPH ROBERTS, OWNER OF RALPH ROBERTS REAL ESTATE IN WARREN, LEADS ALL U.S. REAL ESTATE AGENTS IN SALES, ACCORDING TO THE NATIONAL ASSOCIATION OF REALTORS. HIS BOOK, *WALK LIKE A GIANT, SELL LIKE A MADMAN,* LED *TIME* MAGAZINE TO DUB HIM "AMERICA'S SCARIEST SALESMAN."

wanted it to be the most beautiful. Kahn obliged them with fantastic Persian-style mosaics, and patterned walls and floors crafted from forty varieties of marble. The resulting structure is considered Michigan's largest artwork.

Also in 1928 the exuberantly rococo Fox Theatre opened on Woodward Avenue. Flagship of the nationwide Fox chain, the building was the work of

Albert Kahn gained fame as the premier architect of the megalithic factories that sprang up around Detroit as part of Michigan's industrial revolution. When his Willow Run bomber plant was erected by Ford Motor Company between 1941 and 1942, the factory floor alone covered 80.4 acres, and the L-shaped assembly line was a mile long. The enormous plant helped boost American morale

after Pearl Harbor. But the crown of Kahn's career had come earlier when his masterpiece, the Fisher Building, opened in 1928. The Fisher Building was the biggest commercial structure of its time; but the Fisher brothers, flush with money from inventing the enclosed car, also

BENCHMARK

THE FIRST WOMAN TO SERVE AS A FEDERAL JUDGE WAS CORNELIA KENNEDY OF DETROIT, NOMINATED BY PRESIDENT NIXON AND APPOINTED IN 1970.

GOOD INVESTMENT

THE FIRST PUBLIC AUCTION OF MICHIGAN LAND OCCURRED ON 6 JULY 1818, WITH PARCELS BEING SOLD FOR AN AVERAGE OF FOUR DOLLARS PER ACRE.

Detroit architect C. Howard Crane, who made a name designing picture palaces across the country. Detroit's Fox, restored in 1988 to its original splendor, is an oriental melange of peacocks, Buddhas, Greek masks, Egyptian lions, and anything else Crane could think of.

On the opposite end of the decor spectrum are the starkly elegant buildings designed by father and son architects Eliel and Eero Saarinen. Originally from Finland, they made the Cranbrook Academy of Art in Bloomfield Hills their head-quarters and won national recognition for buildings such as the National Gallery of Art in Washington, D.C.; New York's CBS Tower; the TWA Passenger Terminal at Kennedy International Airport; and the General Motors Technical Center in Warren.

Minoru Yamasaki, who opened his Detroit firm in 1959, took the Saarinens' sim-plicity a step further with his famous World Trade Center in New York, the Michigan Consolidated Gas skyscraper, and Saudi Arabia's Royal Reception Pavilion. Although Yamasaki died in 1986, his firm, now located in Rochester Hills, continues to design buildings around the world.

Michigan's own building boom is being shaped by local architects with international reputations. The SmithGroup, a Detroit-based diversified architectural and engineering firm, designed Chrysler's stunning world headquarters in Auburn Hills and is now at work on Metro Airport's new Northwest Airlines terminal, and downtown stadiums for the Lions and Tigers. Giffels Associates of Southfield designed Kellogg's Institute for Food and Nutrition Research in Battle Creek. General Motors' Renaissance Center renovation, the work of Dearborn's Ghafari Associates, has prompted national investors to begin snatching up many of the older Detroit office buildings for renovation.

In Grand Rapids a landscape architect reviews plans for the grounds of a new office complex. © Bill Lindout

New schools and school renovations, three Detroit casinos, airport expansion, sports stadiums, road improvements, major retail facilities, and countless new housing projects across the state will keep contractors and construction workers busy well into the new century.

The construction industry has produced some of Michigan's best-known companies. Masco, based in Taylor, was founded in 1929 by Alex Manoogian who made a fortune with his innovative washerless faucet. From its Delta Faucet Company, Masco expanded into other home building products including cabinetry, decorative hardware, and computerized security systems, growing into an international organization, now run by Richard Manoogian, which earns nearly $4 billion in annual sales. Among the Manoogians' many contributions to the Detroit area is the Manoogian Mansion, the Mayor of Detroit's official residence.

Michigan's prefabricated housing industry had its beginnings in the 1880s, when Saginaw lumber mills cut boards to the exact specifications of particular structures. Today Champion Enterprises in Auburn Hills is one of the nation's leading builders of manufactured homes, operating fifty-six factories in thirty-three locations. The nation's largest on-site homebuilder is also headquartered in Michigan. Pulte Corporation of Bloomfield Hills has built more than 175,000 homes in twenty-five states since 1950, when Bill Pulte built his first home in a Detroit suburb at the age of eighteen.

UNLOCKING THE FUTURE

The financial, professional services, real estate, and construction sectors are significant contributors to, as well as beneficiaries of, Michigan's economic expansion.

Wayne State University's College of Engineering has 215,000 square feet of new or renovated classroom, office, and library space. The college offers degrees in nine major engineering fields.
© Dwight Cendrowski

Michigan can finance, plan, and build a bright tomorrow with the abundance of talent and initiative evident in these sectors. They are the keys that open the door to continued prosperity.

Courtesy, State Archives of Michigan

IN 1941 RICHARD AUSTIN BECAME MICHIGAN'S FIRST AFRICAN AMERICAN CERTIFIED ACCOUNTANT. THIRTY YEARS LATER HE TOOK OFFICE IN LANSING AS THE NATION'S FIRST ELECTED AFRICAN AMERICAN SECRETARY OF STATE. AUSTIN SERVED IN THAT OFFICE FROM 1971 TO 1994, MAKING HIM THE LONGEST-SERVING AFRICAN AMERICAN ELECTED STATE OFFICIAL IN THE UNITED STATES.

The Detroit skyline rises behind Hart Plaza. © Andre Jenny/International Stock

PROFESSIONAL SERVICES

FLAGSTAR BANK

Flagstar Bank, headquartered in Bloomfield Hills, offers the One Hour Home Loan[SM], which makes possible loan application results within an hour. Flagstar was granted the prestigious Computerworld Smithsonian Award for visionary use of information technology.

I t didn't take long for Flagstar Bank to become one of the biggest financial institutions in the state of Michigan. Chartered less than two decades ago, in 1987, as First Security Savings Bank, the Bloomfield Hills, Michigan–based entity already is the largest independent savings institution headquartered in the state. Its network of more than two dozen bank branches is spread throughout southern and western Michigan.

Much of Flagstar's success can be attributed to the institution's decision to remain a strong community-oriented bank despite its phenomenal growth. As the bank enters the twenty-first century, it is poised for even more growth. Since Flagstar Bancorp, Inc., the holding company, took its stock public in 1997, Flagstar Bank has positioned itself to raise capital in

Flagstar Bank is the largest independent savings institution headquartered in Michigan and one of the largest wholesale originators of residential mortgage loans in the United States.

a cost-effective manner, to continue to expand its businesses further.

"It is all part of the bank's commitment to service," says Mark T. Hammond, Flagstar's president and a member of the family that founded the bank. "Superior customer service is a Flagstar hallmark. We recognize that our success is driven by catering to the interests of the communities we serve and by treating every person, whether he or she be one of our customers, an employee, or a member of our board of directors, as the most important person on the Flagstar team." Emphasizing this maxim, Flagstar has adopted the "sit-down teller" concept in its new banking centers to provide consumers with a personal banking environment, giving them more privacy and attention while conducting routine transactions. Flagstar's expanded banking hours for its drive-through window has proven to be another welcome convenience for consumers.

Flagstar also has achieved status as one of the nation's leading originators of residential mortgage loans. It serves not only individual home buyers, but also thousands of mortgage companies, banks, and credit unions in all fifty states through nearly three dozen loan origination

centers in Michigan, Ohio, California, and Florida, and more than a dozen correspondent lending offices across the United States.

In addition to providing conventional home loans to the communities it serves, the bank has made a strong commitment to making housing affordable to all individuals, regardless of their economic status. In 1997 Flagstar received an award by the Federal Home Loan Bank Board for its contributions to Jackson Affordable Housing. Flagstar also has been, and continues to be, the largest financial institutional contributor to the Family Neighborhood Empowerment Initiative, a group that provides services to low-income families in Pontiac, Michigan. The bank consistently is one of the leading lenders to people with low and moderate incomes in Pontiac, Jackson, Lansing, and Grand Rapids, Michigan, as well as throughout the metropolitan Detroit area.

Flagstar continually seeks and uses innovative state-of-the-art technology to improve the efficiency and the breadth and depth of its services. For example, providing the service of On-line Banking allows Flagstar's customers to access their bank account via the Internet twenty-four hours per day. The

Flagstar Bank provides convenience by making available extended banking hours at its full-service banking centers and by offering a wide variety of home, consumer, and commercial loans through its retail loan-origination offices.

bank also employs automated underwriting technologies and videoconferencing facilities that enable a home buyer, regardless of where he or she lives, and a loan underwriter in one of Flagstar's Michigan offices to meet face to face and have loans approved quickly, often within an hour.

The bank's extensive use of modern technology won it the prestigious Computerworld Smithsonian Award in 1997. The award recognizes individuals, businesses, and institutions that benefit society by their innovative applications of technology. Flagstar was honored for its visionary use of information technology in the finance, insurance, and real estate category. Flagstar's future, like that of its home state of Michigan, appears to be a secure and prosperous one.

Flagstar's slogan, Convenience you can count on, is illustrated by the bank's policy of providing exemplary customer service. Continually striving to accommodate customers who apply for home loans, Flagstar is committed to service.

JACKSON NATIONAL LIFE INSURANCE COMPANY

Although Jackson National Life Insurance Company (JNL®) now conducts business in all fifty states, its roots—and its home—remain in Michigan.

Headquartered in Lansing, Jackson National® employs more than 1,100 people, placing it among the top-ten employers in the Lansing area. Jackson National, named after the seventh president of the United States, was started in 1961 by the late A. J. (Tony) Pasant, a graduate of Michigan State University. In just thirty-eight years, Jackson National has grown to become the eighteenth-largest life insurance company in the United States (ranked by total assets), and an industry leader in the areas of fixed and variable annuities, as well as term and permanent life insurance.

The world headquarters of Jackson National Life Insurance Company is located in Lansing, Michigan.

Jackson National's first home office was in the National Bank Building in Jackson, Michigan. Before the company could begin selling insurance, it needed a license from the state. Because Michigan hadn't licensed an insurer in twenty-seven years, granting Jackson National a license was a slow, painstaking process. But Jackson National persevered, and this trait became one that has characterized the company ever since.

Jackson National sold its first policy on 5 September 1961 to a prominent Michigan restaurateur, Win Schuler. But sales were few in those early years for the young, unknown company. Jackson National now sells more insurance in a single day than it did in its entire first year of full operation.

During the 1970s, Jackson National abandoned a company-owned agency workforce and began working directly with independent producers. This allowed producers to work directly with Jackson National through one of its several regional offices. It was a risky decision at the time, but the company was able to eliminate the tremendous costs associated with individually recruiting and training new salespeople. These

Jackson National is building a 300,000-square-foot world-class headquarters facility, as shown in the architect's rendering at left, on eighty acres of land in the Lansing area. Occupancy is planned to take place in 2000.

savings helped the company price its products competitively, and sales began to skyrocket.

Jackson National's continued growth resulted in another move—this time to Lansing, in 1976. The company's growth over the next decade would attract the attention of Prudential Corporation plc, the largest life insurance company in the United Kingdom (unrelated to Prudential Insurance Company of America). Prudential was seeking to enter the United States market and was looking for an established, well-managed company with growth potential. In 1986 Jackson National became a wholly owned subsidiary of Prudential. Today Jackson National is Prudential's most significant business outside the United Kingdom, representing more than 40 percent of Prudential's total operating profit.

With Prudential's backing, Jackson National continued its phenomenal growth. Its three-story headquarters was no longer adequate, so a six-story addition was built in 1989. No one anticipated that the company would once again outgrow its office space. Jackson National has quickly filled its new headquarters building and, over the past several years, has rented office space in six other Lansing locations.

In 1998 Jackson National made plans to construct a 300,000-square-foot headquarters building, a world-class

Robert P. Saltzman (second from the right), Jackson National president, is joined by (from left) John Engler, governor of Michigan, David Hollister, mayor of Lansing, and Marvin Lott, supervisor of Alaiedon Township, in announcing Jackson National's plan for development of a new headquarters facility.

facility on eighty acres of natural wooded area near the intersection of I-96 and Okemos Road in the Lansing area. The company plans to occupy the building in 2000.

Much of Jackson National's growth has come since Robert P. Saltzman joined the company as president and chief executive officer in 1994. A year before his arrival, Jackson National's assets stood at $19 billion. Today assets have nearly doubled, to nearly $38 billion.

Before Saltzman joined Jackson National, fixed annuities were the company's most successful product. Fixed annuities are a deferred savings vehicle that can provide owners with a monthly income for life, if desired. Jackson National is still one of America's leading fixed annuity writers, but Saltzman saw that Jackson National was competing in an environment of low interest rates that favored equity-based products.

Saltzman's philosophy was to diversify. One way to do that was to strengthen and expand Jackson National's portfolio of life and annuity products. Jackson National has always been a pioneer in developing life insurance products that not only protect against the death of a breadwinner, but also can help with other needs, such as meeting college expenses.

Jackson National's regional marketing staff spends a good deal of time on the road meeting with independent producers and cultivating strategies for continued business growth and success.

Jackson National was among the first to offer a new type of life insurance with living benefits—life insurance you didn't have to die for—which pays a portion of the policy's face value if the insured is diagnosed with a life-threatening illness.

Jackson National also has expanded its line of annuity products to include variable annuities and equity-indexed annuities. These two new types of annuities help policyholders respond to changes in the economy. Unlike traditional fixed annuities, which pay a fixed rate of interest, equity-indexed annuities give clients the opportunity to earn a rate of return linked to a stock index without risking their principal.

In addition to diversifying products, Jackson National has diversified the way it brings products to market. For example, a few years ago, people did not go to banks to buy life insurance or an annuity. Today 70 percent of banks offer life insurance and annuity products through insurance affiliates. In fact, Jackson National is currently among the top-seven underwriters of individual annuities sold through banks in the United States.

Because of such diversification, nearly three-quarters of Jackson National's new sales now come from products that didn't exist five years ago. The company believes that a fully diversified, world-class financial services organization needs to

Jackson National Life Insurance Company is wholly owned by England's Prudential Corporation plc, the largest life insurance company in the United Kingdom and one of the largest insurers in the world (not affiliated with Prudential Insurance Company of America).

offer world-class service. Special service groups, such as a specialized bank service unit, help the firm respond to the unique service challenges of a diversified market. Customer service representatives have also become better trained and better equipped to deliver prompt, accurate information. To attract and keep the best people in the industry, training and education have become an integral part of company associates' work life. Jackson National not only provides on-site training and tuition reimbursement, it offers associates up to $10,000 a year per child for their children's college education.

Diversification is the strategy that will drive Jackson National into the next century. Michigan has provided Jackson National with resources to make that happen—a supportive community, access to talented workers, and room to grow.

Friendly, well-trained customer service representatives help answer policyholders' questions.

MICHIGAN ECONOMIC DEVELOPMENT CORPORATION

A waterfront view of the Detroit, Michigan skyline as seen across the Detroit River from the vantage point of Belle Isle. © Don Simonelli

THROUGH ITS

INNOVATIVE

PROGRAMS, THE

MICHIGAN ECONOMIC

DEVELOPMENT

CORPORATION

HELPS BUILD JOBS

AND BUSINESS-

EXPANSION

OPPORTUNITIES,

WHICH ARE ENHANCED

BY THE HEALTHY

WORKING AND LIVING

ENVIRONMENT OF

THE STATE

The change that has pushed Michigan to the forefront of national attention is by no means a stroke of luck. Michigan has become not only an excellent destination for a vacation but also a great state in which to live and raise a family.

With the help of the Michigan Economic Development Corporation, Michigan offers an abundance of opportunities for jobs and business expansion. Michigan has succeeded in becoming a national leader in many arenas by strengthening the state's already distinguished programs and policies.

Michigan offers a wealth of activities and entertainment. With 11,000 lakes, ninety-nine state parks and recreation areas, forty ski resorts, and more golf courses than any other state, Michigan is a premier place for recreational activities. The state also is justly proud of its professional and collegiate sports as well as its visual and performing arts scene.

Michigan also has much to offer individuals and families as a place to live: a healthy, expanding economy, low taxes, affordable housing, flourishing communities, and a strong commitment to education.

Also, through the efforts of the Michigan Economic Development Corporation, Michigan ranks among the best states in the nation in job and economic development opportunities. Michigan had more new plants and expansions than any other state in both 1997 and 1998, earning the coveted Governor's Cup awarded by *Site Selection* magazine two years in a row. Michigan has added more than 700,000 new jobs since April 1991, making it number one among the eleven largest states. Michigan received an additional four prestigious honors in 1997 and 1998:

- *Plants, Sites and Parks* magazine ranked Michigan number one on their 1998 "bizsites" list for attracting new business sites;
- the National Alliance of Business named Michigan number one for its workforce development system in 1997;
- Coopers & Lybrand and *Corporate Locations* magazine named Michigan's investment promotion agency the best in the nation in 1997; and
- the National Association of State Development Agencies named Michigan number one in private-public partnership in 1997.

Additional information on the Michigan Economic Development Corporation may be found on its Web site: www.michigan.org, which also provides Travel Michigan's many travel and tourism opportunities listings.

Downhill skiing provides fun for the whole family in Thompsonville, Michigan. © Crystal Mountain Resort

DETROIT TEACHERS CREDIT UNION

The mission statement of Detroit Teachers Credit Union is: "To provide programs and services that will enhance our members' ability to meet their present and future financial needs successfully."

When Detroit Teachers Credit Union (DTCU) was founded more than seventy years ago it was with this mission in mind and through the years its mission has remained the same.

DTCU has prospered and grown because of the inherent strength of the fundamental credit union concept of people helping people, while maintaining standards of excellence with the best in personnel, services, training, and facilities. The success of DTCU is built on a foundation of mutual trust and cooperation among its members.

DTCU began in 1926 when a group of dedicated educators, including the first secretary/treasurer of the credit union, J. C. Howell, met at Howell's home and formed a group whose members would pool resources and create a fund to lend money at reasonable rates to other members. A member with financial needs could

Detroit Teachers Credit Union's first official home, in 1926, was at 1735 Calvert, in Detroit.

borrow money for purchasing a needed item, such as a refrigerator or a car. What began as an investment of $140 by nine teachers has grown into an organization of nearly 60,000 members with assets of more than $280 million.

Organized as a nonprofit entity, DTCU offers a complete array of financial services. Its field of membership includes more than forty-seven different educational organizations. Employees of these organizations can join DTCU. The immediate family of a member, or a person residing in the same household, also may join the credit union.

One of the ways DTCU meets its members' needs is to conduct ongoing member surveys to assess the quality of service and develop new product offerings. Its services range from loan programs to investment seminars.

"In our most recent survey the response was overwhelming," says Ernest Holland, DTCU president/CEO. "Our overall evaluation was very positive, and many of our services received high ratings. However, we realized that we would have

This photograph, taken in 1953, shows DTCU members conducting financial transactions at teller windows.

to make some changes to meet our members' upcoming needs. Using the survey results as a guide, we refined our strategic plan and made a commitment to become the credit union that our members need and want. As we enter the new millennium, we are proud to say that we are continuing to develop new services to save our members time and money."

Recent additions to DTCU services include providing an ATM at each of its four locations, plus a drive-up ATM at its Puritan office. ATMs are available twenty-four hours a day and services are free of surcharges. Members also benefit from DTCU's excellent, highly competitive VISA and MasterCard rates. Other new DTCU service enhancements include 24-Hour Loan-by-Phone, home banking via the Internet, mortgages, a new downtown office, and the Partnering for Education Program.

DTCU stays in communication with its members. It maintains a Web site so members can easily access information.

Under the direction of Ernest Holland, president/CEO of Detroit Teachers Credit Union, the organization has refined its strategic plan and is developing new leading-edge services to further assist its members.

The site includes an electronic edition of the credit union's newsletters, *The Communicator* and *Draft Notes*. DTCU has more than 400 volunteer building representatives to cover each of the participating schools. Representatives are available to answer current and potential members' questions about existing, new, or upcoming DTCU services and events.

DTCU also protects the interests of its members by lobbying on their behalf. For example, it rallied its members to send more than 10,000 letters to Michigan senators requesting support for HR 1151, the Credit Union Membership Access Act. On 7 August 1998, President Clinton signed the act into law. As a result of this legislation, federal credit unions are able to extend membership to small employer groups outside their core membership. This guarantees millions of Americans the right to join a credit union.

"Detroit Teachers Credit Union is a living example of the financial cooperative concept successfully at work in its field of membership," says Ernest Holland. "By definition, cooperation is exemplified by association with others for mutual benefit. This measure of attainment could only come about in today's world with the high level of cooperation that is found in the credit union movement. The stability and strength associated with DTCU is proof of the value of financial togetherness with a common goal. With excellence, together we will strive to reach new heights—and we will continue to succeed with the support of our members."

Detroit Teachers Credit Union

The 1999 headquarters of Detroit Teachers Credit Union is at 7700 Puritan, in Detroit.

CITIZENS INSURANCE COMPANY OF AMERICA

The Citizens Insurance Company staff assembles for a photograph in 1920. Company founder, W. E. Robb, is seated in the front row, at left.

When Citizens Insurance Company of America was founded in Howell, Michigan, in 1915, it pioneered automobile insurance in the state. Since then it has grown to become a major provider of innovative property and casualty insurance.

Still headquartered in Howell, the company is the largest writer of property and casualty insurance in Michigan through independent agents. More than 700 agencies sell Citizens automobile, home, boat, and business insurance in Michigan, Indiana, and Ohio.

In August 1915 the Michigan legislature passed a bill permitting the formation of mutual automobile insurance companies. The bill had been drafted by Howell

Citizen/Care, the company's medical managed care program, offers practical solutions for automobile accident injury and workers' compensation claims. The Citizens Insurance staff of highly trained medical specialists provides insured customers with personal, professional medical care while ensuring their safe and timely return to work.

attorney William Robb, who saw the business potential of insurance for the new trend in automotive transportation. In the same month that the legislature approved "Robb's Law," he obtained a license for his new firm, which he named The Citizens Mutual Automobile Insurance Company.

Within a year the new company had 15,000 members and more than 300 agents. By 1921 Citizens had issued more than 50,000 insurance policies. Initially Citizens provided fire, theft, and liability coverage in an automobile policy. It later expanded its auto insurance to include collision and medical coverage. By 1955 the company had added fire and extended coverage for homes, general liability and property insurance, and workers' compensation for businesses. In 1963 the name was changed to Citizens Mutual Insurance Company, reflecting the company's commitment to serve Michigan as more than an automobile insurer.

In 1974 policyholders voted to change Citizens from a mutual firm to a stock company. Today the company is a wholly owned subsidiary of Allmerica Financial Corporation. During the last quarter of a century Citizens has consistently grown in premiums and market share and in the number of policies in force. Citizens extended its boundaries in 1985 when it began writing insurance in Indiana and in 1995 when the company entered Ohio. Citizens has branches in Howell, Grand Rapids, and Gaylord, Michigan, as well as in Indianapolis, Indiana.

Citizens cultivates a close working relationship with its independent agents by providing products, sales support, ongoing training, and incentive programs. This relationship fosters a sense of partnership and cooperation, with the end result of better service for customers. The agents' efforts are supported by the 1,500 employees of Citizens.

Nearly half of Citizens annual premiums are comprised of group programs in commercial and personal lines, which are at the heart of the company's success in innovation. Comprehensive commercial coverages and discounts are offered to businesses and organizations grouped in a variety of professions and industries. Many prominent associations and companies have selected Citizens group insurance for their employees' personal automobile and homeowner needs.

"We have long provided insurance for affinity groups, such as professional societies, and we are now also focusing on employer group programs. By providing targeted programs for people who share common insurance needs, we are able to increase cost effectiveness through group purchasing," says James R. McAuliffe, president of Citizens Insurance Company of America.

Citizens personal insurance includes automobile, homeowner, manufactured/mobile home, rental dwelling, watercraft, and personal umbrella policies.

Commercial coverages include commercial multiperil package, business owner protection, workers' compensation, commercial auto (fleet), contractor protection, inland marine, and special coverages, such as governmental liability, liquor liability, day care center, and campground liability.

Additionally, the company's subsidiary Citizens Management Inc. provides self-insurance administration to help companies set up and maintain their own self-insured workers' compensation programs, tailored to their specific needs.

Business owners insured with Citizens can expect fast and fair claims service from the company's team of professional adjusters.

With decades of experience in providing commercial coverage, the Citizens loss control division helps businesses reduce injuries and control accident and work-loss expenses.

Citizens's overall strategy for the future is to pursue growth in existing markets and in new markets that offer long-term growth potential. Today the company is meeting clients' needs by providing an integrated approach in which several forms of insurance are offered to each client.

As Citizens moves forward into the future it will continue to grow by applying the innovative approach that began at its founding. "We offer programs that integrate our property and casualty products with employee benefits coverage," says McAuliffe. "These integrated programs can include corporate-owned insurance programs, such as workers' compensation and group life and health coverage. In addition, Citizens offers voluntary benefits programs to employers that enable employees to purchase their automobile and home or other voluntary products. By adding these unique programs, our agents are able to better serve their clients because they can offer a menu of products through one well-coordinated source."

FARM BUREAU INSURANCE

As an affiliate of the Michigan Farm Bureau, Farm Bureau Insurance has been protecting members and clients since 1949. After its beginnings as an auto insurance provider for thousands of Farm Bureau members, the company introduced the first Farmowner's package policy in the nation in 1960 and has been the leader in Michigan farm protection ever since.

The company's Farmowners package was the first ever to cover all the needs of a farm business in one policy. Today Farm Bureau Insurance provides life, home, auto, farm, business, and retirement insurance for 350,000 policyholders in rural, urban, and suburban areas throughout Michigan.

With its corporate headquarters in Lansing, the company has agents and claims offices throughout the state, including more than 400 insurance agents, 100 claims adjusters, and more than 500 staff employees. Farm Bureau Insurance provides protection for more than 100,000 lives, 90,000 homes, 25,000 farms, 16,000 businesses, and 250,000 automobiles.

The company's highly trained and experienced agents work with clients so that clients' individual goals can be defined and reached.

Farm Bureau Insurance continually researches its customers' needs and creates new ways to provide coverages that protect clients against risks.

When the company developed the first Farmowners policy in the United States in 1960, the policy was designed specifically for the Michigan farmer. The package was created by asking Michigan Farm Bureau member-farmers what coverages they wanted—an example of the company's responsiveness to clients and a big reason why it is the state's largest farm insurer today.

Farm Bureau Insurance sponsors high school sports, scholarships, and Michigan's longest-running essay contest to benefit the state's young people. At left, the top-ten winners of the company's annual America & Me Essay Contest gather at the State Capitol before meeting with the governor.

A familiar sight, Farm Bureau Insurance billboards have been part of the Michigan scene for many years. The billboard above was named "Most Creative Painted Billboard in Michigan" in 1992 by the Michigan Outdoor Advertising Association.

Farm Bureau Insurance continues to respond to the needs of clients through all of its products. As one of the largest automobile insurers in Michigan, the company offers safe-driver credits and other discounts that encourage long-term client loyalty.

One of Michigan's largest home insurers, Farm Bureau Insurance offers high-quality homeowners protection and a variety of discounts that provide many ways to trim home insurance costs.

Dedicated to Michigan families and Michigan's future, Farm Bureau Insurance has helped thousands of Michigan families achieve financial security through life insurance. Its life insurance company (Farm Bureau Life Insurance Company of Michigan, organized in 1951) was the first company ever to specialize in the rural life insurance market in Michigan. Today Farm Bureau Life offers a variety of life insurance products that protect families and businesses. Its annuity products guarantee secure retirements for thousands of Michigan residents.

Attesting to Farm Bureau Life's strength and stability, it has earned the "Excellent" rating from A. M. Best Company for several years in a row. Farm Bureau Life also has the distinction of being named one of the top-performing life insurance companies in the United States by Ward Financial

Group. Ward has chosen the company for several consecutive years as one of the nation's top-fifty life insurance companies based on outstanding achievement in the areas of safety, consistency, and performance. "This puts us in very elite company, and that's where we feel Farm Bureau Life belongs," says Larry Thomas, executive vice president of Farm Bureau Insurance.

Farm Bureau Mutual Insurance Company of Michigan and Farm Bureau General Insurance Company of Michigan also have earned ratings of "Excellent" from A. M. Best. "This rating reflects the efforts that we have made to provide our clients with the best possible products and service," Thomas says. "It is based on our profitable operating results, favorable liquidity position, and strong market presence here in Michigan, as well as the tremendous customer loyalty we receive through our relationship with Michigan Farm Bureau. An A. M. Best review takes into account a company's financial statements, its economic outlook, markets, and distribution systems. We believe our rating is an indication that our property and casualty insurance companies are the kind of strong, solvent insurance organizations that deserve an 'Excellent' rating by Best."

Through its own in-house agency (Community Service Acceptance Company), Farm Bureau Insurance also provides a number of other products, including Blue Cross/Blue Shield health insurance, long-term care insurance, crop insurance, and many other coverages.

Farm Bureau Insurance serves Michigan communities through more than just high-quality insurance coverage. The company also sponsors many community programs that benefit Michigan's young people and families. These programs incorporate the company's core values, which center around outstanding service, trust, learning, innovation, and families.

As a major sponsor of high school sports in Michigan, Farm Bureau Insurance awards twenty-four $1,000 scholarships each year to Michigan's top scholar-athletes. The company is a long-time partner with the Michigan High School Athletic Association in working with young people. In the fight against cancer, Farm

Nearly 100,000 Michigan families are protected by life insurance from Farm Bureau Life, which has been named by Ward Financial Group as one of the fifty most-outstanding life insurers in the nation based on safety, security, and financial performance.

Bureau Insurance has helped raise millions of dollars by sponsoring several American Cancer Society golf tournaments each year. The company also is proud of its annual America & Me Essay Contest, which since 1968 has been encouraging Michigan eighth-grade students to explore their roles in America's future.

"We serve only Michigan, so we care deeply about the people and the communities of this state," says Larry Thomas. "We invest in programs that strengthen Michigan's families and young people because we believe that is the best way to strengthen the state's future. As Farm Bureau Insurance marked its fiftieth anniversary in 1999, we renewed that commitment and continue it today."

Farm Bureau Insurance, with agents located statewide, offers Michigan residents a full range of insurance services: life, home, auto, farm, business, retirement, annuities, and more. Visit the company's Web site (www.farmbureauinsurance-mi.com) for more information about its many products, services, and agents.

With combined assets that have grown to $1.5 billion, Farm Bureau Insurance is no longer the small firm it was in 1949. However, its roots in the farming community are still the basis for the values that guide it today. The company's slogan, Making Your Future More Predictable, is a promise that it continues to keep to the people of Michigan.

Indicating the company's stability, Farm Bureau Insurance has had just three executive vice presidents in more than fifty years of history. They are, from left, Nile Vermillion (1949–1974), founding CEO and charter inductee in the Michigan Insurance Hall of Fame; Robert Wiseman (1974–1989); and Larry Thomas (1989–present).

AMERISURE COMPANIES

Michigan-based Amerisure Companies can trace its roots back to a historic act of the Michigan State government.

When the Michigan legislature approved a workers' compensation law in 1912, a small group of members of the Michigan Manufacturers Association (MMA) responded by joining together and forming Michigan Mutual Insurance Company for the specific purpose of writing the first workers' compensation insurance plan in the state.

Today, nearly ninety years later, the group, now called Amerisure Companies, maintains its strong partnership with the Michigan Manufacturers Association. The successful Amerisure-MMA workers' compensation program has returned more than $20 million in the form of dividends to participating MMA members.

While workers' compensation insurance still accounts for 43 percent of its business, Amerisure Companies, with its subsidiary firms—Amerisure Inc., Amerisure Insurance Company, Amerisure Re (Bermuda) Ltd., and Amerisure Business Solutions, Inc., also provides businesses with insurance coverages for general liability, automobile, property/casualty, and umbrella and employee administration services.

Amerisure's business has grown well beyond Michigan's borders. Through a strong network of highly skilled independent insurance agents, Amerisure has evolved into a premier property/casualty insurer, particularly in the Midwest and South and is licensed to market its products in all fifty states.

From 1935 to 1951 the headquarters of Michigan Mutual was located on Madison Avenue in downtown Detroit.

With ninety years of service and strong ties to the manufacturing industry, Amerisure Companies maintains a unique understanding of the challenges and opportunities faced by today's manufacturers.

"Amerisure is still committed to its original beliefs and objectives, providing innovative products, unsurpassed service quality, and treating policyholders, agents, and employees as true partners," says Amerisure's president and chief executive officer, Richard F. Russell. Through its independent insurance agents and a dedicated staff of service professionals, Amerisure continually responds to the unique needs of its policyholders. Among the innovative and custom-designed insurance programs Amerisure offers to manufacturing, contracting, retail, and wholesale distribution businesses are the Manufacturers Advantage Program (MAP), the Contractors Advantage Program (CAP), APEX, Command Coverage, and Flagship Gold programs.

Amerisure's MAP was created specifically to protect today's manufacturing operations. It provides additional and expanded liability and property/casualty coverage tailored to meet manufacturers' product-coverage requirements. MAP includes coverage that is not typically offered in standard insurance programs, such as insurance for product recall, product repair or replacement, and specification errors and omissions.

CAP coverage was created for general contractors and trade contractors who have superior management, financial strength and hazard control. CAP goes beyond standard insurance policies to protect contractors from daily risks.

APEX was developed to meet the sophisticated property/casualty needs of large businesses. It has programs in place to help identify workplace hazards and create safer working environments for clients in a variety of industries.

Command Coverage, designed specifically for manufacturing, industrial, contracting, institutional, and other commercial operations, offers expanded commercial property coverage at a competitive price.

Flagship Gold allows qualified Amerisure customers the ability to lock in rates and coverage for up to three years.

In addition to its broad range of products, Amerisure also provides an array of business-enhancing services to policyholders, including loss control, exceptional claims service, managed care, and return-to-work programs.

Amerisure's sophisticated loss-control programs and experienced loss-control professionals find solutions to on-site safety issues by evaluating a customer's workplace, analyzing and investigating current accidents and loss records, and recommending ways to reduce risk.

The company's managed care program controls costs and helps employees return to work as quickly as possible without sacrificing the treatment they need.

Amerisure's claim-service quality is consistently ranked outstanding by A. M. Best Company. By working directly with medical providers and staying involved in the return-to-work process, Amerisure processes claims quickly and pays medical bills promptly. Amerisure also is proud of the fact that it saves policyholders millions of dollars by detecting, investigating, and eliminating fraudulent claims.

Partnership and teamwork are critically important to Amerisure. Amerisure recruits, retains, and rewards professionals and support personnel who demonstrate teamwork, creative problem-solving, initiative, effective communications, and responsibility. Its independent insurance agents are treated as peers and receive unsurpassed service, support, and reward through

The headquarters of Amerisure Companies has been located in Farmington Hills, Michigan, since 1993.

Amerisure's Partners for Success program. Amerisure takes a hands-on approach to conducting business with policyholders to keep employees safe, reduce claims, and keep premiums low.

To assist agents in the field and serve its policyholders, Amerisure maintains core service center offices in Farmington Hills and Grand Rapids, Michigan, plus eight other locations in the midwestern and southern United States.

It's all part of Amerisure's commitment to providing service to business.

In Michigan, Amerisure is endorsed by the Michigan Manufacturers Association, Associated General Contractors, and Associated Builders and Contractors.

Visit the Amerisure Web site at www.amerisure.com for more information.

Amerisure has established an impressive track record in the contracting industry. The company continues to specialize in programs that protect contractors, their business, and their employees.

FRANKENMUTH MUTUAL INSURANCE COMPANY

FRANKENMUTH

MUTUAL INSURANCE

COMPANY MOVES

FORWARD AND

INVESTS IN

THE FUTURE, WHILE

BUILDING ON ITS

RICH HISTORY THAT

SPANS MORE THAN

130 YEARS

OF SUCCESS

Frankenmuth Mutual Insurance Company's 100,000-square-foot architecturally acclaimed corporate office building is at One Mutual Avenue in Frankenmuth, Michigan.

A major financial force throughout the Midwest, with assets of $411 million, Frankenmuth Mutual Insurance Company carries more than 250,000 policies in Michigan, Indiana, Ohio, and Wisconsin. It has 450 employees and is represented by more than 420 independent agencies. Recently licensed in Illinois, Iowa, Minnesota, Kentucky, Tennessee, and Virginia, the company is mapping out a strategy to offer insurance in all forty-eight contiguous states. A. M. Best Company has given Frankenmuth Mutual an A+ rating for eighteen consecutive years, and Ward Financial Group has ranked it for the last six years among the top fifty property and casualty insurers in the nation, citing a healthy balance between solvency and profitability. "Growth alone doesn't mean profit to us. We never measure our success by premiums but by financial security," explains Gerald L. Stanton, president and CEO of Frankenmuth Mutual.

That the company consistently manages to enjoy both growth and security is clearly expressed by its 100,000-square-foot headquarters located in Frankenmuth, Michigan.

The spacious interiors of the Frankenmuth Mutual headquarters building center around an atrium filled with greenery and light.

Surrounded by beautifully landscaped grounds and flower gardens, the architecturally acclaimed complex includes an 18,000-square-foot subterranean Emergency Operations Center designed to be tornado-resistant, fireproof, and self-sufficient in the event of disaster. The claims division is moving to a 27,000-square-foot building now undergoing renovation in downtown Frankenmuth. Blueprints for the $1.5 million project call for the installation of fiber-optic cables linking the site with headquarters. Frankenmuth Mutual has also purchased a 190-acre parcel on the Cass River, just outside the city limits, for a future campus.

Frankenmuth Mutual's forward-thinking management has also staked out cyberspace for future growth. "Electronic commerce (E-commerce) presents unique opportunities for Frankenmuth Mutual," says Gerald C. Webb, senior vice president. "We believe insurance products and the proper technological infrastructure, when combined, can deliver unprecedented efficiencies. Not only can we reduce costs, but we will also deliver levels of customer service previously unattainable."

Through Frankenmuth Mutual's Web site (www.fmins.com), agents will be able to access policy, billing, and claims information. If the underwriting criterion is met, the system can automatically initiate the policy issuance function. "Ultimately, our point-of-service goal is to provide automated insurance solutions, which will improve speed and accuracy in risk assessment, enhance productivity, expedite policy issuance, and reduce costs for both the agent and Frankenmuth Mutual," says Webb.

Agents also will be able to go on-line to enter first notice of loss—a key advantage for a company that agents already consider to be a leader in claims processing. (Just hours after a tornado hit Frankenmuth in June 1966, company representatives were busy scouring the city on golf carts to write checks to policyholders.)

Electronic data interface (EDI) and electronic information management (EIM) will streamline "document" processing and provide Frankenmuth with improved information handling and interdepartmental communications. EDI and EIM will allow electronic or "imaged" information such as notices of loss, digital pictures, E-mail confirmations, medical evaluations, and litigation summaries to be electronically disseminated and filed. "More cost-effective claims processing and customer service will be achieved, and an enhanced standard for work flow, storage, and retrieval of claims information will be enacted," says Jim Wilds, manager of the claims division. Ideally the new imaging system will result in same-day payment of claims.

In 1868 a group of German farmers in Michigan's Saginaw Valley planted the seeds of what is now Frankenmuth Mutual. Joining together in the spirit of neighbor helping neighbor, they formed the *Deutschen Frankenmuther Unterstüzungs Verein* (German Frankenmuther Aid Association) to insure one another against fire, lightning, and other perils. Although the association's name was changed to Frankenmuth Fire Aid Association in 1924, the switch from German to English record keeping wasn't completed until 1939. At that time, the association's only employee was Carl Nuechterlein, its offices were located in the back room of the Nuechterlein Mortuary, and its records were stored in a coffin.

In 1941 Frankenmuth Mutual Fire Insurance Company assumed operations of the association, ushering in six decades of tremendous change and steady growth. Within seven years the company more than doubled the amount of its insurance in force,

The visitors' entrance to Frankenmuth Mutual Insurance Company's corporate office building balances bold linear architecture with lavish flower gardens and graceful landscaping.

with more than 10,000 policyholders. A decade later it merged with Frankenmuth Mutual Auto Insurance Company (which Carl Nuechterlein had helped to found in 1921).

From farsighted leaders like the Nuechterleins—first Christoph, then his son Carl, and grandson Arnold—to today's capable management, generation after generation has made its contribution to this growing, financially strong company. "We have a corporate responsibility to the community. The people who were here before us left us this business, and we owe it to them to build on that," says Stanton.

Sixty years after switching its bookkeeping from German to English, Frankenmuth Mutual is already communicating fluently in the language of the twenty-first century. As technology makes the world smaller and faster paced, Frankenmuth Mutual Insurance Company can respond to clients' needs more quickly and efficiently than ever, while it continues to demonstrate pioneering initiative and a deeply rooted tradition of neighbor helping neighbor.

FRANKENMUTH
MUTUAL INSURANCE COMPANY

Seen at dusk, the massive structure with soaring roof and walls of glass evokes Frankenmuth Mutual's strong foundation and its spirited outlook and future-oriented strategies.

DETROIT REGIONAL ECONOMIC PARTNERSHIP

The Detroit region . . . singular region, multiple choices.

There is no question that the Detroit region is the global leader in the automotive industry. Since Henry Ford rolled the first vehicle off his assembly line, the area has led the world in innovative automobile design, cutting-edge technology, and highly skilled employees. The region's long history in the automotive industry has allowed it to build the foundation that sets standards for the rest of the world.

DaimlerChrysler, Ford Motor Company, General Motors Corporation, Mazda, and Volkswagen of America all have headquarters in the area. More than 11,000 companies within Michigan supply technology or parts to the automotive industry. It is apparent that key decision makers in the industry are located in the Detroit region.

But the Detroit region has much more to offer than its world-class automotive industry. It offers a kaleidoscope of opportunities in a variety of industries and an outstanding quality of life.

A century of experience in high-tech manufacturing and research and development has created one of the most

More than 200,000 designers work in twenty-seven research and development centers in the Detroit region.

Regional Detroit's five border crossings create the busiest section of the Canadian border in the United States.

powerful knowledge centers in the world. This knowledge has been tapped and applied to the medical industry. The results are phenomenal. The medical industry in the Detroit region is the sixth largest in the United States, with gross revenues of more than $11.2 billion, and represents one-seventh of the region's economy. The region's unique history of manufacturing, with the ability to take products from concept to reality, adds further value for medical technology companies. A strong supplier network, highly skilled engineers, and advanced manufacturing methods provide a foundation for bringing products to market.

The Detroit region has a well-developed transportation infrastructure that is able to handle movement of goods quickly and efficiently. The city's location in the middle of the nation's industrial heartland means that virtually all major industries have plants or facilities within 500 miles of the metropolitan area, and more than 50 percent of the population of North America lives within the same radius.

Detroit Regional Chamber
Powering the economy for Southeast Michigan

The region's location positions it as a center for the North American Free Trade Agreement. Michigan is Canada's number-one trading partner. Twenty-seven percent of all merchandise traded between the United States and Canada crosses the Ambassador Bridge in downtown Detroit. Michigan is Mexico's number-three trading partner.

Detroit is home to a wide range of world-class museums, including the Detroit Institute of Art, the sixth-largest fine arts museum in the United States; the world famous Museum of African American History; the Henry Ford Museum and Greenfield Village; and the Motown Museum. In addition, the city is home to the Detroit Symphony Orchestra, one of the finest symphonies in the nation. With the second-highest number of live-theater seats in the United States, regional Detroit offers an array of ballets, musicals, operas, and plays for everyone's taste.

In addition to an abundance of cultural and recreational attractions, the quality of life in the Detroit region is enhanced by state-of-the-art medical, educational, and research centers. The Detroit region is home to eight universities, eight colleges, and eighteen community colleges. The area has been ranked twenty-first out of 351 metropolitan areas in North America for overall quality of education.

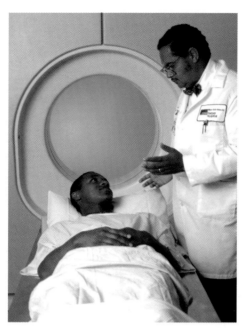

The Detroit region's medical market is the sixth largest in the United States. One in seven individuals within the region is employed in the medical industry.

Companies that locate in or expand to regional Detroit have access to a wide variety of economic development–assistance programs, including workforce development grants, community finance assistance, tax-reduction programs, land transfers, and block grants.

The Detroit Regional Economic Partnership recognizes that making a business location decision or seeking new trade opportunities is a challenging and time-consuming process. The partnership was formed to make this process easier.

To find out how the partnership can be of assistance, contact: The Detroit Regional Economic Partnership, One Woodward Avenue, Suite 1700, Post Office Box 33840, Detroit, Michigan 48232-0840; telephone toll-free in the United States: (888) 519-7177; outside the United States: (313) 596-0341; Fax: (313) 964-0168. Or send E-mail to drep@detroitchamber.com or visit the partnership's Web site at www.detroitchamber.com for more information.

The world headquarters of General Motors Corporation is located in the heart of downtown Detroit.

Detroit Regional
Economic Partnership

THE DETROIT REGION
Singular Region — Multiple Rankings

- Number-One Trade City in the United States — *WorldTrade* magazine
- Number-One Region for New Corporate Facilities and Expansions — *Site Selection* magazine
- Fastest-Growing Market in the United States — The Society of Industrial and Office Realtors
- Number-Two Large City in the United States for Small Business — *Entrepreneur* magazine
- One of the Top-Eight Best Communities in the World for Manufacturing — *Industry Week* magazine

AUTO-OWNERS INSURANCE COMPANY

The evolution from birth to maturity of successful corporations is dependent on a number of factors. One of the most important is leadership. The quality of leadership is what has made Auto-Owners Insurance Company one of the largest property and casualty insurance firms based in Michigan and one of the largest in the nation.

The company's success can be traced back from its present management to the early leadership of Vern V. Moulton who, in 1916, organized Auto-Owners Insurance Company in Mt. Pleasant, Michigan. Within a year, Moulton moved his company to Lansing, Michigan, where it remains today.

During the Great Depression and through the economy's ups and downs since, the company has always demonstrated its corporate toughness and retained its financial stability. From its original one-man operation, which was begun with no capital and housed in one room of a bank building, Auto-Owners Insurance has grown to serve approximately 4,300 independent insurance agencies, marketing personal and commercial property/ casualty and life as well as disability and annuity insurance in twenty-two states. Today the Auto-Owners Insurance Group has more than 2.6 million policies in force. The company also enjoys the highest possible ratings assigned by nationally recognized independent rating authorities.

The Auto-Owners corporate headquarters is located in the Verndale business and residential complex in Delta Township, on the west side of

The corporate headquarters of Auto-Owners Insurance is located in the Verndale complex in Lansing, Michigan.

Lansing. The building, constructed in 1975, has been expanded twice to keep pace with company growth, increasing its size to 284,000 square feet. In 1998 construction was completed on the 108,900-square-foot Moulton Building, named for company founders. This building, located across the street from the corporate headquarters, is home to Auto-Owners' Michigan regional operation.

The Lansing corporate office services not only Auto-Owners Insurance Company, but also its subsidiary companies: Auto-Owners Life Insurance Company, Home-Owners Insurance Company, Owners Insurance Company, Property-Owners Insurance Company, and Southern-Owners Insurance Company.

The source of Auto-Owners Insurance growth is its loyal associates, agents, and policy-holders. Its more than 2,300 associates include 1,100 in the Lansing area. The firm also has full-service offices in White Bear Lake, Minnesota; Peoria, Illinois; Montgomery, Alabama; Marion, Indiana; Lima, Ohio; Lakeland, Florida; Brentwood, Tennessee; West Des Moines, Iowa; Charlotte, North Carolina; Mesa, Arizona; Appleton, Wisconsin; and Duluth, Georgia; and claims offices in thirty-four additional cities. Auto-Owners is already planning further expansion, during mid-1999, into Colorado, its twenty-third operational state.

Auto-Owners Insurance
Life Home Car Business
The 'No Problem' People®

The Moulton Building, named for Auto-Owners founding fathers, is home to the company's Michigan regional operation.

Michigan insurance company representatives discuss ways to expand their products and services to meet the growing needs of their customers. © PhotoDisc

THE POLK COMPANY

The world headquarters of The Polk Company is located in Southfield, Michigan.

Based in Southfield, Michigan, The Polk Company is one of the nation's premier providers of multi-dimensional marketing information solutions to corporations worldwide. From humble beginnings, Polk has grown to more than 4,000 employees, with annual revenues exceeding $450 million and offices throughout the United States, Canada, Europe, Costa Rica, and Australia.

It began in 1870, when twenty-one-year-old Ralph Lane Polk founded R. L. Polk & Company and published a small directory of the residents and businesses in the towns along the Detroit and Milwaukee Railroad. During the early years, the company grew by acquiring existing directory companies and by initiating directories in cities across the nation. One hundred years later, approximately 1,300 directories were being published, referencing more than 6,500 communities in the United States and Canada.

In 1922 the company launched its motor statistical operations when the first automobile registration reports were published for General Motors Corporation. Realizing that automobile owners represented a significant audience for marketers, Polk acquired three mailing list companies and offered lists of automobile

At far left is legendary R. L. Polk & Company founder, Ralph Lane Polk. At near left, inset, is his great-grandson Stephen Polk, the company's current chairman and chief executive officer.

owners classified by state, county, and make of automobile owned.

In 1988 the company acquired National Demographics & Lifestyles, Inc. (NDL), and established itself as an industry leader in the collection of consumer lifestyle information. Polk's premier list product, The Lifestyle Selector®, is one of the direct marketing industry's preeminent offerings in the self-reported lifestyle information segment. Along with TotaList® and a host of other list products, including outdoor and packaged goods information, Polk is leading the way with its roster of data offerings.

Today Polk compiles data on more than 106 million households and 180 million individuals, reports on some 200 million cars and trucks in operation, supplies specific-consumer analysis to more than 100 consumer goods companies, and publishes city directories. Polk also provides detailed mapping and clustering systems.

In keeping with the entrepreneurial spirit of the company, Polk continues to concentrate on globalization, including China and other countries throughout Asia. A strong focus on innovation, technology, research, analysis, and the needs of customers has cemented Polk's position as a marketing information leader. And with Stephen Polk, great-grandson of the founder and current chairman and chief executive officer, leading the way, Polk is positioned to sustain that status as it enters the next millennium.

CITIZENS BANK

CITIZENS BANK IS A FAMILY OF COMMUNITY BANKS OFFERING PERSONAL BANKING WITH A FULL RANGE OF FINANCIAL SERVICES TO BUSINESSES AND INDIVIDUALS

Tracing its roots back to 1871, Citizens Bank takes pride in its long-standing tradition of community banking. In its early days, it helped provide the financial muscle to build Michigan's lumber and automotive industries. Today each of its community banks is an active community member, dedicated to serving local clients, helping local businesses grow, and meeting local needs through civic leadership and involvement.

Citizens Bank is part of Citizens Banking Corporation (NASDAQ: CBCF), a diversified financial services company headquartered in Flint, Michigan, with assets of more than $4.5 billion. Its network of 124 offices and more than 130 ATMs extends throughout the state of Michigan and suburban Chicago, Illinois. Citizens consistently ranks among the top Midwest banking companies.

"We are pleased with our earnings, the implementation of our technological resources, and the reaffirmation of our Clients First!SM strategy," says Robert J. Vitito, chairman, president, and CEO of Citizens Banking Corporation. "We look forward to the future as we strengthen our commitment to fully understanding and exceeding our clients' financial needs and expectations."

A commitment to focusing on client needs, delivering superior service, and building lasting relationships, that's the **Clients First!** strategy. It is what sets Citizens apart from other banks, and it plays an integral role in Citizens' drive to become the single source of financial services for all its clients. A majority of the bank's client households has been assigned Personal Bankers who act as financial consultants and advisers, monitor portfolios, and

Citizens Bank's three-building corporate complex is a key architectural landmark in downtown Flint, Michigan. The elegant, spacious lobby features marble accents in the client reception area.

Citizens Bank
You're A <u>Client</u> First.SM

facilitate transactions. Through Citizens Financial Services, clients find a one-stop source for trust and investment services, retirement plans, asset management, and other services. And business clients can look to Commercial Relationship Officers for everything from loans and cash management services to sophisticated investment options.

Community branches, commercial financial centers, private banking offices, ATMs, workplace banking, and automated telephone and computer-based programs make it possible to deliver products with more convenience than ever. Citizens Bank's client-centered approach is further enhanced by the latest on-line technology with Internet banking. In addition to providing account balance information, account transfers, and bill payment service, Clients First On-LineSM at the Citizens Web site (www.cbClientsFirst.com) posts the bank's recent financial statements, and offers product and service information, all at the click of a mouse. From local communities to the World Wide Web, Citizens is committed to ensuring easy access to financial services of every kind.

Citizens Bank is committed to building long-term relationships with its clients to help them achieve their financial goals. In a recent survey, clients gave Citizens Bank Personal Bankers high marks. More than 90 percent felt comfortable discussing their financial goals with a Personal Banker.

The Lansing Regional Chamber of Commerce's Capital Choice Program and the Regional Economic Development (RED) Team are partners in promoting the Lansing region

the Place for Futures

Picturesque Beaumont Tower, on the Michigan State University campus in East Lansing, is a beautiful backdrop for student discussion groups.

The Lansing Regional Chamber of Commerce and the Regional Economic Development (RED) Team, Inc., are devoted to improving the greater Lansing community and its business climate. The chamber's Capital Choice Program fosters economic growth by attracting new businesses to the region. Members of the program are part of the RED Team, a coalition of local governments, utilities providers, school districts, and development professionals. Together their retention and attraction efforts draw worldwide companies to Lansing's unique expansion opportunities. The RED Team and the Capital Choice Program are making the Lansing region the Place for Futures.

Small-town charm and big-city amenities are hallmarks of the Lansing region. Located just ninety miles west of Detroit in south central Michigan, the three-county region has a population of 430,000. Lansing, the capital of Michigan, and East Lansing, home to Michigan State University, are at the center of a region composed of Clinton, Eaton, and Ingham counties. They are surrounded by smaller communities with historic downtown centers and picturesque rural areas. The Lansing region is at the junction of major highways, rail lines, waterways, and air services— linked together and connected to the world.

The Lansing region has a vibrant economy anchored by good jobs in manufacturing, education, state government, computer technology, and biotechnology. Lansing has the fourth-largest workforce in the state. The region's highly talented and stable workforce is well educated and skilled. Extensive business and education partnerships create a solid base for training workers. Educational innovations in the Lansing region give the area dynamic growth.

The Lansing region is more than a great place to work—it offers plenty of opportunities to play! The area is amply supplied with golf

Flowering apple trees, a reminder of the state's rich agricultural heritage, frame the historically renovated state capitol in Lansing.

courses, movie theaters, bowling and ice skating centers. There are parks with soccer, football, and baseball fields. There also are numerous horse riding stables, lakes and streams for boating and fishing, and nearly 300 indoor and outdoor tennis courts. The Lansing region has exciting Big Ten college sports, minor league baseball, and a professional golf tournament.

The region is rich in live theater, dance, and music performances. The Wharton Center for Performing Arts at Michigan State University offers touring Broadway shows, leading dance troupes, and lecturers. The Breslin Events Center hosts the nation's hottest country, rock, and contemporary music performers. Coffeehouses and restaurants maintain the area's strong tradition of live folk music. Art galleries, symphonies, museums, and community fairs round out the region's cultural and entertainment offerings. The Lansing region also has premier facilities for hosting conferences and other events.

The Lansing Regional Chamber of Commerce's Capital Choice Program and the Regional Economic Development (RED) Team, Inc., are partners in developing the Lansing region. Find out more about the Place for Futures by contacting Capital Choice by telephone at (517) 487-6340; fax (517) 484-6910; or visit its Web site at www.lansingchamber.org for more information.

The Lansing State Capitol building has been restored to its 1879 beauty. © D. E. Cox/Tony Stone Images

Traffic zooms past historic Tiger Stadium in Detroit. © SuperStock

REAL ESTATE, DEVELOPMENT, AND CONSTRUCTION

BLACK & VEATCH

This 90,000-square-foot office building constructed in Ann Arbor was designed by Black & Veatch Advanced Technology Division.

Founded in 1915, Black & Veatch is a full-service global engineering and construction firm specializing in the fields of energy, environment, process, and construction.

"The mission of Black & Veatch is to provide quality engineering, architectural, management, and related services and facilities with creative and innovative solutions that are responsive to client and public needs," says CEO Len Rodman. The firm offers a local presence and a hands-on approach to each of its clients while drawing on the expertise of its 8,000 professionals to handle any size project, whether it be small in scale or large and complex. In addition to outstanding people, Black & Veatch offers state-of-the-art management information technology, world-class project controls, and industry-recognized safety programs.

The company's Detroit and Ann Arbor operations are part of its global network of approximately ninety offices. The Ann Arbor office employs about 230 people and has moved to new facilities to accommodate its growth. Engaged in projects worldwide, this office also has many local clients, including DTE Energy, Consumers Energy, University of Michigan, Michigan State University, DaimlerChrysler, and Pharmacia & Upjohn. Internationally, the office is responsible for energy projects in Latin America. Its staff consists of skilled personnel with extensive experience in power plant design and upgrades and modernization of power and utility facilities.

The firm's Detroit office works extensively with the City of Detroit and Chrysler Corporation. The Detroit office also provides environmental engineering and construction services throughout the Great Lakes region. With primary responsibility for project management and customer support, the office works closely with process specialists from the company's Kansas City, Missouri–based headquarters to provide the highest standard of environmental design and project services.

True to its motto, If you can imagine it, we can build it, Black & Veatch brings innovative solutions to every project and maintains the highest standards of quality.

BLACK & VEATCH
the imagine·build **company™**

BLACK & VEATCH RANKINGS

Engineering News Record
Top 500 Design Firms
- First–Fossil fuel, water supply, semiconductor plants
- Second–Power
- Third–Sewerage/solid water
- Fourth–International markets

Top 200 International Design Firms
- First–Water • Second–Power • Third–Sewerage

Top 400 Contractors
- Second–Fossil fuel
- Third–Telecommunications, power

Top 200 Environmental Firms
- Second–Top-twenty firms by state/local clients
- Third–Water quality
- Fourth–Design/consulting

McCoy Power Reports
U.S. and worldwide leader in project awards for electricity generation, for the past ten years

Environmental Business Journal
Third–Top Environmental Consulting/Engineering Firms

Environmental Business International Inc.
Fourth–Top Water/Wastewater Consulting Firms

Private Power Executive
- Top–U.S. Engineering Designer
- Second–U.S. Constructor
- Third–U.S. Engineer/Constructor

SIGNATURE ASSOCIATES, MICHIGAN'S REPRESENTATIVE OF ONCOR INTERNATIONAL, PROVIDES COMPREHENSIVE SERVICES FOR CLIENTS WITH MULTIMARKET REAL ESTATE NEEDS

Worldwide Real Estate Services

One has to get up early to keep pace with the team of real estate professionals who make up Southfield, Michigan–based Signature Associates, a full-service, commercial real estate firm.

The Signature team, made up of the Detroit area's top industrial, office, retail, commercial, and high-tech real estate brokers, frequently can be found in their offices before dawn, fielding telephone calls from current and prospective clients and preparing for an early morning staff meeting.

Indeed, the nearly three dozen full-time brokers and thirty-five support-team members who make up the company are firm believers in the old adage that the early bird gets the worm. These highly trained and motivated professionals, who have an aggregate of more than 350 years of real estate experience, consistently get the lion's share of them.

Because of their efforts, Signature Associates already is southeast Michigan's leading commercial real estate firm, even though the firm has been in existence for just ten years. In fact, since its inception in 1989 the firm annually has led all other area commercial real estate firms in total real estate leasing and sales. In 1998 alone Signature sold and leased more than sixteen million square feet of commercial real estate.

Signature Associates • ONCOR International's offices are located in Southfield, Michigan.

Long hours put in by Signature's staff are just part of the reason, of course, for the firm's success. Market knowledge and close relationships with customers also play a big part. The fact that the company is more service-oriented than dollar-driven also is significant. Indeed, members of Signature's sales force pride themselves on being not just good salesmen but also good consultants.

"The key here is the camaraderie and sharing of information among our staff members that allows us to tap all the resources of our company," says Steve Gordon, Signature's founder and chief executive. "We then take those resources and go out and turn them into successes for our clients." Signature provides clients with industrial, office, commercial, and retail brokerage services; property management; tenant representation; investment sales; and comprehensive real estate market research.

As Michigan's only representative of ONCOR International—an umbrella group of forty-nine independent commercial real estate firms covering more than 225 markets in twenty-nine countries—Signature offers clients with multimarket real estate needs the highest quality in global real estate services.

IN TOUCH WITH THE WORLD

CHAPTER EIGHTEEN

MICHIGAN ALWAYS HAS BEEN A CROSSROADS FOR TRANSPORTATION AND COMMERCE AND, AS TECHNOLOGY DEVELOPED, IT BECAME A COMMUNICATIONS HUB AS WELL. SIX MONTHS AFTER SAMUEL F. B. MORSE'S FIRST SUCCESSFUL DEMONSTRATION OF THE ELECTRIC TELEGRAPH, THE NEW TECHNOLOGY WAS INTRODUCED IN DETROIT. MICHIGAN'S FIRST REGULAR TELEGRAPH SERVICE LINKED DETROIT AND YPSILANTI IN 1847. WITHIN SIX

months telegraph messages were traveling between Detroit and Chicago.

The telephone has a similar story. Only months after Alexander Graham Bell first demonstrated his invention at the Philadelphia Centennial Exposition in 1876, telephone service arrived in Michigan. Initially adopted mainly by businesses and a few wealthy families, phones had become normal home fixtures by the turn of the century. By 1920 there were telephones on nearly half of all Michigan farms. The state soon became a leader in the new industry. In 1879 Detroit customers became the first in the nation to be assigned telephone numbers. The first Yellow Pages phone directory was issued in Detroit in 1906. In 1965 Michigan Bell customers in Jackson became the first in the nation to use the new "trimline" phones featuring a dial mounted in the receiver.

Michigan Bell was absorbed into Ameritech in 1984, and today more than 85 percent of the state's local

telephone service is provided by Ameritech's five million lines. These lines are part of the most advanced telecommunications infrastructure in North America. By 1996, 90 percent of Michigan's population could dial the Internet by a local phone call, making Michigan the most Internet-connected state in the Midwest. More than 425,000 miles of fiber-optic cable were in the ground by then, connecting virtually every city in Michigan. The groundbreaking 1992 Michigan Telecommunications Act made Michigan the first large state to deregulate its business telecommunications services, allowing for increased competition and pricing flexibility.

FIRST CAME THE WORD

Long before the arrival of the telegraph and telephone, news circulated around Michigan via newspaper. Michigan's first paper appeared in Detroit in 1809, and, although that publication expired after a single issue, many more were soon cropping up across the territory.

OPPOSITE: *A technician in a long-distance switching station examines a fiber-optic bundle. Fiber-optics use light impulses to transmit information down fiber lines, replacing copper wire, and are fast becoming the standard telecommunications transmission medium.* © HMS Images. ABOVE: *The* Detroit Free Press *is Michigan's oldest continuing newspaper. Here, in the early 1900s, workers pause for a moment among the turning presses to check their work and catch up on the day's events.* © Detroit Free Press

Today Michigan's oldest existing newspaper is the *Detroit Free Press,* which began in a small log cabin in 1831. The *Kalamazoo Gazette* is the state's oldest continuously published daily outside Detroit, dating back to 1835. Perhaps the most famous name in Michigan journalism history is Scripps. In 1873 the Scripps family founded the *Detroit News,* which grew into the nation's largest evening newspaper. Once a cornerstone of the Scripps-Howard newspaper chain, the *Detroit News* is now owned by Gannett Corporation. Crain is another prominent name in Michigan publishing. The Crain magazine empire, overseen from the company's Detroit offices, includes business journals in New York, Chicago, Cleveland, and Detroit, as well as *Advertising Age* and *Automotive News.*

Michigan's publishing industry success is not limited to journalism. Zondervan Publishing House in Grand Rapids is the leading international Christian communications company. Founded in 1931 by brothers P. J. and Bernie Zondervan, the company currently publishes more than eight hundred authors, and has two thousand Bible, book, and other product titles in its catalog translated into

The Kalamazoo Gazette *is the oldest ongoing Michigan daily outside Detroit. Shown here, the Gazette building circa 1930. Courtesy,* Kalamazoo Gazette

eighty-five languages, including the *New International Version of the Bible (NIV),* which has sold more than 100 million copies. Zondervan is now a division of HarperCollins Publishers.

Gale Research, founded in Detroit in 1954, is one of the country's oldest and most respected publishers of reference materials. Now headquartered in Farmington Hills, Gale publishes about five hundred academic, educational, and business reference books a year for libraries, educational institutions, and businesses the world over. The company recently merged with Information Access Company, the California-based electronic publisher best known for its InfoTrac SearchBank used in libraries, and Connecticut's Primary Source Media, which specializes in unique and rare research materials.

BORDER CROSSING

THE WORLD'S FIRST INTERNATIONAL TELEPHONE LINE OPENED BETWEEN DETROIT AND WINDSOR ON 20 JANUARY 1880.

This merger makes The Gale Group the world's number-one reference provider.

Valassis Communications of Livonia is the nation's largest printer of the coupon booklets that come tucked inside Sunday newspapers. Fully 90 percent of all coupons distributed in the United States are through Valassis Free-Standing Inserts (FSIs), totaling 250 billion coupons each year. Since 1993 Valassis has ranked among Fortune's "100 Best Companies to Work for in America" thanks to generous benefits, an open communications policy, and amenities such as an on-site physician and automated teller machine (ATM).

THE MOTOWN SOUND

Michigan's most famous publishing business was not involved with newspapers, books, or magazines, but with music. During the thirteen years that Motown Record Company was based in Detroit it published hundreds of songs, dozens of which were million-sellers. Berry Gordy, once an aspiring professional boxer, founded the company in 1959 after other music publishers denied him the royalties he felt he had earned

Motown publisher and producer Berry Gordy. © Archive Photos/ Lawrence Siskind

from writing and producing songs such as "Lonely Teardrops" for his friend Jackie Wilson. Gordy sought out and found talented African American musicians, many of them teenagers from the Detroit projects, and molded them into stars, creating a "Motown Sound" whose popularity cut across racial barriers. Motown artists such as Smokey Robinson and the Miracles, Diana Ross and the Supremes, Marvin Gaye, Stevie Wonder, Mary Wells, the Temptations, Martha Reeves and the Vandellas, and Gladys Knight and the Pips created twenty-two number-one rock hits and forty-eight number-one rhythm and blues hits by 1970. At Motown's peak in 1966, 75 percent of the company's releases made the charts, while the industry average was 10 percent. Drawn by the movie industry, Motown relocated to Los Angeles in 1972, and its creative spark gradually dimmed. But it remains one of the nation's largest African American–owned businesses. And the memories of its glory days keep a steady stream of tourists wandering through the Motown Museum, housed in the original Hitsville, U.S.A., headquarters on Detroit's West Grand Boulevard.

RADIO AND TELEVISION TRAILBLAZERS

Nearly forty years before the birth of Motown, on 20 August 1920, the *Detroit News* inaugurated WWJ, the nation's first commercial radio station. Set up in a corner of the newspaper's sports department, WWJ's original twenty-watt transmitter broadcast over a range of just 100

MediaOne provides cable services to many Michigan communities and digital television service in a growing number of areas. © Dwight Cendrowski

MediaOne
2505 SOUTH INDUSTRIAL DRIVE

Carmen Harlan, WDIV Channel 4 news anchorwoman, is a respected reporter in the Detroit community. © Dennis Cox/ D. E. Cox Photo Library

miles to about three hundred set owners who listened in on the political primary results that made up the first program. Within a week, however, programming expanded to cover campaign news, foreign affairs, and baseball scores. Detroit remained a national leader in the new medium. In 1922 WWJ and the Detroit Symphony Orchestra broadcast the first complete symphony concert presented on radio. When WXYZ began broadcasting in 1930, it pioneered a new market niche with radio dramas. The owners were partial to westerns, so they tossed around ideas for a program about a hero of the

Wild West, a sort of lone operator, maybe even a former Texas Ranger. Thus the Lone Ranger was born. From 1932 until 1954 the masked man and his noble steed, Silver, rode out on their western adventures broadcast live from a studio in Detroit. WXYZ soon added *The Green Hornet* and *Sergeant Preston of the Yukon* to its offerings, putting Detroit in the forefront of radio entertainment.

The *Detroit News* also gets the credit for introducing television to Michigan. The state's first station, WWJ-TV, another *News* affiliate, began operation on 4 March 1947. WWJ, now NBC-affiliate WDIV, racked up an impressive number of television firsts: the first telecast stage show, the first televised bowling match, and the first complete university extension courses by television. In 1951 the station was responsible for the first international television broadcast, live coverage of a reception given across the river in Windsor for then Princess Elizabeth of Great Britain.

Today Michigan is home to more than three hundred commercial radio and television stations as well as public radio, television, and cable, placing it among the top ten broadcast states. For advertisers Detroit is the seventh-largest media market in the country. Michigan continues to serve as a news and information hub. The CNN bureau responsible for covering much of the Midwest and Canada is located in Detroit.

A highly skilled telephone technician uses a remote-control device and a TV monitor to adjust a long-distance switch. © HMS Images

AT THE CENTER OF IT ALL

With the latest in telecommunications technology, a vigorous publishing industry, and a history of broadcasting leadership, Michigan is dialed in to continued eminence in information transmission.

LEFT: *Workers construct a telecommunications tower, a functioning symbol of our interconnectedness. © Andrew Sacks.* BELOW: *A technician inspects fiber-optic cable in the glow of a computer circuit board. © HMS Images*

Fiber-optic cable bundles are used to transmit telephone signals. © *HMS Images*

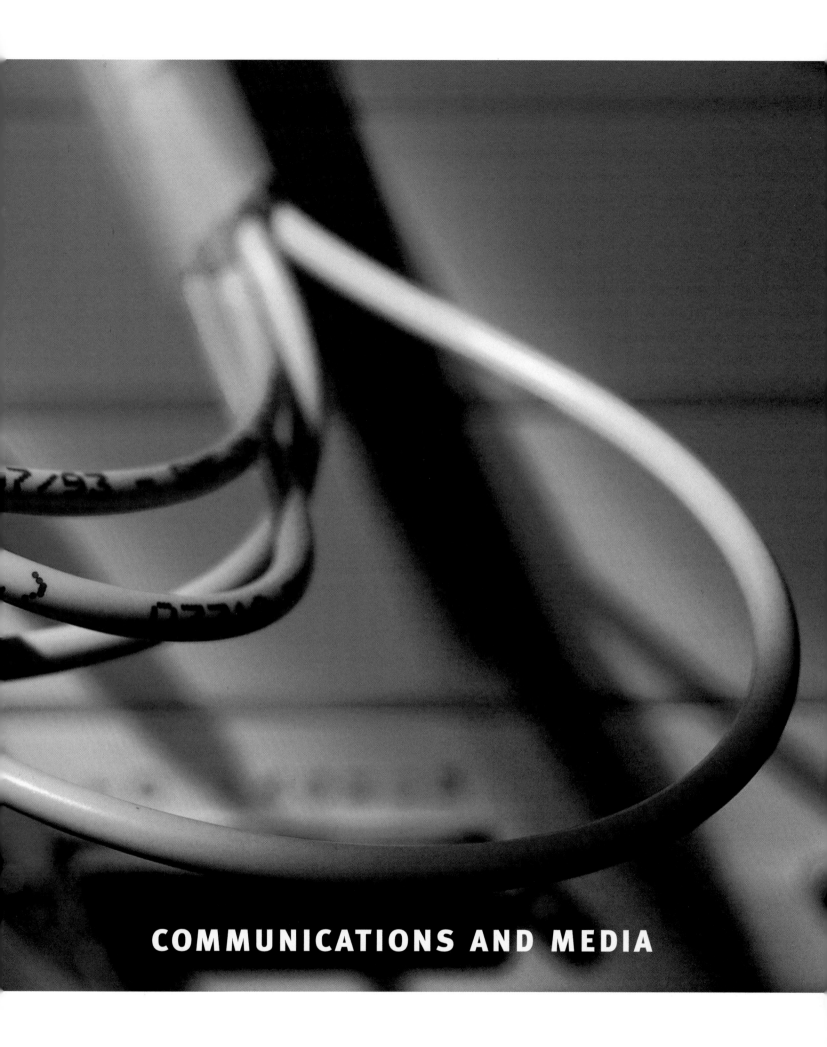

COMMUNICATIONS AND MEDIA

THE OAKLAND PRESS

LEFT: *A nineteenth-century photograph shows the offices of the* Pontiac and Oakland Gazette, *launched in 1844, which became* The Oakland Press.

ABOVE: *The building that houses* The Oakland Press *today dates back to 1914.*

For more than 150 years, *The Oakland Press* has not only recorded history but also has helped make history itself in Oakland County, Michigan.

Since its inception, it has raised Cain through its political commentaries and rallied for such civic improvements as the Pontiac Silverdome through its editorials. It has enlightened and entertained readers through its features. And it has investigated wrongdoing by politicians and others who placed themselves above the law.

But most of all, *The Oakland Press* has kept the citizens of Oakland County informed about the day's events, from the goings-on within the county's schools, police departments, and courts to the halls of Congress to the seats of government abroad.

Today *The Oakland Press* serves more than 80,000 subscribers in the suburbs north of Detroit on Monday through Saturday and more than 100,000 on Sunday. In addition to its regular news, business, features, and sports sections, it offers a host of special news and advertising sections with targeted appeal for its readers, such as an annual auto show section; a senior living section; and a special boat, sport, and fishing section, along with golf.

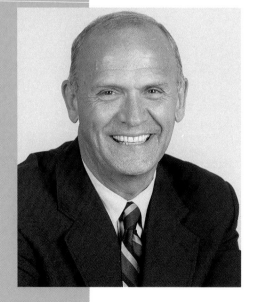

Frank Shepherd is president and CEO of 21st Century Newspapers, which includes The Oakland Press.

The roots of *The Oakland Press* reach deep into Pontiac and Oakland County's past.

The newspaper traces its origins to 1844, when businessman J. Dowd Coleman combined his publishing, editing, and printing skills and founded the *Pontiac and Oakland Gazette*, a weekly newspaper that catered to the Whig Party, and later the upstart Republican Party. In 1860 the *Gazette* endorsed Abraham Lincoln for president.

More than a half-century later, in 1900, the *Pontiac and Oakland Gazette* merged with a weekly newspaper founded in 1868 by William P. Nesbitt, the *Pontiac Bill Poster*, which catered to the Democratic Party. The two newspapers were political opposites, nonetheless, their marriage, which created the *Pontiac Evening Press*, proved to be a success. As a result, Oakland County had its first daily newspaper, the forerunner of today's *Oakland Press*. Over the next fourteen years the *Pontiac Press* established a firm foothold in Oakland County under the able leadership of Harry Coleman, a University of Michigan alumnus who devoted his entire life to journalism.

In 1914 members of the Fitzgerald family, who had made their mark in the newspaper business in Flint, Michigan, acquired the *Evening Press*, and for the next fifty-five years the family shaped the newspaper into the successful and highly acclaimed journalistic enterprise that it is today.

Between 1914 and 1969, the pages of Pontiac's newspaper were overseen by three generations of Fitzgeralds. Under their watch, Pontiac grew from a town without much of an identity to an industrial Mecca, and automobiles bearing the town's name cruised the nation's highways.

The Fitzgerald reign began with Howard Fitzgerald and his brother, Harry, who, along with George Gardner, a seasoned newspaperman, bought the *Pontiac Press* in 1914 for $140,000. Next came Howard's son, Harold A. Fitzgerald, who not only became the newspaper's most prominent editor and publisher but also one of Pontiac's all-time major power brokers. And finally, in 1966 Harold's son, Howard Fitzgerald II, took over. Three years later the family sold the *Evening Press* to Capital Cities Broadcasting for $16 million.

Robert Hively, at right, is publisher of The Oakland Press, *and Roger John, at left, is its facilities and packaging manager.*

Under the ownership of Capital Cities, in 1972, *The Oakland Press* assumed its current name, to reflect the broadening base of the newspaper's subscribers.

Ownership of the newspaper again changed hands in 1996 when Capital Cities/ABC was acquired by the Walt Disney Company. Disney, in turn, sold *The Oakland Press* in 1997 to the newspaper's current owners, 21st Century Newspapers Inc., an investment group formed by publishing industry veteran Frank H. Shepherd.

Throughout the ownership changes in recent years, *The Oakland Press* has remained steadfast to the journalistic principles established for it by men like Harry Coleman and Harold A. Fitzgerald—"to report the news, especially local news, without color or bias and to avoid playing favorites or selecting enemies to punish."

The Michigan Press Association presented its "Newspaper of the Year" award to the editorial staff of The Oakland Press *five times during the 1990s.*

GOOD TIMES, GREAT BUSINESS

CHAPTER NINETEEN

WITH MORE THAN $8.5 BILLION SPENT ON TRAVEL IN MICHIGAN EACH YEAR—THAT'S ONE MILLION DOLLARS EVERY HOUR OF EVERY DAY—FUN IN THE GREAT LAKES STATE IS BIG BUSINESS. IN NORTHERN MICHIGAN IN PARTICULAR, WHERE THREE-QUARTERS OF THE WORKFORCE IS EMPLOYED IN TOURIST-RELATED JOBS, TOURISM IS A MAINSTAY OF THE ECONOMY. ABOUT THIRTY-EIGHT MILLION DOMESTIC VISITORS AND TWO MILLION

international visitors come to Michigan each year. For visitors and residents alike there is plenty to see and do when the object is having fun.

Michigan's 3,200-mile shoreline is the longest of any state except Alaska—longer than the entire Atlantic seaboard of the United States. About one-quarter of Michigan's shoreline is open to the public as beaches or other access sites. It's no wonder that this is the number-one boating state, with nearly one million registered pleasure boats. Along with sailing and cruising there is sea kayaking on Lake Superior, parasailing on Grand Traverse Bay, and scuba diving to explore shipwrecks at nearly a dozen underwater preserves.

THE TOP TEN

According to Travel Michigan, the state tourism agency, the following are the ten most-visited of Michigan's many attractions:

- Frankenmuth: Michigan's "Little Bavaria" has German food, microbreweries, and the world's largest Christmas store.
- Sleeping Bear Dunes National Lakeshore: Thirty miles of spectacular Lake Michigan shoreline offer camping, hiking, and water sports.
- Henry Ford Museum & Greenfield Village: The world's largest indoor-outdoor museum complex has more than eighty historic homes, workplaces, and buildings.
- Motown Historical Museum: The original "Hitsville, U.S.A.," features a preserved recording studio and Motown memorabilia.
- Tahquamenon Falls State Park: In terms of waterfalls, only Niagara is larger east of the Mississippi.
- Pictured Rocks National Lakeshore: Multicolored sandstone cliffs, waterfalls, sand dunes, beaches, inland lakes, and the forest of the Lake Superior shoreline make up the nation's first national lakeshore.

OPPOSITE: *Sleeping Bear Dunes National Lakeshore, with its glorious sunsets and its bluffs rising as high as 480 feet, is one of Michigan's top-ten tourist destinations. People come from all over Michigan and the United States to fish, canoe, hike, cross-country ski, or just sit and stare at the clouds blanketing Lake Michigan. © Andre Jenny/International Stock.* ABOVE: *This chubby fellow has plenty to smile about. The Elias Brothers' Big Boy System has restaurants around the world and is still growing. © Dwight Cendrowski*

Lake of the Clouds in Porcupine Mountains State Park looks like a piece of fallen sky. © Ron Goulet/Dembinsky Photo Associates

- Michigan International Speedway: This two-mile super speedway hosts NASCAR, Indy Car, ARCA, ASA, and IROC races.
- Mackinac Island: No cars are allowed on this picturesque summer resort island steeped in history.
- Mackinac Historic Park: Three settlements have been restored and preserved to showcase two centuries of Michigan history.
- Soo Locks: Some of the world's busiest locks raise and lower freighters twenty-one feet to link the Great Lakes with the oceans of the world.

AND THERE'S MORE

But the state offers many other unique attractions whose appeal cannot be measured in numbers. Visitors to Michigan can stalk elk in the Lower Peninsula and moose in the U.P., view the world's largest Saran Wrap bubble, pan for gold, get their face on a corn flakes box, tour an open-pit iron mine, discover where magic is made, tour America's only Ice Museum, or watch the nightly show at the second-largest bat cave in North America.

Those seeking a place to stay in Michigan find not only the largest number of prepared campsites in any state, but also a hotel industry that offers visitors a broad range of accommodations, from lighthouse bed-and-breakfasts to world-class luxury resorts. Probably the state's most famous inn is the historic Grand Hotel on Mackinac Island. Upon its completion in 1887, the Grand Hotel ranked as the world's largest summer hotel and the world's largest pine building, boasting the world's longest porch—records that remain unchallenged to this day.

Michigan's busy hotel and convention industry is

Passengers of the tall ship Malabar *enjoy a cruise on Grand Traverse Bay's pristine waters. © Ross Frid*

switching into hypergear with the planned construction of three Detroit casino-hotels by gaming giants such as MGM Grand and Circus Circus. These casinos will join the twenty others located around the state, which are operated by various Native American tribes. Mount Pleasant's Soaring Eagle Casino and Resort is currently the largest casino between Las Vegas and Atlantic City, the second-biggest Indian casino in the world after Foxwood's Casino in Connecticut. The addition of the Detroit casinos will place Michigan among the top five gaming states.

FOOD, GLORIOUS FOOD

Restaurants are another popular form of recreation in Michigan. Gourmets across the nation recognize the names of renowned local chefs such as Jimmy Schmidt and restaurants such as The Lark in West Bloomfield and Tapawingo in tiny Ellsworth, which consistently make it onto every list of the top restaurants in the country. But while Michigan ranks high in the fine-dining category, it is family dining that gave the state's restaurant industry national prominence. In 1952 Detroit's Elias family opened the first Big Boy franchise in Michigan. Within just a few years they were among the largest franchisees in the country, and, in 1987, Elias Brothers became the exclusive worldwide franchiser for the International Big Boy System. Headquartered in Warren, Elias Brothers Corporation and its young mascot sporting the red-and-white checked overalls preside over seven hundred restaurants worldwide.

One hot day in 1875 a clerk at Fred Sander's Detroit dairy bar ran out of the sweet cream used to make sodas. Quick thinking prompted him to substitute ice cream.

The ice cream soda was born and immediately became a Sanders phenomenon. Another Michigan chain took Sanders's idea and added its own twist—root beer. Root beer floats became a staple at A&W Restaurants, along with another Michigan specialty—Coney Island (chili) hotdogs, all served by roller-skating carhops. Today only the carhops are gone. The Farmington Hills–based chain, founded in 1919, has nearly one thousand restaurants in forty-six states and fifteen countries.

Forget Italy: Michigan is quickly becoming the pizza capital of the world. Home base for the world's number-two and number-three pizza makers—Domino's and Little Caesar— in 1998 the state also became the new headquarters for one of the largest

This A&W employee proudly proffers a classic meal: a Coney, fries, and root beer. © Dwight Cendrowski

WATER MUSIC

GRAND HAVEN IS THE HOME OF THE WORLD'S LARGEST MUSICAL FOUNTAIN, FEATURING 2,600 SPRAY NOZZLES PUMPING 40,000 GALLONS OF WATER UP TO 125 FEET IN THE AIR. THE ACCOMPANYING HALF-HOUR RECORDED CONCERT OF POP FAVORITES (HYMNS ON SUNDAY) CHANGES EACH NIGHT, BROADCAST OVER A 12,000-WATT STEREO SYSTEM, ONE OF THE WORLD'S LARGEST PERMANENTLY INSTALLED SOUND SYSTEMS.

companies. Michigan resident Jeff Daniels uses his Hollywood expertise and his Purple Rose Theater in Chelsea to encourage new actors and playwrights. Michigan also has some of the most advanced movie theaters in the country, many owned by Loeks Star Partners of Grand Rapids. The Loekses, a husband and wife team, create megaplex theaters nationally recognized for unique design and sophisticated technology, such as stadium seating, state-of-the-art sound systems, and reclining chairs. They designed two of the world's most attended theater complexes, Michigan's Star Southfield and Sony Theatre Lincoln Square in New York. The Southfield complex features original costumes from favorite Hollywood movies and replicas of famous Detroit buildings.

Palace Sports and Entertainment is one of the state's largest entertainment conglomerates. It operates Pine Knob Music Theatre, the nation's largest outdoor amphitheater when it opened in 1972; Meadow Brook Music Festival, summer home of the Detroit Symphony Orchestra; and the Palace of Auburn Hills. When it opened in 1988, the Palace was named "best new venue," and was chosen "arena of the year" six out of the following nine years by *Pollstar* and *Performance* magazines. While the Palace is a national favorite for musical performers and audiences, it is also one of the nation's highest-rated sports arenas, home to Detroit Pistons basketball, Detroit Safari soccer, Detroit Vipers hockey, and the new WNBA Detroit Shock.

Not far away, the Pontiac Silverdome has been home to the Detroit Lions since 1975. Also considered one of

franchisers of number-one Pizza Hut. Ann Arbor–based Domino's sells nearly $3 billion in pizzas each year from six thousand stores in sixty countries. Founder Thomas Monaghan created the company in 1960 and is credited with such pizza business innovations as dough trays, the corrugated pizza box, and insulated pizza transport bags. With more than four thousand stores around the world, Little Caesar is right behind Domino's in the race for global pizza domination. Chairman Michael Ilitch didn't stop after making his fortune from pizza. He has gone on to become Michigan's major sports and entertainment mogul as owner of Detroit's Tigers and Red Wings and the Fox Theatre.

Speaking of Entertainment...

The Fox, which opened in 1928, remains the largest movie house in existence, with 5,041 seats. Now primarily used for live theater, it regularly leads the list of the nation's top-grossing venues. The Fox is just one of a dozen Detroit theaters, auditoriums, and concert halls making up the largest theater district in North America outside New York City. The performing arts thrive outside Detroit as well. Cities and campuses across the state draw big-name performers and support local theater

LIVE AND WIRED

THE CALUMET THEATRE OPENED IN 1900 AS THE FIRST MUNICIPALLY OWNED THEATER IN AMERICA. DURING THE COPPER BOOM THE 1,200-SEAT FACILITY (WITH UP-TO-THE-MINUTE ELECTRIC LIGHTING, STEAM HEATING, AND INDOOR LAVATORIES) RIVALED STAGES OF NEW YORK AND SAN FRANCISCO FOR LUXURY AND BIG-NAME ENTERTAINMENT.

Ann Arbor's three concurrent art fairs attract more than 1,000 exhibitors and turn the downtown area into a pedestrian mall for several days each July. © Dennis Cox/D. E. Cox Photo Library

Brewers 14 to 13 on 25 April 1901. The new stadiums are part of a downtown revitalization initiative spearheaded by Tigers and Red Wings owner Michael Ilitch, who recognized that sports both promote civic pride and are good business. Tickets to see the Stanley Cup champion Red Wings are always sold out, making it easier (theoretically) to get a seat on the Space Shuttle than in Joe Louis Arena to watch the Red Wings pass a puck.

Michigan's sports business is not limited to arenas. The Great Lakes State leads the nation in the number of public golf courses (more than 750) and in the annual number of new courses opening and under construction (about 30 per year). Michigan's forty ski resorts make it one of the nation's leading ski states. Michigan leads the nation in the number of registered snowmobiles, and enthusiasts can travel the length and breadth of the state on more than 4,000 miles of snowmobile trails.

THE MICHIGAN MARKETPLACE

Around here, shopping is considered an indoor sport. In many ways, Michigan invented the game. The Greeks had their agora and the Romans had their Forum, but the modern shopping mall is a concept that originated in Michigan. Northland, the nation's first regional shopping mall, opened in the Detroit suburb of Southfield in 1954. Five years later, Kalamazoo became the first

the nation's finest sports facilities, the Silverdome has the second-largest seating capacity of all National Football League stadiums. In 1982 it hosted the first Super Bowl to be played in a northern city and, in 1994, was the first indoor venue for the World Cup soccer tournament. Credited by the *Guinness Book of World Records* as having the largest air-supported roof in the world, the Silverdome's future is yet to be determined after the Lions depart for their new downtown stadium around the turn of the millennium. The new Lions stadium will be adjacent to another new stadium, one that will replace historic Tiger Stadium, a Detroit landmark since 1900. Originally called Bennett Park, then Briggs Stadium, it was the scene of the first American Baseball League game ever played, when the Tigers rallied for ten runs in the bottom of the ninth to beat the Milwaukee

Great Lakes Crossing Mall in Auburn Hills is one of many fine shopping centers scattered throughout the state. © Dwight Cendrowski

OPPOSITE: *The Presque Isle River tumbles through Porcupine Mountains State Park. © Bob Firth/Firth Photobank.* ABOVE: *Dawn brings a fiery glow to Squaw Bay. © Rod Planck/Tony Stone Images*

community in the country to close off city streets in its shopping district and turn them into a permanent pedestrian mall. With twenty-six properties scattered across the United States, the Bloomfield Hills–based Taubman Company is the nation's preeminent developer and manager of giant regional shopping malls. A. Alfred Taubman founded the company in 1950 and continues to serve as its chairman, chief executive officer, and director. In 1993 Taubman also assumed leadership of Sotheby's, the world-famous art auction house. Taubman is a major philanthropist supporting a myriad of arts, education, medical research, and Jewish causes. He is the principal benefactor of the Taubman Center for Public Policy and American Institutions at Brown University and the Taubman Medical Library at the University of Michigan.

The state also has supplied the nation with a number of famous individual retailers. Niles native Montgomery Ward began his career clerking in a general store in Saint Joseph. Sebastian S. Kresge opened his first eponymous store in downtown Detroit in 1899. In 1976 the S. S. Kresge company changed its name to Kmart Corporation. The Troy-based company is one of the

world's largest mass-merchandise retailers, with about two thousand stores in all fifty states as well as Puerto Rico, Guam, and the Virgin Islands. One of Kmart's major competitors is Meijer. The Grand Rapids company was founded in 1934 when Hendrik Meijer couldn't rent out the space adjoining his barber shop, so wound up buying $338 of merchandise and opening a grocery store. In the 1960s Meijer pioneered the notion of combining groceries and general merchandise under one huge roof. Today, with stores in five states, Meijer is the fifth-largest discount retailer in the country. Among the nation's specialty retailers, Borders Group, Inc., is a standout. Over the course of twenty-five years the Ann Arbor–based chain grew from being that university town's favorite bookstore into the nation's second-largest retailer of books, music, videos, and other informational products.

BUSINESS IS BOOMING

Michigan's tourism and leisure sector is among the most vibrant in the nation, and chambers of commerce across the state predict even more growth. Next on the horizon: reintroducing the cruise ship industry to the Great Lakes. The state tourism office has inaugurated a new organization called Cruise Michigan to promote Michigan ports as vacation destinations for cruise tourists. The market for Michigan's own brand of fun is just about limitless.

South Haven's South Pier Lighthouse glitters at night. © Terry Donnelly

HOSPITALITY, TOURISM, AND RETAIL

BORDERS GROUP, INC.

Borders began in 1971 when Tom and Louis Borders opened a bookshop in the heart of Ann Arbor, an academic community in southeast Michigan. As business grew, the first Borders store became known as one of the finest bookshops in the world—a place where customers could rely on a friendly, well-informed staff to find the book they were looking for, or browse uninterrupted for hours through shelves stocked with books about everything from Africa to Zoroaster.

The Ann Arbor shop was so successful that the Borders brothers decided to open more stores. They felt that there was a need for bookstores for so-called serious readers in communities across the United States. After opening a few stores in suburban markets, they found that serious readers were everywhere. Borders became an instant hit. In the early 1990s the company began selling music recordings in addition to books. As the company and its inventory expanded, competitors and investors took notice, and the Borders brothers decided to expand nationally. Today Borders is one of the nation's leading book and music retailers.

"The original Borders store was an institution," says Borders chairman Robert F. DiRomualdo. "People would visit from hundreds of miles around to shop there; that's how great an appeal it had. We've been able to adapt that concept nationwide, and now we're expanding internationally."

Borders bookstores, such as the Birmingham, Michigan, store above, offer a relaxing atmosphere in which customers are encouraged to browse at their leisure.

Now a publicly owned independent corporation, Borders Group, Inc., is the world's second-largest retailer of books, music, videos, and other informational, educational, and entertainment products. The Borders Group includes Borders, Inc., which owns and operates more than 250 superstores nationwide, offering what is widely regarded as one of the broadest selections of books and multimedia titles anywhere. It also is the parent company of Borders.com (Web site: www.borders.com), an electronic commerce site with 10 million books, music, and video items ready to ship immediately. Through Borders (UK) Limited, Borders Group, Inc., also operates twenty-six Books etc. and three Borders stores in the United Kingdom. In addition, Borders Group, Inc., owns Walden Book Company, Inc., the nation's leading mall book retailer with approximately 900 Waldenbooks stores in malls,

The original Borders Book Shop, on State Street in Ann Arbor, Michigan, is shown here circa 1971.

BORDERS®

BOOKS, MUSIC, VIDEO, AND A CAFE.

www.borders.com

shopping centers, and airports across the United States. Together, these companies operate in more than 1,100 locations in the United States, Singapore, the United Kingdom, and Australia. The company still retains its strong local roots in Ann Arbor, with its corporate headquarters, a Borders Books and Music store on Liberty Street, a Waldenbooks store, and a second Borders Books and Music location, which opened in spring 1999.

Borders has excelled at making the shopping experience a pleasure. Borders superstores feature a vast inventory of books, music, and videos and host in-store appearances by authors, musicians, and artists. A Borders superstore averages 27,500 square feet, and carries about 200,000 book, music, video, and periodical titles. Most Borders stores also offer a Borders Cafe Espresso℠. Borders music departments carry a broad assortment of music, including blues, jazz, classical, world beat, New Age, and stage production and movie soundtracks.

"Our employees make a tremendous contribution to our success," DiRomualdo says. "We rely on full-time book and music sellers. At any point of customer-service contact, people are dealing with someone who knows what they're talking about, who loves books and music."

Every Borders store has its own distinct character and makes outreach efforts to gain strong roots in the community. A sophisticated inventory system and expert buyers allow books to be stocked to reflect local tastes.

"We have competition across the board, from competing bookstores to other types of retailers that offer books, on-line Internet businesses, or music and book clubs," says DiRomualdo.

The second Birmingham, Michigan, Borders Books • Music • Cafe, above, opened in September 1997.

"As we have from the very beginning, each store has a community relations coordinator. What differentiates us over time is the assortment we provide. The books we offer in each store are custom-picked for the community. We have developed an in-house inventory management system that uses artificial-intelligence technology that allows us a clear picture of consumer demand in each location. A store in Alaska may get Russian language books or pilot books. A store in New England gets more ice hockey books in September than in March. Many factors are measured, which allows us to offer a more focused, community-based assortment. We are international in scope, but locally oriented in response to our customers."

International expansion and on-line Internet services, the newest ventures of Borders, are the basis of its strategy for future growth.

"Our business is becoming increasingly complex as a result of international expansion and Internet selling," says Philip M. Pfeffer, chief executive officer. "As we approach the twenty-first century, we are looking forward to the challenge of building on the success that the company has achieved and continuing it well into the future."

Most Borders superstores include a Borders Cafe Espresso℠.

KMART CORPORATION

When Sebastian Spering Kresge opened a modest five-and-ten-cent store in downtown Detroit in 1899, little did anyone realize that his fledgling enterprise would one day blossom into a retail giant of more than 2,000 discount retailing centers extending halfway around the globe.

But blossom Kmart did, into one of Michigan's and the world's major corporations.

By 1912, a little more than a decade following the opening of the first store, S. S. Kresge expanded his operation to eighty-five stores with annual sales of more than $10 million. By 1966, less than seven decades later, the company he founded grew to 753 Kresge stores and 162 Kmart discount department stores, with sales topping the $1 billion mark. And by 1981 the Troy, Michigan–based firm opened its 2,000th store.

Today Kmart Corporation, which changed its name from

Big Kmart stores make shopping easier through a better and brighter layout and the added convenience of the Pantry, where they can stock up on everyday basics and consumables.

Kmart's Web site at www.Kmart.com offers on-line Internet shopping with a product assortment that ranges from music to nutritional supplements to Kmart Cash Cards.

the S. S. Kresge Company in 1977, has 2,160 Kmart, Big Kmart, and Super Kmart stores, with locations in all fifty states, Puerto Rico, Guam, and the United States Virgin Islands.

Since the arrival in 1995 of its current president, chairman, and chief executive, Floyd Hall, Kmart also has taken steps to ensure continued growth and success. Under Hall's leadership, the company embarked on a successful major reorganization, which, in turn, led to a three-year, $3.7 billion bank financing of the firm and a $1 billion convertible preferred-stock offering to the public that was completed in June 1996.

Along with its phenomenal growth, Kmart Corporation has, since its founding, made a habit of being a model for the retailing industry.

In the mid-1930s it pioneered the concept of having a major retail establishment anchor a suburban shopping mall when it opened a store in the nation's first suburban shopping center—Country Club Plaza in Kansas City, Missouri. In 1962 it took the concept of self-service shopping to a new level with the opening of its first Kmart discount department store in Garden City, Michigan. In 1976 it became the first-ever retailer to launch seventeen million square feet of sales space in a single year, with the opening of a record number of 271 Kmart stores.

In 1991 Kmart took self-service retail shopping to an even higher level with the opening in Medina, Ohio, of the first of its 102 Super Kmart stores. The stores offer groceries in addition to general merchandise twenty-four hours a day, seven days a week.

More recently, the company has become a retailing pioneer on the Internet. In 1995 it established a general information Web site (www.Kmart.com), and in 1998 it added a secure on-line shopping network that provides an array of virtual shops, offering Internet shoppers such items as National Football League novelties, household products, music recordings, and gifts for all occasions.

Other recent Kmart innovations include a Kmart Cash Card, an electronic-swipe card that replaced paper gift certificates in 1997; and Kmart Solutions, an electronic shopping service in select stores that provides customers with touch-screen access to a wide range of products and services such as floral delivery and money orders.

During its storied history, Kmart briefly entered the specialty retailing market, acquiring in 1984 one of the nation's largest bookstore chains, Walden Book Company, Inc., and the home improvement retail chain Builders Square, Inc. In 1990 Kmart purchased the sporting goods specialty retailer Sports Authority. And in 1991 it acquired 90 percent of the discount office-supply retail chain OfficeMax. These specialty retail firms were sold in the late 1990s as the company focused on its core businesses.

Kmart also briefly entered the retail market in the Czech Republic and Slovakia and formed joint ventures in Mexico and

The Kmart Kids Race Against Drugs combines the excitement and fun of racing with the opportunity to educate young people about the dangers of drug abuse.

Singapore before selling its overseas and Mexican and Canadian operations in the late 1990s.

Despite its growth, Kmart has adhered strictly to the mission that S. S. Kresge set forth for his company more than a century ago: to be the discount store of choice for middle-income families with children by satisfying their routine and seasonal shopping needs as well as or better than the competition.

Kmart employees, who today number more than 265,000 associates, also faithfully have adhered to Kresge's pledge of putting customers first, "every day and in every way," including matching competitors' prices to ensure that the company will always remain a United States price leader and striving to give shoppers ease in securing refunds and exchanges.

Moreover, the company and its employees continue to follow Kresge's example when it comes to philanthropy and community service to help children and families. Each year they donate millions to charitable causes. Since 1996 Kmart also has taken an active role in the fight against youth drug abuse through the Kmart Family Foundation.

Were he alive today, S. S. Kresge would unquestionably be pleased with what he started.

Open twenty-four hours a day, seven days a week, Super Kmart stores offer the ultimate shopping experience, combining a full assortment of fresh groceries with a broad selection of general merchandise.

THE MICHIGAN CHAMBER OF COMMERCE

The Michigan Chamber of Commerce was established in 1959 to represent employer interests by working to promote conditions favorable to economic development in the state. Located a few blocks from the state capitol in Lansing, the chamber represents small businesses as well as some of the largest companies in the world. About 7,000 businesses, local chambers of commerce, and trade and professional associations are members of the chamber.

Harry R. Hall was the president of the Michigan Chamber of Commerce from its inception until 1976, when James Barrett took over as president and CEO. Thirty-two years old at the time, Barrett became the youngest president of any state chamber in the nation. He still leads the chamber and has developed it into one of the most powerful and respected business organizations in Michigan.

One of the main reasons the Michigan chamber was created by employers was to provide the business community with a voice in public forums. Over the years the Michigan chamber's Government Relations and Political Affairs programs have grown into an effective team effort in support of job creation and economic development.

In 1978 Michigan Chamber Services was formed as a subsidiary of the chamber to serve as an educational resource for executives from companies of all types and sizes. Chamber Services keeps the business community current

The Michigan Chamber of Commerce clock tower, shown here in an artist's rendering, looks out over some of Michigan's most prominent companies and organizations.

Michigan Chamber of Commerce

on such important issues as changing labor laws, environmental and safety regulations, taxes, and technological development. Chamber Services publishes books and posters, sponsors dozens of seminars and conferences each year, and provides a Web site with continually updated information for subscribers. Chamber Services also has developed a consulting group to provide employee benefit programs for small- to medium-size businesses around the state.

The Michigan Chamber Foundation is another subsidiary of the chamber, formed in 1985 to support special programs of interest to businesses across the state. Among these programs is Leadership Michigan, a nonprofit leadership program. In 1992 Michigan Business Leaders for Education Excellence (MBLEE) was created in association with the foundation to act as a catalyst for systemic education reform for kindergarten through twelfth grade, with a focus on high levels of achievement. In 1995 the foundation began the statewide Drugs Don't Work program to assist businesses in establishing a drug-free workplace.

With members of every size and type in all eighty-three Michigan counties, the Michigan Chamber of Commerce represents a broad cross-section of the state's economy. As it prepares to enter the twenty-first century, the chamber continues its advocacy and educational efforts to ensure Michigan's prosperity in the increasingly global marketplace.

Michigan's world-class meeting and convention facility, Cobo Conference/Exhibition Center is the centerpiece of downtown Detroit's Civic Center. Located at the foot of Washington Boulevard, alongside the Detroit River, the center encompasses 2.4 million square feet and boasts one of the biggest contiguous floor spaces in North America. Nine elegant banquet rooms command spectacular views of the river, Ambassador Bridge, and the Windsor, Ontario, skyline.

Named Cobo Hall when it first opened its doors in 1960, the convention center was then the largest facility of its kind in the United States. The complex was rededicated in 1989 as Cobo Conference/Exhibition Center following a $225 million expansion that doubled its size. Today it offers 700,000 square feet of prime exhibit space. Cobo's flexible design allows the adjoining four halls on the main floor to form a total of 600,000 square feet of contiguous exhibit space, plus an additional 100,000 square feet on the lower level that is accessible via two sets of escalators. All five exhibit halls offer easy access to eighty meeting rooms that accommodate from 30 to 3,300 people.

The adjacent 12,191-seat Cobo Arena and the 20,525-seat Joe Louis Arena, home of the Detroit Red Wings hockey team, are also available for conventions. Linking the whole complex to hotels, restaurants, parking facilities and entertainment throughout the central business district is Detroit's 2.9-mile elevated railway, the People Mover.

"Cobo Center's physical capabilities are surpassed only by the unrivaled level of care and customer service that exhibitors find here," says Lou Pavledes,

Cobo Conference/Exhibition Center offers four exhibit halls with 600,000 contiguous square feet of exhibit space and an adjoining hall of 100,000 square feet.

Cobo Conference/Exhibition Center in downtown Detroit is one of the nation's premier trade show and conference facilities, with 2.4 million total square feet, including 700,000 square feet of prime exhibit space.

the center's director. "Management, staff, and suppliers are prepared to handle the unique demands of any event, from initial planning stages to its successful conclusion."

To promote the highest level of customer service, the center maintains a model labor-training program. In addition, special arrangements allow trades and service contractors to adapt their crews to better serve exhibitors' needs and to reduce labor costs. Center management also works in close cooperation with city, county, state, and federal agencies, the local business community, and the Metropolitan Detroit Convention and Visitors Bureau to ensure the success of events held at the facility. Everyone from exhibitors to conventioneers benefits from Cobo Center's experience in handling high-profile events such as visits by United States presidents and foreign heads of state, the International G-7 Jobs Summit, the annual North American International Auto Show, and Society of Automotive Engineers International Congress.

Along with a premier location, spacious facilities, and stunning views, it is proven commitment to service that makes Cobo Conference/Exhibition Center one of the most flexible and user-friendly convention centers in the nation.

TOWARD THE NEW MILLENNIUM

PART FOUR: REFLECTIONS

Leading figures in Michigan's economy—visionaries in their field—are perfectly positioned to reflect upon the expanding parameters of our world. In this section several of them take us along with them, through personal essays, on a journey back to the turning points in their sector— to those moments that changed the status quo forever. First reflecting on the course of events and what it meant for Michigan and the world, they then turn their attention to the future, giving us a unique perspective on what might lie ahead.

Each essayist recalls developments that changed our lives, brought a new reality to society. And each looks to the pioneers of the new century to carry the vision forward. Just as Ransom Olds, Henry Ford, and Billy Durant dreamed and sweated the American car industry into prominence at the turn of the century, so a new generation of globally minded leaders will transform the social and economic landscape of Michigan in the new millennium.

Our essayists agree that as the world moves inexorably toward instant access and communication, Michigan will maintain its lead in the global economy by keeping a finger on good judgment. Rather than fast-forwarding at an ever-accelerating pace, one key to success in the coming years will be the ability to step back, view the big picture, and assess what works and where the opportunities for improvement lie. As industry, government, and academia collaborate more and more, the results are bound to be a quality-oriented, competent, creative workforce . . . and the joy of new products and experiences we can only imagine.

The sun rising over Lake of the Clouds, in Porcupine Mountains Wilderness State Park, illuminates the lake's edge, offering just a hint of what is to come. A perfect time for reflection, the opening of a new day brings both new perspectives and new opportunities. © Bob Firth/Firth Photobank

FUELING PASSION THE WORLD OVER

KEITH CRAIN
Chairman, Crain Communications Inc

Keith Crain is chairman of Crain Communications, one of the country's largest trade, consumer, and business publishing companies. With his publishing and business expertise, Crain helped take the family-owned company from four titles in 1971 to thirty today. As publisher of *Automotive News* and *Crain's Detroit Business,* he uses his two weekly columns to address issues and support causes that concern Detroit and the automotive industry. An active participant in civic and business organizations, Crain serves as chairman of the board of the Center for Creative Studies and on the boards of directors of United Way Community Services, the Community Foundation for Southeastern Michigan, Boy Scouts of America, and many others.

Of all the places in the world, Detroit is the most passionate. How can this be? Well, Detroit is the place that fuels passion all over the globe: Detroit makes cars. The men and women who run the auto industry are a famously passionate breed who laugh at fifteen-hour days. They'll do whatever it takes to bring cars and trucks to the world.

But it's not just automotive executives who are passionate about Detroit's wares. Almost every American with a heartbeat has special feelings about this car or that truck. Perfect strangers ask how you like your new car. From the next lane, a driver gives you the thumbs-up, the ultimate seal of approval for the dramatic sculpture of that new sedan or sport-utility.

Pittsburgh has steel; New York has finance; and Silicon Valley has software. Important? Yes. Passionate? No. Those places hawk products; Detroit makes the car, the machine that transformed America and the world and that says more about its owner than any other material thing.

> **IMMIGRANT AUTO WORKERS, BORN WITHOUT PROSPECTS, PUT THEIR CHILDREN THROUGH MEDICAL SCHOOL**

THE GREATEST DEMOCRATIZER

It wasn't always thus. The Germans started making cars before the Americans. And Cleveland, Buffalo, Chicago, or Indianapolis might have become the center of American car making. But Michigan had bicycle makers, and metal benders for the furnace and stove industries. And most important, it had Ransom Olds and Henry Ford and Billy

Designers determine a seat's safety, comfort, and environmental impact.
© Jeff Corwin/Tony Stone Images

Durant, men of vision and relentless energy. The new manufacturing jobs in Michigan attracted people from all over, from Poland and Italy, Alabama and Kentucky. Michigan was the greatest democratizer the world has ever known. In Michigan, immigrant auto workers, born without prospects, put their children through medical school, a jump all but impossible anywhere else in the world.

Detroit so dominated this amazing industry that it became synonymous with the car. Even in World War II, when that genius at making things was funneled into defeating Hitler and Tojo, everyone knew what Detroit was. And when the war ended and a generation of men and women who had sacrificed some of the best years of their lives found themselves with good jobs and new houses, Detroit and Michigan leaped to the task of giving them the cars they hankered for, big dream machines for even the common man.

NEW SPIRIT, NEW GENERATIONS

Times and tastes changed, and that '59 Cadillac may have come to seem a piece of excess. Thirty years ago the environmental and safety movements drew new limitations and possibilities for the car. Just a few years ago, a shortage of gasoline redesigned the economy car and sent buyers by the millions to importers' showrooms.

NOW, JOINING NAMES LIKE DURYEA AND SLOAN, KNUDSEN AND CHRYSLER, THERE'S A NEW PANTHEON OF INTERNATIONAL DETROITERS

People who had never much liked the auto industry or Michigan gleefully wrote off Detroit. But a funny thing happened on Detroit's way to the dustbin of history. A new generation of globally minded automotive leaders injected new spirit into the auto industry and created whole new generations of cars and trucks that Americans wanted to buy. And, wonder of wonders, at the new millennium Detroit is still synonymous with world automotive leadership. Now, joining names like Duryea and Sloan, Knudsen and Chrysler, there's a new pantheon of international Detroiters with names like Lutz, Trotman, Petersen, and Smith.

And Detroit is still a place of passion. Drive to that great, rowdy car parade called the Woodward Dream Cruise, take a peek at the research and development center of a seat supplier, tour an engine plant. You'll see a glorious industry with a glorious past. And perhaps amazingly, as it starts a new millennium, it's in the midst of a golden age, with more decades to come.

A new generation of American cars, inspired by global-minded automotive leaders, takes shape on robotic welding lines such as this.
© Michael Rosenfeld/Tony Stone Images

READY FOR THE NEW MILLENNIUM

ARTHUR C. JOHNSON

President, Michigan Bankers Association
President and Chief Executive Officer, United Bank of Michigan

Fondly referred to as "the chief" by colleagues and staff at Grand Rapids–based United Bank, Art Johnson has provided the leadership that sparked his organization's transformation from a rural bank into one of Michigan's most experienced SBA lenders over the course of his twenty-five-year career at the bank. Johnson has long served as a spokesperson for the banking industry through his service with the Michigan Bankers Association and as an active member of the American Bankers Association Government Relations Council.

In 1806 the territorial authorities authorized the organization of Michigan's first bank. The second one was incorporated by the territorial Legislative Council in 1817, but it had to wait two years to open its doors until the stockholders finished paying in the initial $10,000 in gold as the bank's capital.

In the early days, however, most Michigan banks were private banks operated by an unincorporated proprietor or partnership. Often they were just a separate drawer in the safe of a local merchant. Incorporated national banks began to appear in Michigan during the Civil War, primarily to issue sound paper money. That is why the regulator of national banks is still known as the comptroller of the currency.

> **IN THE EARLY DAYS, MICHIGAN BANKS OFTEN WERE JUST A SEPARATE DRAWER IN THE SAFE OF A LOCAL MERCHANT**

PROGRESS BRINGS CHANGE

The first national banks were unable to offer many of the financial services required by economic development and population growth. To better satisfy these needs, Michigan voters created a Banking Department in 1888 to charter and supervise state banks. When the Banking Department began operating the following year, many national banks converted to state banks. All private banks were required to obtain charters from the department and submit to its supervision and regulation in order to continue doing business.

For the next forty years, development of the banking industry in Michigan closely paralleled the development of the industry in other states. Then the Great Depression wreaked havoc among Michigan's banks, just as it did in every state in the Union. A majority of the state's banks survived those troubled times, although virtually all of them found it necessary to recapitalize

Prior to traveling abroad, a business owner buys foreign currency at one of Michigan's many strong, progressive banks. © PhotoDisc

themselves. During the following thirty years, Michigan banks rebuilt their businesses on the three-legged stool of federal deposit insurance, strictly limited competition, and regulated interest rates. In time, a sound and progressive banking system regenerated itself in Michigan.

The modern era of banking in this state began with a revised banking code in 1969 and the Michigan Bank Holding Company Act of 1972. The new banking code replaced the old Banking Department with a Financial Institutions Bureau capable of supervising major institutions with national and international operations. The Bank Holding Company Act allowed individual banks to affiliate with each other under the same corporate ownership.

PERHAPS THE MOST INTERESTING DEVELOPMENT IS THE DRAMATIC SUCCESS OF NEW COMMUNITY BANKS IN THE STATE'S LARGEST MARKETS

Today the structure of Michigan's banking industry is much like a barbell. At one end there are a small number of very large interstate banking companies. Along the bar are a number of smaller holding companies and branch banks that operate in multiple markets across the state. At the other end are scores of independent community banks.

The largest corporations that need the services of the nation's largest banks will find them available at numerous Michigan banking offices of these large interstate banking companies.

The smaller multibank holding companies and branch banks that have most, if not all, of their operations in Michigan are now known as super community banks. They offer an array of both traditional services and innovative products in the state's smaller communities and compete aggressively with independent community banks.

Michigan's independent community banks are thriving. They have achieved sufficient size to attract able management and acquire the technology they and their customers require. Perhaps the most interesting development in the Michigan banking industry today is the dramatic success of new community banks in the state's largest markets: twenty-three have been chartered since 1995, mostly in metropolitan Detroit and the Greater Grand Rapids area.

These community banks have come to fill an important niche in the urban markets dominated by very large interstate banks. Many of the owners and managers of small and midsized corporations, as well as individual consumers, prefer the more personal service they provide and have no need for the sophisticated services of a large interstate institution. The success being enjoyed by these institutions explains why at least a dozen additional community banks are now being organized.

READY, WILLING, AND ABLE

As we move toward the beginning of the third millennium, Michiganians can be confident that strong and progressive banks will be ready, willing, and able to provide any financial services they might need or want. In fact, the high level of service that our state's citizens and business organizations have come to expect over nearly 200 years should only get better in the years ahead.

A customer prepares to use the ATM at one of Michigan's thriving community banks, each a blend of technology and service. © Corbis

STRENGTH THROUGH DIVERSITY

CURTIS J. TOMPKINS, PH.D.
President, Michigan Technological University

Dr. Curtis J. Tompkins became the eighth president of Michigan Technological University in 1991, after serving as dean of engineering at West Virginia University for eleven years. He is a fellow and past president of both the American Society for Engineering Education and the Institute of Industrial Engineers and a fellow of the Michigan Society of Professional Engineers. Tompkins earned B.S. and M.S. degrees at Virginia Tech and a Ph.D. from Georgia Tech. He is a member of the Council on Competitiveness and the Governor's Workforce Commission and sits on the boards of directors of Michigan Technologies, Inc., the Michigan Chamber of Commerce, and Oak Ridge Associated Universities.

Since higher education began here in 1817 with the founding of the University of Michigan, the state of Michigan has grown a rich mix of private and public institutions of higher education. Eight of its fifteen public universities were created prior to 1900, including the nation's first land-grant university, Michigan State University, in 1855; a national research university in a major urban setting, Wayne State University, in 1868; and the only public doctorate degree–granting technological university in the upper Midwest, Michigan Technological University, in 1885. Half of the thirty private baccalaureate degree–granting colleges in the state were created prior to 1900. Since the turn of the twentieth century, twenty-six community colleges, seven public universities, and fifteen private baccalaureate-granting colleges have been started in Michigan, along with dozens of other private institutions offering postsecondary education. One of the substantial strengths of our state is the impressive diversity in higher education, a diversity that has been appreciated and supported for more than a century by the citizens of Michigan.

Some of the world's best research has been conducted on the campuses of Michigan's research universities during the twentieth century. Faculty of the doctorate degree–granting universities have made significant breakthroughs in medicine, engineering, agriculture, and science.

> **THE USE OF THE INTERNET WILL FACILITATE COLLABORATIVE EFFORTS BETWEEN INDUSTRY AND ACADEMIA**

POWERFUL COLLABORATIONS

Michigan's colleges and universities used powerful information technology to transform education and research methods during the latter years of the twentieth century. The use of the Internet and telecommunications during the early twenty-first century will facilitate collaborative efforts between industry and academia to foster technology transfer and continuing professional development of engineers, technologists, and managers with particular emphasis on manufacturing, information technology, and biotechnology-related businesses.

Faculty members at one of Michigan's renowned research universities examine a computer logic board wafer in their efforts to achieve an engineering breakthrough. © Dwight Cendrowski

Globalization of the marketplace has affected higher education in Michigan in several ways. Top students from 130 countries other than our own choose to pursue undergraduate and graduate studies at Michigan universities and colleges. Increasing numbers of Americans enrolled in Michigan institutions—such as the 85 percent of the students at Kalamazoo College—include study abroad in their academic programs. Michigan's sister state in Japan, the Shiga prefecture, developed the Japan Center for Michigan Universities in 1988, and hundreds of Michigan students have studied there, learning the Japanese language and culture. Collaborative research and education programs with universities in other countries, particularly in Asia and Europe, are increasing.

Having strong autonomous colleges and universities has positioned the state of Michigan well for the twenty-first century. Governor John Engler created Michigan Technologies, Inc., to help guide the state's strategy to assure that higher education, industry, and government collaborate appropriately and that state resources are wisely invested in research and education. He also created the Michigan Virtual University in 1998, comprising all private and public colleges and universities in the state, to provide continuing education through the Internet for employees of Michigan corporations.

Future leaders of higher education in Michigan will be challenged by the acceleration of the growth of knowledge and information, especially in science and technology. More than 80 percent of the science and technology that will be known in the year 2025 is unknown at the turn of the century. Funding for information technology and scientific equipment and facilities on Michigan's campuses will increasingly need private support from individuals, foundations, and corporations. Collaboration among institutions will increase, especially on issues related to the environment, health, and global competitiveness. Michigan students increasingly will study abroad, and foreign students increasingly will study in Michigan.

MICHIGAN'S INVESTMENT IN HIGHER EDUCATION WILL PAY HANDSOME DIVIDENDS, FROM WORKFORCE CREATIVITY TO ENTREPRENEURIAL INITIATIVES

INNOVATION ESSENTIAL

A predominant theme emerging at the turn of the century in Michigan, perhaps reminiscent of the theme of 100 years ago, is that innovation and the capacity to innovate are essential to Michigan's position as a leader in the world economy. Graduates of Michigan's colleges and universities must be able to transform knowledge and ideas into new products, processes, and services with an emphasis on creativity and competence as well as competitive cost and productivity. Entrepreneurship must be fostered as part of the educational process.

Michigan's continuing investment in higher education will pay handsome dividends during the twenty-first century. The returns on that investment will include the creativity of the workforce; the entrepreneurial initiatives of leaders in technology and science; innovations in health care, advanced materials, hardware, electronics, communications and software; and graduates with global, futuristic perspectives.

The turn of the century is an exciting time of transformation in Michigan. One of the great benefits of living and working here is the rich array of opportunities for education and for collaboration with our colleges and universities. Higher education is an essential ingredient in the state's transformation.

One of the many top foreign students studying on Michigan campuses shares a proud day with his father. © Bill Lindhout

MANUFACTURING

THE ESSENCE OF TIME

Jack H. Miller
President and Chief Executive Officer, Howard Miller Company

Jack H. Miller is the second-generation owner of the Zeeland-based Howard Miller Company, the world's largest manufacturer of grandfather clocks and other fine furniture. A graduate of Hope College in Holland, Michigan, he began working for the company in 1954. Beginning in 1983, Miller led an effort to diversify Howard Miller Company through the acquisition of three complementary companies: Hekman Furniture, Woodmark, and Kieninger. Miller participates in numerous organizations such as Aquinas College, Pine Rest Christian Mental Health Services, the Grand Valley State University Foundation, Davenport College Foundation, and Rest Haven. He also serves as chairperson of the Michigan State Chamber of Commerce.

A recent study noted that "contrary to established thinking, it is not steel, labor, or technology that is the most important resource for the global automobile industry—it is time." The study, compiled by Deloitte & Touche Consulting Company and a University of North Carolina professor, pointed out that rapid product development, speed to market, and quick response to customers would make or break car makers and their suppliers over the long term.

As I pondered the study, it became increasingly apparent just how universal these statements are for all manufacturers today. As the millennium winds to a close, we are part of a manufacturing age that is taking the old phrase "Time is money" to new extremes. Customers expect more than ever before. They want to be fully involved, from product development to supply-chain management to distribution and logistics. And they expect results sooner rather than later.

In a way, this is nothing new. Customers have always had high expectations for quality, value, and delivery. They want to feel like the product they are buying was built specifically for them, whether it be a $30,000 car or a $5,000 grandfather clock. They want to believe we still make products one at a time, as if the era of craft production that marked the 1800s never ended. The difference today is that they want it now.

Perhaps that's why so many Michigan manufacturers are rediscovering their roots as product- and customer-driven companies and, in the process, leading the global change in manufacturing.

> # WE ARE PART OF A MANUFACTURING AGE THAT IS TAKING THE OLD PHRASE 'TIME IS MONEY' TO NEW EXTREMES

SHAPING THE BASIC IDEAS
Throughout this century, companies in Michigan's main manufacturing

A Michigan furniture maker approaches his work as creative art rather than a manufacturing process. Photo, courtesy Howard Miller

industries—the automotive and furniture businesses—have shaped our most fundamental ideas about how to manufacture products. From Henry Ford's 1908 Model T, which gave birth to mass production techniques, to the current work in the office furniture business, where new products are being designed by a customer and salesperson as they meet, Michigan's leading companies have always focused on finding a way to build it faster, better, and more productively.

The paths of Michigan's two top industries over the past century, of course, were vastly different. Beginning with Henry Ford's assembly line, the automakers focused their efforts on designing cars that could be built, driven,

SUCCESS IN THE NEW MILLENNIUM WILL GO TO THOSE WHO MANAGE TIME, AND THAT SOMETIMES MEANS TAKING A STEP BACK TO ASSESS WHAT WORKS

and repaired by almost anyone. Ford and others, notably General Motors' Alfred Sloan, created a revolution in mass manufacturing, earning the auto business plaudits like "the industry of industries," as management guru Peter Drucker dubbed it a half-century ago. Over the years, Detroit's Big Three car makers—General Motors, Ford, and Chrysler—poured billions of dollars into factory automation and even more into diversification outside the auto business.

The furniture business, on the other hand, remained steadfastly—some would say stubbornly—true to its workbench origins and the single focus of making furniture. In a period when the primary strategy of American industry was mass production and standardization, West Michigan's furniture makers focused on building very high quality items in lower volumes. Nearly 150 years after cabinetmaker Deacon Haldane first set up shop in Grand Rapids, many of the area's furniture companies still approach making furniture more as creative art than manufacturing process.

An adhesive manufacturing plant employee quickly seals boxes on an assembly line. © Dwight Cendrowski

FINDING THE DIAMONDS

Along the way, the two industries looked across the state at each other and learned a few lessons. Today, after decades of diversification, Michigan's automakers have refocused themselves on designing and building cars that excite and delight customers. And the furniture business, particularly the office furniture segment dominated by Steelcase, Herman Miller, and Haworth—Michigan's other "Big Three"—has adopted automotive-style production techniques that are enabling companies to lower costs, improve quality, and speed up product development.

As our Michigan manufacturers move into the future, we need to guard against confusing motion for progress. The key to success in the next millennium may very well have to do with time, but success won't necessarily go to those who get caught up in the ever-accelerating pace. Rather, success in the new millennium will go to those who manage time. And that sometimes means taking the time to step back, to assess what works and where the opportunities for improvement exist. That has been the strength of Michigan's manufacturing companies over the past century and will no doubt be the hallmark of the future. Some lessons are as timeless as they are successful.

TRAVEL 2000

R. D. (Dan) Musser III
President, Grand Hotel

R. D. Musser III is president of Grand Hotel, built in 1887 on Mackinac Island. Along with his sister, Mimi, he represents the third generation of Musser family ownership and operation of the Grand. He began full time there in 1986, working his way up through every department. He was named president in 1989. Active in the industry, Musser is former chairman and current vice chair of the Michigan Hotel, Motel and Resort Association and a member of the Resort Committee of the American Hotel and Motel Association. In addition, he is president of the Mackinac Island Community Foundation and serves on the boards of the Mackinac Island Chamber of Commerce and the Michigan Chamber of Commerce.

Tourism in the state of Michigan began early on, when travelers passing through the state discovered its unique natural beauty, endless coastlines, and spectacular woods. The same is true today.

One hundred years ago the Straits area was converting from a fishing community and fur-trading outpost into a destination resort. The idea for a resort of this type was conceived, as well as serviced, by rail and steamship concerns. Following the Second World War, quality roads were finally completed—along with automobiles that worked and could travel them—making the beauty of northern Michigan available to the traveling public. Later the Mackinac Bridge was constructed, connecting the upper and lower peninsulas and making tourism possible in a way that it had not been before. With plentiful transportation and the postwar boom in the economy, tourism flourished and basically has ever since.

The transportation infrastructure that has been set up in Michigan over the twentieth century has enabled the traveling public from the two largest metropolitan centers in the Great Lakes area, Detroit and Chicago, to see our beautiful state.

MICHIGAN HAS BEEN CARED FOR BY STEWARDS IN GOVERNMENT WHO MAINTAINED ITS NATURAL BEAUTY

In Good Hands

I feel that there were two people who helped significantly in pushing tourism along during this century.

First, to the south of those of us on Mackinac Island, was Everett Kircher, whose drive and vision were the catalyst in bringing quality skiing and recreation to the state in the wintertime. Perhaps even more important, he brought quality golf to northern Michigan and then to the rest of our state.

Closer to home, I see my father, R. D. Musser Jr., as the driving force in pushing for and seeking quality in the travel experience. While certainly uniqueness is the top

Hoping (praying?) for perfect form, a skier descends Suicide Hill ski jump in Ishpeming, one of the state's top ski areas. © Tom Buchkoe

priority in a travel destination, quality sells if one sticks to the basics. In our case, the resort business, a beautiful, pleasant atmosphere is of course important, but the traveling public enjoys, acknowledges, and must have quality rooms that are clean, nicely appointed, and attended to, and quality meals that are professionally prepared, served hot, and presented in a gracious and friendly manner. Fortunately, in our case, this philosophy has served us well when combined with the unique historical nature and character of Mackinac Island.

The ideas of these two men were the driving force behind the great growth and popularity of the vacation and tourist destination spots in our state within this century.

All of this success, however, could not have been possible without the foundation that our state has. Fortunately, Michigan has been cared for over the past century by stewards in our government who maintained the natural beauty that is Michigan. Our limitless coastline, the beautiful northern woods, and scenic beauty are unparalleled in the Great Lakes region.

THE TRAVELING PUBLIC WILL BE EAGER TO GET AWAY FROM ALL THAT IS MODERN — YET INCREASED AWARENESS WILL BRING A DEMAND FOR QUALITY

KEEPING THE PRIORITIES STRAIGHT

In the next century, as it becomes easier for all of us to communicate, easier for all of us to travel, easier for all of us to be aware of the opportunities and experiences around us, I expect certain things to happen. First, I think there is going to be eagerness by the traveling public to get away from all that is modern, such as major metropolitan areas and instant access and communication. And yet, because of this very increase in knowledge and awareness of what is around us, there will be a surge in demand for unique quality vacation spots.

So, if there is a lesson to be learned from the twentieth century, it is this: Now that we have set up the infrastructure, we must focus in on quality in our tourist destination products. We must also take great care to maintain the natural beauty that we have been afforded. We can use it to our advantage, promoting its uniqueness, yet we must also keep to the basics: quality food, quality experiences, quality atmosphere, and quality treatment of our guests, no matter which aspect of the tourism business we are in. If we do this, not only will tourism improve but so will our economy and quality of life.

Lake Superior laps at the rocky shore of Union Bay, in Porcupine Mountains Wilderness State Park—part of Michigan's treasured natural beauty. © Terry Donnelly

A year-round playground, Old Mission Peninsula on Grand Traverse Bay is a favorite vacation spot. © Don Smetzer/Tony Stone Images

BIBLIOGRAPHY

1997 Grand Rapids/Kent County Convention and Visitors Bureau Guide.

"About Michigan." <http://www.virtualmichigan.com/aboutm.htm> (28 August 1998).

Abraham, Molly. "Town to Honor Cats, Kitty Litter Inventor." *Detroit Free Press,* 7 July 1998.

American Automobile Association. *Michigan/Wisconsin Tour Book.* Heathrow, Fla.: AAA Publishing, 1997.

Bacon, John U. "Final Four's Floor is Michigan Made." *Detroit News,* 23 March 1998.

Bald, Frederick Clever. *Michigan in Four Centuries.* New York: Harper & Brothers, 1954.

Barfknecht, Gary W. *Mich-again's Day.* Davison, Michigan: Friede Publications, 1984.

———. *Michillaneous.* Davison, Michigan: Friede Publications, 1982.

———. *Michillaneous II.* Davison, Michigan: Friede Publications, 1985.

———. *Ultimate Michigan Adventures.* Davison, Michigan: Friede Publications, 1994.

Bissell, Inc. "BISSELL News and History." <http://www.bissell.com> (27 May 1998).

Blashfield, Jean F. and Newcomb, Annette. *Awesome Almanac: Michigan.* Fontana, Wisconsin: B&B Publishing, 1993.

Borders Online, Inc. "About Borders." <http://www.borders.com> (5 August 1998).

Brennan, Mike. "Computer Firms Report Record Earnings." *Detroit Free Press,* 5 May 1998.

Brown, Alan S. "One Hundred Years of Dow." *Michigan History Magazine,* Vol. 82, No. 3, May/June 1998, p. 50.

Brown University. "A. Alfred Taubman." <http://www.brown.edu/Departments/Taubman_Center/taubio.html> (9 August 1998).

Carpenter, John Allan. *The New Enchantment of America: Michigan.* Chicago: Childrens Press, 1978.

Couch, Ernie and Jill. *Michigan Trivia.* Nashville: Rutledge Hill Press, 1995.

Crain's 1998 Book of Lists. Vol. 13, No. 52, 29 December 1997.

Detroit Country Day School. "Achievements." <http://www.dcds.edu> (14 July 1998).

"Dow Corning to Trim 1,000 Jobs Worldwide." *Detroit Free Press,* 20 May 1998.

DTE Energy Company. "Who We Are." <http://www.detroitedison.com> (3 July 1998).

DuFresne, Jim. *Michigan: Off the Beaten Path.* Old Saybrook, Connecticut: The Globe Pequot Press, 1996.

Dunbar, Willis F. and Hay, George S. *Michigan: A History of the Wolverine State.* Grand Rapids: William B. Eerdmans Publishing Company, 1980.

Ellis, Eileen. "Making Economic Headlines." *Michigan Health and Hospitals,* Vol. 34, No. 1, January/February 1998, pp. 18–19.

Gargaro, Paul. "Light at the End of the Runway." *Crain's Detroit Business,* Vol. 14, No. 16, 20 April 1998.

Hamilton, William L. "Boomers Kick Back; La-Z-Boy Does Rest." *Detroit Free Press,* 17 April 1998.

Henderson, Tom. "Snyder Helps High-Tech Firms." *Detroit News,* 16 July 1998.

Henze, Doug. "Success by Design." *The Oakland Press,* 5 April 1998.

Howes, Daniel. "World Leaves Flint Buick City Behind." *Detroit News,* 17 May 1998.

Hunt, Mary and Don. *Hunts' Guide to Michigan's Upper Peninsula.* Albion, Michigan: Midwestern Guides, 1997.

———. *Hunts' Highlights of Michigan.* Third Edition. Albion, Michigan: Midwestern Guides, 1996.

Jenkin, Denise. "Beaumont Hospital No. 1 in State for Admissions, Surgeries." *The Oakland Press,* 26 April 1998.

Jones, Stephen. *Michigan: Travel+Smart Trip Planner.* Santa Fe: John Muir Publications, 1997.

Kmart Corporation. "Fun Facts." <http://www.kmart.com> (5 August 1998).

Lazar Productions. "Marlo Thomas: That Woman!" <http://www.gigaplex.com/celebs/marlo.htm> (1995).

Lewis, Eugene W. *Motor Memories.* Detroit: Alved Publishers, 1947.

Lewis, Ferris E. *Michigan Yesterday and Today.* Hillsdale, Michigan: Hillsdale Educational Publishers, 1980.

———. *Our Own State Michigan.* Hillsdale, Michigan: Hillsdale Educational Publishers, Inc., 1989.

Lloyd/Flanders Industries, Inc. "All Weather Wicker." <http://www.lloydflanders.com> (27 May 1998).

"Major Drug Wholesaler in Ohio to Buy Troy-based Scherer," *The Oakland Press,* 19 May 1998.

Malan, Allan and Deanna. "Mabel's Magic Mixes." *Michigan History Magazine,* Vol. 82, No. 1, Jan./Feb., 1998, pp. 22–27.

May, George S. *Michigan: An Illustrated History of the Great Lakes State.* Northridge, California: Windsor Publications, Inc., 1987.

McConnell, David B. *Michigan's Story.* Hillsdale, Michigan: Hillsdale Educational Publishers, Inc., 1996.

Meijer, Inc. "Welcome to the History of Meijer." <http://www.meijer.com> (6 June 1998).

Mercer, Tenisha. "Amid Gizmos and Robots, VSI Conducts Meeting." *Crain's Detroit Business,* Vol. 14, No. 15, 13 April 1998.

Michigan Dental Association. "About the MDA." <http://www.michigandental.org> (9 July 1998).

Michigan Department of Agriculture. *Michigan Food and Fiber Facts.* Lansing, 1997.

Michigan Department of Commerce Travel Bureau. *Michigan: It's Wonderful to Know.* Lansing, 1987.

Michigan Education Association. "About MEA." <http://www.mea.org> (13 July 1998).

Michigan Health and Hospital Association. "1997 Hospital Performance Report." <http://www.mha.org> (4 June 1998).

Michigan Jobs Commission. *Michigan Data Book: A Reference Text for Economic Development Professionals.* Lansing, 1996.

Michigan State University. "The College of Human Medicine." <http://www.chm.msu.edu> (7 July 1998).

Michigan Travel Bureau. *Michigan Travel Ideas.* Lansing, 1997.

"New Ranking," *The Oakland Press,* 7 May 1998, chart p. A–11.

"Off-Beat Attractions." <http://www.michigan.org/factsb.html> (5 August 1998).

Powers, Tom. *Michigan in Quotes.* Davison, Michigan: Friede Publications, 1994.

Rector, Sylvia. "Honey-Baked Ham's Upward Spiral." *Detroit Free Press,* 17 December 1997.

Ross, Pippin. "On Track." *Disney Magazine,* Fall 1998, pp. 45–48.

Roush, Matt. "Bringing it Back Home." *Crain's Detroit Business,* Vol. 14, No. 18, 4 May 1998.

———. "State Wins Award for Y2K Problem-Solving." *Crain's Detroit Business,* Vol. 14, No. 43, 26 October 1998, p. 2.

———. "Venture Capital." *Crain's Detroit Business,* Vol. 14, No. 23, 8 June 1998.

Rust, Betsy V. "A Family-Friendly Focus." *Michigan Health and Hospitals,* Vol. 34, No. 2, March/April 1998, p. 36.

Semion, William. *Michigan Family Adventure Guide.* Old Saybrook, Connecticut: The Globe Pequot Press, 1996.

Shay, Harry, ed. *All About Michigan Almanac.* Hartland, Michigan: Instant Information, 1993.

Singhania, Lisa. "Gerber Products Goes Global." *Detroit News,* 26 July 1998.

Sirvaitis, Karen. *Michigan.* Minneapolis: Lerner Publications Company, 1994.

Stapler, Harry. *Pioneers of Forest and City.* Lansing: Michigan Historical Commission, 1985.

Stimson, Melissa and Chatfield, M. F. *Michigan's Capital Cities.* Leland, Michigan: Thunder Bay Press, 1997.

Stopa, Marsha. "Publishing Group Struggles with Its Growing Pains," *The Oakland Press,* 2 October 1998.

Struthers, Nancy. "Health in Michigan Communities." *Michigan Health and Hospitals,* Vol. 34, No. 3, May/June 1998, pp. 24–28.

Thompson, Kathleen. *Michigan.* Austin, Texas: Raintree Steck-Vaughn Publishers, 1996.

UMI Company. "UMI Names New President." <http://www.umi.com> (15 June 1998).

University of Michigan. "About UMHS." <http://www.umich.edu> (5 May 1998).

Wayne State University. "Wayne State Best of Profile." <http://www.wayne.edu.> (13 July 1998).

Wayne State University School of Medicine. "The Detroit Medical Center." <http://www.phypc.med.wayne.edu> (5 May 1998).

"Welcome to Michigan—The Great Lakes State!" <http://www.inetmi.com/mi/index.html> (1998).

Who's Who Among African-Americans 1996–97. Detroit: Gale Research Inc., 1996.

Woodard, Inc. "About Woodard." <http://www.woodard-furniture.com> (27 May 1998).

The Web sites of the following companies and electronic publications also were consulted for this book: ABC News and Starwave Corporation Celebsite, 1998; *Compton's Encyclopedia Online* version 3.0, 1999; Comshare Corporation; Compuware Corporation; DaimlerChrysler; Ford Motor Company; General Motors Corporation; Kelly Services; Pulte Corporation; Valassis Communications, Inc.

The Fist, by sculptor Robert Graham, stands at the corner of Woodward and Jefferson Avenues in downtown Detroit as a tribute to world heavyweight champion Joe Louis. © Andre Jenny/International Stock

Built in 1907, Holland Harbor Lighthouse, affectionately known as "Big Red," is one of the premiere landmarks of Holland, Michigan. The twin-gabled structure stands at the end of a long pier that connects Lake Macatawa to Lake Michigan. © Vito Palmisano/Tony Stone Images

SPONSOR

MICHIGAN CHAMBER OF COMMERCE
Contact: Elisabeth Weston
600 South Walnut Street
Lansing, MI 48933-2200
Telephone: (517) 371-7677
Fax: (517) 371-7228
Web site: www.michamber.com

PATRONS

ERIM International, Inc.
Contact: Dr. Peter M. Banks
1975 Green Road
Ann Arbor, MI 48105
Telephone: (734) 994-1200
Fax: (734) 994-6070
Web site: www.erim-int.com

Kheder & Associates
Contact: Noble Kheder
201 North Washington Square,
Suite 905
Lansing, MI 48933
Telephone: (517) 482-2896
Fax: (517) 482-9423

Mead Paper Division
Contact: Kelvin Smyth
7100 County 426 M.5 Road
Escanaba, MI 49829
Telephone: (906) 786-1660
Fax: (906) 789-3252

Michigan Technological University
Contact: Curtis J. Thompkins, President
1400 Townsend Drive,
Room 500 Admin. Bldg.
Houghton, MI 49931-1295
Telephone: (906) 487-2200
Fax: (906) 487-2935
Web site: www.mtu.com

Universal Forest Products, Inc.
Contact: Amb. Peter F. Secchia
2801 East Beltine North East
Grand Rapids, MI 49525
Telephone: (616) 364-6161
Fax: (616) 364-5558

INDEX